LOCAL DEVELOPMENT IN THE GLOBAL ECONOMY

# Local Development in the Global Economy

## The case of Pakistan

PERVAIZ NAZIR
*University of Bristol*

Avebury

Aldershot · Brookfield USA · Hong Kong · Singapore · Sydney

Published by
Avebury
Gower Publishing Company Limited
Gower House
Croft Road
Aldershot
Hants GU11 3HR
England

Gower Publishing Company
Old Post Road
Brookfield
Vermont 05036
USA



ISBN 1 85628 106 X

Printed and Bound in Great Britain by
Athenaeum Press Ltd., Newcastle upon Tyne.

# Contents

# Tables

Thanks are due to Avtar Brah, Tariq Salim, Peter Townsend, Paddy Hillyard, Alan Tuppen, Nigel Harris, Fahmida Nazir and Ian Cunnison for their help and encouragement in completing this book. I remain responsible for any shortcomings.

# 1 Introduction

The present study seeks to analyze local development in Pakistan and the way this development is connected with and shaped by the national and international economy. This is indicated by the fact that both the pre-conditions and the results of local development have been Pakistan's further integration into the international economy. National and local development in Pakistan relies increasingly on the international economy for production technology and intermediate equipment, as well as raw materials. These in turn are financed in part through export earnings but depend mainly on loans from international agencies and rich countries. The country is thus, to a large extent, externally dependent for its development process. In fact, as we shall see, there seems to exist, and not just for Pakistan, an inverse relationship between the degree of integration into the international economy and the level of structural independence and self-reliance of the national economy.

The study of local development is useful in that, to a significant extent, local development mirrors national development; by focussing at this level the process of development can be amenable to a relatively detailed empirical analysis, which is often not possible in macro-level studies.

My main argument in this study is that local and national development in Pakistan, and other similarly placed developing countries, can only be understood if it is seen in relation to the international and national economy of which it is an integral part. Secondly, the capital goods and technology producing sectors, which are weak in Pakistan, are the most important determinants of the development of an integrated and self-reliant national economy - whether or not the development strategy is based on large-scale production units, or on a smaller scale using 'appropriate technology.' Third, the process of integration into the national economy facilitates development in the short-term, but restricts development in the long-run.

However, acknowledgement of the international economy's significance for national development is not to assert that external relationships are the only determining factors in local development; rather that in combination with the national and the local economy, the internatuional economy structures a framework and creates a situation that conditions the limits and possibilities of local development.

In this study development is defined as a process which is reflected in the attainment of levels of socio-economic equity sufficient to ensure equal opportunity and individual self-realization, taking cultural factors into account. It should be noted, however, that the attainment of either aspect of development does not mean the attainment of the other. No rigid criteria is offered to quantify development; though conventional indicators such as gross national product per capita and income distribution can be used in conjunction with the structural indicators such as sectoral analysis of the economy, quality and quantity of the labour force, and the degree of self-reliance of the national economy.

Since the internal dynamics of the local economy has taken different forms in response to changes in the structure of the national and international economy, local, national and international development processes have to be seen as different moments of a complex and multivariate process; a result of the complex configuration of the internal dynamics of a developing country and the increasing internationalization of capital. It is in this sense that local development has to be explained in terms of the penetration of, and incorporation into, the larger structures. A focus on local development enables one to see concretely the effects of this incorporation, and vice versa.

Of course, this is a contested terrain which I shall discuss in chapter 2: whether the primary cause of development or underdevelopment is to be sought in the world economy, or factors internal to a national economy, or varying degrees of each. This is an old problematic which has reappeared rather sharply in the wake of significant changes in the international and Third World economies: especially industrialization in the so-called newly industrializing countries which include among others, Mexico, Brazil and the 'four little tigers', South Korea, Taiwan, Hong Kong and Singapore; and changes which are also related to the global relocation of industry since the 1970s. This, plus the momentous transformation in the socialist bloc has, for many, made it necessary to question and reevaluate some influential theories of development, in particular those within a broadly Marxist framework of dependent development. As I indicate in chapter 2, there is a tendency for both the Marxist-inspired theories, and those operating within a neo-classical framework, either to establish or dismiss *a priori* the possibility of Third World development within the contemporary world economy. Be that as it may, I shall argue the necessity for a concrete analysis of a concrete situation, as I have attempted in this study, rather than a priori theorising on the causes or possibilities of development or underdevelopment at a local or national level.

The structure of national and local development of Pakistan of course is rooted in history and is the outcome of a complex interaction between Pakistan's development policies and its location within the international economy dominated by a small number of developed industrial countries. It might be objected that Pakistan's development policies themselves have been determined in the first instance by the international division of labour established under colonial rule, whereby the sub-continent completed the British economy by providing it with raw materials necessary for its industry and at the same time provided markets for Britain's manufactured goods. This objection, however, is only partly valid, as it ignores the fact that a few, sometimes rather narrow, options did (and do) exist for alternative development policies, some of which I shall discuss below and in chapter 4.

Since independence in 1947, the role of the state in Pakistan's development has been crucial: with a series of five year plans and state provided infrastructure, it has attempted to facilitate development through encouraging private capitalism. This process of development has relied heavily on the international economy for resources, and the state also mediates this relationship between the national and international economies.

Two development strategies in particular have accelerated Pakistan's integration into the international economy and established the parameters and characteristics of its development. First adopted in the 1950s, import-substitution industrialization (ISI) depended on imported machinery for producing consumer goods which were previously imported. The ISI for producer goods was clearly an alternative that might have made Pakistan's (and other developing countries) economy deeper and more self-reliant, but it called for sacrifices which the combination of dominant class interests in the country ruled out in favour of quick profits through ISI for consumer goods.

The ISI strategy did not generate the much hoped for dramatic improvement in levels of national development; or in the structural transformation of the economy. On the contrary, this strategy institutionalised the almost perpetual trade deficit and acute shortage of foreign currency, combined with a relatively low rate of investment, that has been a significant feature of Pakistan's, as well as that of other developing countries economies, who have followed a similar strategy. But as we shall see, these features are not the cause, rather they are symptoms of the economy's underlying structural problems, characterized by relatively low productivity in agriculture, and a weak industrial base. The high growth rates registered sporadically in the economy over the last four decades did not reflect any deep structural transformation of the national economy, as I shall indicate later in this work.

The strategy of agricultural development in Pakistan since the 1960s has largely been technicist, which relied on increased input of fertilizers, machinery such as irrigation technology, tractors, and fertilizer-responsive High Yielding Variety seeds, to increase output. These inputs too, were imported, or were produced locally with imported technology and raw materials. In any case, the supply of these inputs to agriculture has been both costly to the country, and wholly inadequate in quantity for cultivators, as we shall in our local study.

The rapid growth in agriculture which followed under this strategy came to be known as the 'green revolution', which I shall discuss in detail later in the work. Of course, as in industrial development (import substitution for consumer or for capital goods), alternative policies for agricultural development could have been followed, by fostering the development of an indigenous industry producing inputs for agriculture. The small-scale indigenous industry that did develop as an adjunct to the green revolution was miniscule compared to the need, and in any case the most important component of the green revolution package, fertilizer, was either imported or produced locally using imported technology and raw materials.

However, the agrarian policies that were adopted in Pakistan meant that agricultural development also depended on external financing, including that from the World Bank, and this was crucial to the process of internationalization of Pakistan's agriculture during the green revolution phase. This internationalization manifested itself locally, in areas of our empirical study, through the consumption by cultivators, of products and equipment manufactured by multinational corporations of the developed countries, or by their subsidiaries. For the national and local economy this process of internationaliztion represented several fold increases in the use of chemical fertilizers, pesticides, irrigation technology, diesel and electric-powered engines, tractors, and combines.

Whilst this represented an increase in the process of capital accumulation by the multinationals and the developed countries, for the local economy and Pakistan it meant a drain on scarce resources and a slow rate of capital accumulation, though the larger owners of land benefitted from this penetration of foreign capital in the form of inputs, which were often heavily subsidized by the government.

For the poor cultivators and the landless, this development has resulted in greater unemployment partly because of the capital-intensive nature of the technology used (and greater income inequalities which this technology has engenderd), but mainly because of the lack of, as well the dependent nature of, the industrialization process, which has been slow and has not been able to re-absorb the labour displaced by increased mechanization of agriculture under the green revolution strategy. For example, by the late 1980s almost 200,000 tractors were in operation in Pakistan, and in the main area of our local study, there were 26 tractors operative in 1987. As we shall see in chapter 4, this rather unsystematic and unplanned introduction of modern technology into Pakistan's rural economy has caused the loss of millions of jobs in agriculture without a corresponding increase in jobs in manufacturing industry or other sectors of the economy, except large scale migration of workers to the Middle East.

The strategy of agricultural development never took into consideration the socio-economic context of Pakistan's agriculture, whose basic feature is the unequal distribution of land and the unequal access to resources that this implies. It took a relatively modest influx of imported modern technology to exacerbate an already serious employment situation of the landless and smaller owners of land.

The weakness in Pakistan's agriculture is reflected in the fact that the self-sufficiency in food which has been more or achieved since 1978, is often precarious as it remains dependent to a large extent on climatic conditions and agricultural price support and subsidies on inputs, factors which seriously affect production targets. The export (mainly to the Middle East) of grain and other foodstuff is at the expense of at least 30 percent of the population which is inadequatley nourished. A significant proportion of some food items such as edible oils have still to be imported to meet domestic needs.

In manufacturing industry, inspite of concerted efforts to industrialize, Pakistan's exports rely heavily on the export of rice and cotton and agriculture-dependent manufactures such as textiles. The export of light electrical equipment and surgical goods constitutes less than a quarter of the total exports.

Underlying the state's development strategy for both agriculture and industry was the idea that an autonomous productive structure would emerge through the so-called intersectoral 'forward and backward linkages' which would create self-sufficiency in consumption goods and produce a surplus for export. As we shall see, the goal behind this strategy remains unrealized largely because of the particular development policies that have been advocated.

Far from the development of autonomous productive structures, the three main consequences of the development strategies that I have described is that Pakistan has become technologically and financially dependent on the international economy to a greater degree than comparable countries such as Turkey, Egypt and India. The magnitude of this dependence can be gauged by the fact that over 50 percent of the country's imports consist of capital or intermediate goods, and between 30-40 percent of export earnings go towards debt servicing.

This reflects the fact that Pakistan's economy lacks the strategic sector producing the means of production, which is located out of the country; so that the circuit of national capital is completed only by being linked to the economies producing the means of production, that is the developed countries. Because of this lack, as we shall see in chapter 2, the process of capital expansion occurs mainly in the developed economies. This not only deprives Pakistan's economy of a portion of the surplus which is transferred to the developed economies during the circuit of reproduction; but, more importantly, the moment of capital expansion which occurs during the process of production of technology and capital goods, takes place outside of the national economy.

An effect of this lack is that the country's agricultural and industrial structures have became outwardly directed, that is, integrated into the international, but less so into the national economy. The concept of the national economy of Pakistan, as of other developing countries, may be understood as the interaction between agricultural and industrial sectors, with agriculture providing raw materials and wage goods to industry, and industry providing intermediate goods and production equipment to agriculture. In this sense the structure of agriculture and industry in Pakistan is not only outwardly directed but also asymmetrical. For whilst agriculture provides raw materials such as cotton and food to industry,

industry provides little that is substantial to agriculture in terms of locally produced inputs, as we shall see.

The incorporation of the national and local economy into the global economy has had different consequences for each of these economies, and for the different sectors within these economies. For the international or global economy the process has signalled the further penetration and extension of its capital into, and the realization of surplus value in, the Third World. Conversely, a large part of surplus value produced in Pakistan and other Third World countries is absorbed by international capital. This increasing impingement on the national and local economy of Pakistan (and other developing countries) by the international economy is an aspect of the concentration and centralization of capital at the global level represented by the operation of multinational corporations, who increasingly produce and control machinery and other inputs that go into the process of production in Pakistan.

Pakistan's further integration into the international economy has resulted in some accumulation of capital in the country, but this has been low and has widened the disjuncture between agriculture and industry in the way that I have described briefly already.

Nevertheless the penetration of international capital has resulted in a significant growth and transformation of the socio-economic structures and capital accumulation at the local level; reflected in, for example, increased commercialization and monetization of the economy, in income disparities, social and regional inequalities, extension of the market in agricultural produce, development of new forms of production and labour processes, relative demise of the traditional rural economy, and so on. Inspite of these changes, however, as I shall indicate, the local economy is either excessively outwardly directed and dependent on external sources for its dynamic, or it is excessively inwardly directed and relatively closed; in the latter, both its material conditions of production, and its 'market', which is based largely on barter, lie within the local economy. The local economy therefore presents an internal barrier to the penetration of both the national and international capital and thus restricts the integration of the local economy into these larger structures. Paradoxically, as I shall indicate later in the work, the changes induced by international capital at the local level also effect the transfer of surplus out of the local and national economy, and thus international capital restricts local development as well.

As conceptualized in this study, international capital and the international economy is understood to be synonymous with the economies of the developed countries. The world economy is becoming increasingly internationalized in the sense that the economies in different parts of the globe, which had hitherto remained outside of, or were weakly integrated into, the economies of the developed industrial countries, are now increasingly being incorporated into the developed economies.

As we shall see, this process of enlargement and incorporation of the local economy is reflected in the increasing global mobility and operation of productive units such as the multinational corporations, the transnational banks, and increase in international trade. Other characteristics of the internationaliziation process are the standardization of commodities and production process, and different stages of the production being carried out in different parts of the globe:

> The internationalization of capital as social relation spreads out the labour process on an international scale...[T]he various components of the chain come from the most far-flung parts of the globe:Taiwan, South Korea, USA, France, Britain, Latin America and Africa...[reflecting] a technical division of labour [that] begins to operate on a world scale...(Palloix, 1975:86).

In this sense a single global market is emerging, with this difference: not all parts of the globe benefit equally from this process; and this process in fact has a tendency to subordinate and restrict the development of Third World countries. In such a situation, as I shall indicate in chapter 2, it is necessary to emphasize the dualistic and contradictory nature of the international economy, in terms of its effects on the economies of different countries.

There are other institutions located within the global economy - the world institutions including the World Bank, International Monetary Fund, Food and Agricultural Organization, and the United Nations Industrial Development Organization; these coordinate, regulate and facilitate the internationalization process by setting the agenda and formulating policies that emphasize one or another aspect of development at different times, such as for example privatization and encouragement of capitalist penetration of Third World economies through other means.

One of the major themes in this work is that the main obstacles to local and national development in Pakistan has been the lack of integration between agriculture and industrial development; this in turn can be attributed to the lack of a sufficiently strong capital goods and technology generating sectors, an inevitable consequence of the ISI policies for consumer goods, and an inefficient agriculture. This relationship, between agriculture and industry, and in particular the relationship between agriculture and capital goods and technology generating industries, constitutes the main aim of this study: to analyze agricultural development, concretely, by focussing at the local level, and relating this to the national and international economic processes that shape this development, through their production and control of capital and intermediate goods.

### The agrarian transition

In a situation where agriculture is the dominant sector of developing countries economies, this must take on the role of the engine of development and provide a surplus for the economy in general and industry in particular, in two ways: agriculture must provide a surplus in the form of food and raw materials, that is wage goods and elements of production for industry; and it must also provide a financial surplus (where terms of trade are against agriculture and in favour of industry) to provide for capital formation in industry (Byres, 1974; Ellman, 1979; Johnston and Kilby, 1975). According to Johnston and Kilby (1975: 133):

> The first objective of an agricultural strategy focusses on the need to achieve a rate and pattern of output expansion in the agricultural sector that will promote overall economic...growth and structural transformation and take advantage of positive interactions between agriculture and other sectors.

In order to expand output, developing countries' agriculture must become efficient, based on capitalist production methods, and the backward and relatively inefficient forms characterized by low productivity must be transformed and supplanted by more productive forms (Bharadwaj, 1974; Mellor, 1968, 1976; Berry and Cline, 1979). This process of capitalist development in agriculture is referred to as the agrarian transition, and its importance lies in the fact that it creates the basis for, and is itself reflective of, an efficient and highly productive agriculture based on capitalist production methods. The agrarian transition is therefore of great significance for analyzing development and underdevelopment in Third World countries, and this has been an important object of discourse in the study of socio-economic development in general (Marx, 1974, 1976; Reynolds, 1975;Bagchi, 1970;Dobb, 1960; Johnston and Kilby, 1975).

According to another writer:

> Central to this debate [on the agrarian transition] is the issue of a successful (or otherwise) transition from pre-capitalist agriculture, a process which depends historically on the emergence of generalized commodity production and exchange following the differentiation of the peasantry into large-scale commercial farms owning means of production and non-owning 'depeasantized' proletarians (Brass,1984:108).

The process of transition has been completed in the developed capitalist countries; but the question is the extent to which the agrarian transition is taking place, and the form it is taking, in Third World agricultures, which are located within a process of dependent development characterized by the lack of an integrated national economy and the relative absence of a capital goods sector; issues which I shall come back to in the chapters that follow in this work.

The model of agrarian development that I have sketched briefly, is one that has been followed by a number of relatively recently industrialized countries such as the Soviet Union (Erlich, 1960; Dobb, 1966) and newly industrializing ones such as China (Eckstein, 1979; Howe, 1978). Briefly, this has involved (with modifications vis-a-vis China), attempts at rapid industrialization through transfer of surpluses from agriculture, which is organized on a collective basis, and the introduction of relatively modern and intensive production methods to increase agricultural productivity.

Increase in agricultural productivity and the agrarian transition has also been important in the capitalist development of Japan, so far the only non-western country to have successfully modernized along capitalist lines (not withstanding South Korea, as we shall see in chapter 2), with production based on relatively small-scale, but very intensive agriculture (Ohkawa and Rosovsky, 1960).

The agrarian transition takes many forms, and the appropriation and transfer of agricultural surpluses can be secured by different methods, such as by direct taxation (Japan), direct forcible measures and imposition of centrally controlled terms of trade (Soviet Union), a combination of these (China), and combination of force and the 'free market' mechanism (early modern England).

This study thus is in part (because it is one of three levels of analysis) a study of the agrarian transition at a micro or local level which enables one to analyze this process empirically and relate it to the national and international economy, on which I shall have more to say in chapter 2, in relation to the theoretical concepts that have informed this study.

**The local study**

As I have described in the methodology section in appendix 3, the empirical study is based on a survey carried out in 1978 in a village called Mallian (this is a fictitious name given to keep its anonymity), and its regional economy in the Sheikhupura district of the Punjab in Pakistan. Data were also collected from two other localities (cluster of villages) in the Sahiwal and Sargodha districts of the Punjab. Data from Sheikhupura were updated by a visit to the area in 1987, and this is included where it is of relevance. The conclusions of the research on Sahiwal and Sargodha is contained in the appendix though reference is made to it in the main text.

The object of the research was also to analyze the process of local development in Pakistan by focussing on a village and its regional economy, as well as two other localities in the Sahiwal and Sargodha districts. The intention of the research was to assess the extent of capitalist development over the previous decade, that is from the mid-1960s, which incorporates the period of rapid agricultural change referred to as the green revolution.

In other words, the aim of the research was to ascertain the extent to which capitalist relations of production and exchange had developed and supplanted the non-capitalist, though by no means subsistent, village economy. More concretely, I set out to identify the way capital, wage labour, new productive forces, capitalist labour processes and expanded reproduction had developed in relation to the economy of the previous decade, which was based on sharetenancy, small-scale peasant production, simple technology, and minimal role of capital in the production process (Hasswell, 1961; Bharadwaj, 1974).

The research also undertook to study the demise or otherwise of *sep*, the name given to relationships linking agriculture and artisan production based on traditional feudalistic relations of production and exchange. Also, as part of the study of the regional economy of the village, the effects of interaction between the village and a large modern textile mill was included in the research.

As I shall point out in chapter 2, most studies of development operate at one level of analysis. These are either discrete studies of local development which is not contextualzed or connected systematically to larger processes of which local development is a part. Or the study of development is located at the macro level which has little empirical content; and the analysis does not consider local structures which facilitate or retard development, such as the local class structure, ecological conditions, degree of the local economy's incorporation into the national and international economy, and so on. Our study analyzes local development at three interrelated levels: the international, national and local. Whilst these levels incorporate each other, each level has a specificity which needs to be understood in its own terms as well as in relation to other levels and structures. Thus, the analysis of development in our areas of research includes consideration of local institutions and class structure, the local political economy, as well as ecological and technical factors that facilitate, block, or modify the processes of development.

There are a number of general and specific conclusions of this study. The incorporation of the local into the national and international economy has both accelerated and hindered local development. Development of the local economy, which is mainly, but not exclusively, agricultural, has been accelerated by the large increase in modern inputs, including fertilizers and irrigation technology, which removed some of the constraints on ouput. This has resulted in the growth of both the scale and extent of agricultural production; that is, growth in output due to more productive labour processes, and increase in output due to an increase in area under cultivation.

Small-scale agriculture and artisan production have declined in the local economy, and new forms of social organization of production have emerged. Similarly, sharetenancy, once a dominant form of production relation in agriculture has declined to a large extent. In this regard a theoretical conclusion of this study is that there can be no general theory of sharetenancy as the conditions for its existence are too diverse; this is contrary to attempts at explaining the existence of this phenomenon through constructing a general theory of sharetenancy.

As we shall see, whilst there has been considerable development, the local economy has not been completely transformed along capitalist lines, hence the agrarian transition is not complete. The reasons for this incompleteness are to be sought mainly in the configuration of the distinct but related national and international economies; but there are specifically local factors too, such as the local political economy and the class structure, and adverse ecological conditions such as water-logging and salinity, which hinder development.

The overall conclusion of the study is not that integration of the national and local economy into the international economy is detrimental per se. Rather, this integration needs to be selective and planned so as to optimize national and local development and bring benefits to the majority of the people in Pakistan. And the basis for this can be laid by creating an approprate socio-economic and political context and by adopting policies that enable surplus produced in agriculture and in other sectors of the economy, to contribute towards capital formation, rather than for a considerable portion of this surplus to be absorbed by international capital in the form of imported capital inputs for domestic agriculture. This can be achieved by creating a national economy in which agriculture and industry are integrated and where the international economy has a supplementary, rather than the dominant role.

The book is divided into ten chapters, with three appendix chapters. In chapter 2, I discuss some of the main theoretical concepts that have informed this study: the different phases of capitalist production, the meaning of the agrarian transition, the conceptualization of peasant classes, the nature of dependent capitalist development and the internationalization of the global economy. I also discuss the crucial role of the capital goods and technology generating sector in development as expressed in the relationship between Department 1 and Department 2 in expanded reproduction of the economy.

In chapter 3 some aspects of changes in the international economy are discussed in relation to their effects on development in Third World countries. In particular, the increasing multinational corporations control over the mechanical, agro-chemical and seed production industries, and their penetration into developing countries' agricultures. A process that has increased dependence and 'denationalized' developing countries' agriculture.

In chapter 4, I describe some aspects of Pakistan's development and the policies and strategies that have underlain this development. The consequences of further integration into the international economy are analyzed in relation to both national and local development. This chapter also connects the analysis of the global economy contained in chapter 3 to local development which I discuss in chapter 5 onwards.

Chapter 5 provides a descriptive analysis of the main local area, Mallian, where the survey was carried out. I describe the socio-economic and ecological conditions of the locality, including distribution of land and resources, water availability, crops grown and the regional market. The transformation and development of Mallian's economy and its incorporation into the international economy is the subject of chapter 6; and includes the analyses of increases in agricultural output, increased use of capital in production, emergence of new forms of the labour process, increased mechanization of agriculture, and breakup of the traditional local economy.

In chapter 7 I describe in detail the process of production and the labour process of a representative sample of various producer groups in Mallian, to ascertain the extent of development, or otherwise, of capitalist production.

The interaction between the local agrarian economy and nearby modern industry is analysed in chapter 8. Of particluar interest is the effect of alternative employment on Mallian agriculture, the consequences of a systematic introduction of money into the local economy, and the significance of this for the national and international economy. In chapter 9 I assess Mallian's development in relation to the local as well as the national and international economy. Also analyzed is the extent to which the agrarian transition has been completed, and the reasons for its non-completion are summarized. In chapter 10 I indicate briefly some suggestions for more appropriate development policies and strategies in Pakistan.

# 2 Theoretical perspectives

A theoretically informed empirical study of development at three distinct but interrelated levels of the local, national and international economy, poses a number of problems. For, even though these levels are integrated and overlapping, one has to separate them into distinct entities for analytical purposes. For example, what one calls 'national' economy may itself be comprised of the international economy which is dominated by multinational companies or their subsidiaries; or the domestic companies in the national economy may have large foreign ownership. Nevertheless, it has been found useful to separate the levels because national development policy and development strategy has, relatively speaking, effectivity over particular, delimited, spatial and juridical parameters of a country, in a manner in which the international economy does not.

Another problem, almost endemic to a study of this type, is the perhaps unavoidable, but hopefully slight, disjuncture between the empirical study based on a survey carried out during fieldwork, and the general theoretical framework which connects and explains that data. In other words, this is a theoretically informed empirical study attempting a concrete analysis of a concrete situation; that is, an analysis of local development in its national and international setting.

The theoretical framework which I shall outline in this chapter follows the three interrelated but distinct levels of analysis of development: First, at the local level, the analysis is presented as the problem of capitalist development and the agrarian transition, which is affected by the local, as well the national and international processes. Second, at the national level the concept of dependent development is appropriate in that it links the national and international levels, and raises the issue of the extent to which the latter shapes, facilitates or constrains national development. The third element of the theoretical scheme is the concept of the internationalization of capital, comprised, as we shall see, of three international circuits of capital (commodity, productive, finance) which links the various components of the international economy, and of course the way these incorporate and shape the national and local economy.

*Studies on South Asian rural development*

There are relatively few studies that address the question of the agrarian transition within the larger context - though there is an enormous literature on the politics and socio-economic organization of South Asian villages. In the 1950s and 1960s there was a spate of these 'village studies' (Marriot, 1955; Dube, 1955; Lewis, 1958; Mayer, 1960; Eglar, 1960; Beals, 1962; Berryman, 1963), and the same tradition continues into more recent times (Parry, 1979; Ahmad, 1977).

There are a number of exceptions to the approach adopted in the above studies: Epstein's (1962; 1973) study of two ecologically contrasting (one wet and one dry) villages in South India is located within the context of development policies of Mysore state and changes in the wider Indian economy (1962: 4). Epstein's study is informed by concepts from the 'formalist' school of economic anthropolgy which are concepts more appropriate to a study of developed capitalist societies. Her study is also strongly empiricist, it scarcely goes beyond description of change; it does not tell us in a theoretically meaningful way the nature of economic and social change in her two villages. At the economic level, change is equated with a shift from subsistence to cash economies (ibid:328). Descriptive accounts and correlations of this sort are assumed by Epstein to constitute both cause and explanation of change in the two villages.

Bliss and Stern (1982), attempt to understand the economy of an Indian village through an 'analysis of rural markets and the behaviour of these'(1982:1). They do this by inappropriately applying categories derived from neo-classical economics to a situation where the market is undeveloped. There is no systematic analysis of the relations of production in the village and the local social division of labour of which these are a part. The question of capitalist development, or lack of this in the village, of course, is never posed; the study is therefore limited in theoretical concepts which are adequate for an analysis of social change.

In the wake of the green revolution in the 1960s and 1970s, an extensive body of literature on the nature of agrarian production in India appeared in the Economic and Political Weekly (EPW), that came to be known as the 'mode of production debate'. In brief, there were three main viewpoints expressed on the development or otherwise of capitalist agriculture in India.

The first viewpoint concluded that there was no capitalist development even in states with the most developed agricultures, where the green revolution had developed the strongest, and that Indian agriculture was characterized by basically semi-feudal production relations (Rudra, 1969; 1970; 1971).

The second view holds that Indian agriculture has been capitalist since the colonial period. The problem with this view is that it conflates incorporation into the capitalist colonial economy with capitalist production in the colony itself. This follows from the defining characteristic of capitalist production, which is rather unspecific: the presence of wage labour and commodity production is taken as sufficient condition of the existence of capitalism.

The third view is that there has been capitalist developemt though it is by no means the dominant mode of production in agriculture (Patnaik, 1971; 1972), a conclusion similar to ours, but with one difference: Patnaik does not specify the nature of Indian capitalism which is in part determined by its relationship to the international economy. This is in contrast to our analysis which places local and national development within the context, not of a simple dependency, but within the framework of national development which is not altogether autonomous, but dependent, in important ways, on the internatinal economy, as we shall see later in this chapter.

The mode of production debate in the EPW is important in that it raised issues in theory and method in analyzing capitalist development. That three different viewpoints and conclusions can be expressed on the existence or otherwise of the same phenomena shows the need for a more precise and rigorous understanding and use of theory, method and empirical data in assessing the extent of capitalist development.

A number of criticisms of the mode of production debate are in order. First, the debate scarcely carried any systematic analyses of the labour process or social organization of production that underlies capitalist production. Second, there is no account of *jajmani* (*sep* in Pakistan) which structures relations between agrarian and artisan production and embody the 'unity of agriculture and handicraft production' characteristic of pre-capitalist production relations. This omission renders the focus narrowly on agricultural only, rather than on the rural social formation as a whole. Third, especially in the first and third approaches in the EPW, there is a disjuncture between abstract theory and the statistical evidence which it is supposed to interpret. Fourth, there is little historical dimension in any of the authors' analyses of capitalist development, though the third viewpoint includes some chronological references to Indian agriculture under colonial rule. Fifth, there is little systematic attempt to differentiate between different stages of capitalist development, and the type or quality of capitalism in India which has developed within the constraints of the world division of labour established under colonial rule, and of the increasing concentration and centralization of capital in the contemporary world economy. There is no questioning in the debate as to where the elements of production, on which capitalism was developing in India, were produced; whether these were the products of the domestic capital goods sector in India, or the products of the international economy, in which the valorization of capital took place in the developed countries; and the effect of these on agrarian capitalist development in India.

The EPW debate showed up the problem of operating at too general a level for analyzing capitalist development. A more concrete analysis of rural production systems was needed to show extent of capitalist development - analyses that would complement the EPW studies. This was attempted by a number of studies of local capitalist development: Saith and Tankha, (1972b); Djurfeldt and Lindberg, (1975); Nazir, (1975); Bhalla, (1976); Shivakumar, (1978).

I shall focus on the work of Djurfeldt and Lindberg and Saith and Tankha because their work is theoretically adequate and at the same time a sustained empirical analysis of local capitalist development.

Djurfeldt and Lindberg's problematic is the cause of underdevelopment in a Tamil village, a situation they attribute to a number of factors, but they are not consistent on what these are as I shall point out.

For Djurfeldt and Lindberg, underdevelopment is reflected in, *inter alia*, poor development of the productive forces, low agricultural productivity, extraction of absolute surplus labour and pre-capitalist ground (1975: 172-3). They also find an absence of capital entering into the sphere of production, and the labour process is not even under the formal subordination to capital (ibid: 172). They are of course methodologically correct to stress the primacy of the sphere of production over other spheres of the economy:

> The rich peasantry is not biased towards a technological revolution (and still less, ofcourse, are the big landlords): They are not driven to expand the productive forces of their holdings; they can gain a safe livlihood merely by cultivating their land in the traditional way, or by letting it out to tenants [and] although many observers have been optimistic about the possibilities of 'modernization' (the so-called 'green revolution') to take root among the rich, our analysis makes it doubtful that they are right (1975: 172).

Of course, there are possibilities for raising production by increasing irrigation and other measures, but the ultimate barrier to developemt in the village is that 'the forces of production can be seen as contained by the relations of production' (ibid.: 173). It follows that higher productivity is impossible to achieve because of the opposing interest of classes in the village (ibid.: 169). In my view this argument is untenable: if the subordinate classes are dependent upon rich peasants and landlords, then the latter can put the subordinate classes to work in any form of the labour process, including capitalist, inspite of opposition, as is the case in Mallian.

Djurfeldt and Lindberg's village is underdeveloped, according to them, because it is tied to the national and international markets which are capitalist. The salt and rice produced in the village leaves for the national market and if unequal exchange takes place (and they are not sure whether the exchange is unequal) between these structures then a surplus is appropriated by the national and international bourgeoisie (ibid.: 207). The products which are received in return contributes to underdevelopment too, as these are mainly luxuries and not investment goods.

The puzzling thing about underdevelopment in Djurfeldt and Lindberg's village is that capitalist development had taken place in other villages in the sub-continent with similar class structures, ecological conditions, and distance from the market. Djurfeldt and Lindberg's conclusion of lack of capitalist development in their village is in part due to a misuse of an otherwise appropriate methodology: they have neglected the time factor, the inertia or time lag before the local economy is incorporated into the national and international economy. They have underestimated the way capitalism develops unevenly in different geographical areas, and at different times. After all, their research was carried out in 1969 (ibid.:17), when the new technology of the green revolution had only recently become available. The green revolution gathered momentum in the 1970s, but even in the developed areas of the Pakistani (or Indian) Punjab where capitalist developemt has taken root, some village economies have been transformed more than others, due to diverse factors including empirical conditions such as ecology, the local political economy and the ability to obtain the necessary technology. Djurfeldt and Lindberg's lack of an historical time perspective on the diffusion of the green revolution and its consequences for capitalist development is surprising, given the emphasis they put on the pre-colonial and colonial history of their area.

Saith and Tankha's (1972b) study of a West Uttar Pradesh village in India is another seminal work on local development. The question they pose on agrarian change in a village is theoretically meaningful: the manner in which the differentiation of the peasantry and the agrarian transition is taking place in the village. They point to the rapid disintegration of pre-capitalist relations of production and the emergence of a new social division of labour premissed on capitalist relations: 'The emergence of capitalist relations, catalyzed by the rapid adoption of the new technology [leads] to a marked expansion of the forces of production in agriculture' (op.cit.:723).

The process is spearheaded, according to Saith and Tankha, by the rich peasant households in the village who serve as the chief carriers of the new technology. This is because they own and control sufficient quantity of land which allows them access to credit, markets and other facilities so crucial for capitalist development. And whilst pre-capitalist production relations are still found in the village, the process of differentiation represents a definite tendency for the agrarian transition to take place, a conclusion similar to that of our study.

Saith and Tankha, however, fail to contextualize the agrarian transition; that is, the national and international parameters in which the transition is taking place; in other words, whether the transition in their village is dependent on being incorporated into the national and international economy, and the consequences of this on the pace and nature of the agrarian transition. They fail to specify whether the elements of production on which the agrarian transion is based, is the product of an Indian Department 1, or of one located outside of the national economy; and if so, the effect of this on the nature and possibility of the transition itself.

The different conclusions of Saith and Tankha and Djurfeldt and Lindberg on local capitalist development are indicative: that there may be very specific local conditions that impede development, which one needs to investigate empirically. So that one must not confuse lack of development in a locality, in one particular moment in history, with the impossibilty of capitalist developent altogether; and must not conflate an early, weak or slow development with the impossibility of development in Third World countries (Frank, 1967; 1969; 1978; Amin, 1974).

### Capitalist development and the agrarian transition

As I have said in the Introduction, the agrarian transition is the result of the dominance of the capitalist mode of production (CMP) in agriculture. Under this, capital takes control of, and sets in motion, the labour process in a process of expanded reproduction; and through valorization produces increasing quantities of surplus value resulting in capital accumulation (Marx 1976:302-4). This is reflected in, *inter alia*, the development of productive forces and increased productivity of labour [1].

The labour process is constitutive of a number of elementary factors: 1) objects of work (e.g., land, forests, mines, etc.); 2) tools of work (ploughs, tractors, fertilizers, seeds); and 3) personal activity of persons, that is, work itself (production of knowledge, organization of labour) (Marx 1967: 283-92). Of these 2) and 3) are the means of production which are expended in production and 'disappear' into the product and new elements have to be brought at the completion of every production cycle. It must be noted that the labour process is not the same as production process. The distinction becomes clear when it is understood that while working time is always production time, the converse is not true. The entire time a product or an object of labour exists in the production process is not necessarily working time because of the interruptions in the labour process conditioned by the nature of the product or its production. To give an example: in the raising of timber, once planting and the preliminary work connected with this is completed, the seed may need one hundred years to be transformed into a finished product; during this period, only a relatively insignificant intervention of labour is needed.

A characteristic of the CMP is that it revolutionizes the labour process (ibid.:1021), characterized by qualitative changes in the technical conditions of labour (ibid.:432); that is, by greater application of science and technology, resulting in greater productivity of labour which is signalled by relative, rather than absolute, surplus value appropriation (ibid.:432).

In this situation there is a shortening of the socially necessary labour time required to produce the workers subsistence, so that greater time is devoted to the unpaid part of labour, hence there is greater production and appropriation of surplus value. That is, the exchange of objectified labour (wages, subsistence) for living labour (labour power), takes place (ibid.:1009); without this process the total capital could not valorize itself and so the formation of capital and and the transformation of elements of production into capital could not take place (ibid.:1017).

The labour process which in the abstract, or in its simple elements, is purposive activity aimed at producing mainly the means of subsistence or use-values (ibid.:283,290); under the CMP this process unites the labour process and the process of valorization, the aim of which is the production of exchange-values or commodities (ibid.:304,980).

Of course, this surplus can be, and is, put to different uses in different historical circumstances, but under the CMP it is aimed at producing surplus value and occurs under two conditions: first, the labourer works under the control of the capitalist, to whom his labour belongs; second, the product is the property of the capitalist.

Under capitalist production, capital is both the precondition and the end result of the labour process: the produced means of production such as raw materials and technology, are transformed into capital and enter into the production process as capital. What enters into this process as means of productiion or capital are exchange values or commodities of a previous labour process; which itself is the object of a valorization and production process carried out before, and so on.

This is well illustrated by fertilizer use in agriculture: as capital it is a precondition for the process of, and as a means of, production; but it is also the product of a previous labour process which has produced the fertilizer.

Thus, under capitalist production these are the preconditions and the results of the labour process, and are predicated upon the relative independence but interconnectedness of different branches of industry and agriculture, specializations within industries and in the social division of labour; each of these branches and sectors producing and selling to each other; the existence, that is, of the linkages or upstream and downstream sectors of the economy.

As I indicated in the Introduction, this relationship between different branches of agriculture and industry in Pakištan is weak to the point of being absent in an effective sense; and therefore the cycle of expanded reproduction is completed through the international economy as we shall see in a later section of this chapter.

*The developed capitalist mode of production*

In the fully developed CMP the labour process is under the real subsumption to capital and large scale production ensues where 'capital sums of a certain magnitude have directly taken control over production,'(Marx,1976:1025). Here production is conducted on the basis of a socialized labour process: each individual capitalist brings together a comparatively large number of workers who are separated from their means of production and whose labour is employed in production which is conducted on an extended scale and yields relatively large quantities of products in the form of exchange values or commodities.

In this socialized production the simultaneous employment of a relatively large number of workers and common use of the instruments of production reduces the input of constant (or fixed) capital. Benefits from economies of scale ensue and bring about a lowering in the value of labour power, and hence enabling an increase in relative surplus value. That is, an increase in production based on reorganization of the labour process and its technical conditions of production, as opposed to the production of absolute surplus value which depends on extending working-time (ibid.: 645).

This large-scale production, it must be noted, is not the same as being large in mere quantitative terms: it is a consequence of the centralization and concentration of the means of production. Centralization, where existing but scattered means of production (e.g., scattered units of land) are brought together or consolidated for extensive cultivation; and concentration, where the scale of production is increased by greater inputs of capital and changes in the labour process.

*Capitalist production in agriculture*

A specifically capitalist production in agriculture takes place when it is:

> carried on by capitalists who differ from other capitalists primarily in the manner in which their capital, and wage-labour set in motion by this capital are invested...the farmer produces wheat, etc., in much the same way as the manufacturer produces a yarn or machines...[and] who carries on agriculture for the sake of profit (Marx,1974:614-5).

One of the major preconditions (and results) of the CMP is the conscious scientific application of agronomy which further develops the productive forces (ibid.: 617; Marx,1976:1024). Moreover, other things being equal, application of machinery in agriculture can reduce, relatively, the costs of cultivation; the productivity of the soil can rise thereby cheapening the price of crops.

In agriculture ecological factors condition the process of production in ways that do not affect manufacture. These can be categorized into (1) the natural factor in the means of production (e.g., the fertility of the soil); and (2) the natural instruments or productive forces such as water availability. But these are not static and do change or can be changed, over time, with human effort; as for example in the reclamation of land damaged by water-logging and salinity in areas where our empirical research was carried out.

There are other features of capitalist production which I need only mention briefly: the whole cycle of production, circulation, exchange and distribution of commodities which in turn presuppose a number of conditions: absolute private property in land; division of labour; exchange of commodities; separation of labour, capital and land; market competition (Marx, 1973:259,266-7,295-310,459-644,471-5), and so on; a detailed discussion of which is not of direct relevance.

The process I have described is one that has come under complete dominance of a fully developed CMP, where the agrarian transition is complete. This in itself, however, is the outcome of a long-drawn historical process which in England began in the fifteenth and sixteenth century and was completed in the nineteenth century or even later (Johnson 1979).

Capitalist development is characterized by a number of phases: the primitive accumulation of capital, the early stage where labour is under formal subsumption to capital, and the fully developed stage that I have described. The first two phases characterize the transitional period where the agrarian transition is taking place but the process is not complete, a situation such as one finds in Mallian as well as in Sahiwal and Sargodha.

The process of primitive accumulation of capital precedes capitalist production proper and it is its point of departure which creates the capital-relation (Marx, 1976:873-4). Under this relation the 'free' (because they are separated from their means of production and subsistence) workers' labour power is converted into capital to create more capital. It is a process that brings about two transformations: one, where the workers' elements of subsistence and production are turned into capital; and two, where the immediate producers are turned into wage-labourers (ibid.:874).

Thus the 'so-called primitive accumulation, therefore is nothing other than the historical process of divorcing the producer from the means of production' (ibid.:874-5). Note that this is the starting point of capitalist production and not its end result; a view held by a number of writers who assume that the existence of wage-labour is a sufficient condition for the existence of the CMP (Laclau, 1977:24; Chattopadhyay, 1972a, 1972b).

To put it another way: Marx's analysis of primitive accumulation is premissed on indicating the socio-economic conditions which need to be realized before the CMP can dominate. These are: the separation of the immediate producers from their principal instruments and materials of production; the transformation of these immediate producers into wage-labourers; and the transformation of their instruments and materials of production into capital. Unless these conditions are met masses of potential exchange values are kept out of the domination of capital (e.g., by self-sufficient small producers), and the creation of surplus value and capital accumulation is impeded.

The reasons for the persistence of these relatively self-sufficient petty producers can and do differ for all sorts of reasons, including local empirical factors such as ecological conditions; as well as the lack of, or low development of industry, which in turn may be a consequence of national development policies. The petty producers may also exist because of the conditions under which integration of the national into the international economy took place, and so on; conditions which are similar to those one finds with regard to Pakistan, as we shall see.

It should be noted that both Marx (1974:614), and Lenin's (1960:176-7,191-242) analyses of primitive accumulation presuppose the relative independence and historical variety of the ways in which capitalism develops. As for example, through the transformation of feudal landlords into capitalists (the 'junker' road) or the transformation of well-to-do peasants into capitalists, or a combination of both, as we find in Mallian and in Sahiwal and Sargodha.

*Pre-capitalist agriculture*

This process of primitive accumulation emerges, of course, out of pre-capitalist structures which are not homogeneous and can consist of different social formations (tribal, lineage-based, feudalistic). Pre-capitalist agriculture is carried generally on a small scale where the object of the labour process is to produce for subsistence and localized exchange, though regional specialization, long distance trade and petty-commodity production existed under this economy (Marx, 1976:875; 1974:614-17).

In pre-capitalist agriculture there is unity of agriculture and handicraft industry, as under *sep*, and the immediate producers are not separated from their means of production; though a form of wage-labour is known to have existed in feudalistic modes (as in traditional Mallian), but this was not a generalized phenomena.

In contrast to expanded reproduction under the CMP, pre-capitalist agriculture is characterized by simple reproduction: there is repetition of production on the previous scale and on the previous technical and scientific basis. Though here too, the quantum of technological and economic change fluctuates, but within the parameters circumscribed by pre-capitalist social formations.

*Differentiation of the peasantry and the home market*

The related processes of peasant differentiation and the creation of the home market are an important aspect of capitalist development. Therefore a theoretical understanding of these processes is essential to analyze peasant differentiation and development of the home market in Mallian and to relate these to the national and international economy.

Peasant differentiation refers to the process of the disintegration of independent peasant proprietorship as a result of the penetration and accumulation of capital. This is reflected in, on the one hand, an emerging strata of agrarian capitalists, and on the other, a strata of poor and virtually landless peasant smallholders who are transformed into agricultural labourers by being dispossessd of their means of subsistence:

> The differentiation of the peasantry creates a home market for capitalism. In the bottom group, the formation of a market takes place on account of articles of consumption (the market of personal consumption). The rural proletarian, by comparison with the middle peasantry, consumes less, and moreover consumes food of worse quality...but buys more. The formation and development of a peasant bourgeoisie creates a home market in two-fold fashion: firstly and mainly on account of means of production (the market of productive consumption), since the well-to-do peasant strives to convert into capital those means of production he 'gathers' from both landlords 'in straitend circumstances' and peasants in the grip of ruin. Secondly, a market is also created here on account of personal consumption, due to the expansion of the requirements of the more affluent peasants (Lenin,1960:181).

As we shall see in Mallian, this process occurs simultaneously with the emergence of a new social division of labour, the transition from simple commodity to expanded capitalist production. This process indicates a situation where the process of production is increasingly dominated by capital; now gradualy and slowly, at other times relatively quickly, depending on both endogamous and exogenous factors. Further, this process of primitive accumulation and the higher forms of capitalist development which emerge out of it are concurrent and successive processes and not neatly evolutionary ones. These processes are concurrent, because, looked at synchronically, they share the same historical time and 'co-exist' in our understanding of the term; they are successive in the sense that the predominant tendency is represented by the expanded reproduction (self-valorizing capitalist 'part') which supplants and supercedes the simple reproduction of the non-capitalist 'part.'

It follows that the self-sufficient strata of the peasantry (generally the 'middle peasant') may resist penetration of capital for longer than other strata that participate more in the market, a situation that one finds in Mallian.

*The early phase of capitalist development*

Capitalist agrarian production is a process that emerges out of historicaly given pre-capitalist social formations, consequently the agrarian transition can take a long time: 'the appearance of capital as an independent and leading force in agriculture does not take place all at once and generally, but gradually and in particular lines of production' (Marx, 1974:801).

Capital takes control of production not only in particular lines of production and particular types of cash crops such as cotton and sugar-cane, which are more amenable to commercial production; but also in particular regions because they have or lack the climatic and ecological conditions for specific type of agriculture: as for example the production of cotton, which requires a relatively high humidity count; or wheat, which needs a drier and cooler climate; or the production of rice, which requires higher temperatures and abundant water and which is relatively resistant to damage by salinity.

In the early phase of capitalist development the labour process is formally subsumed under capital, because it merely takes control over the labour process from a previous mode of production without transforming it. Even under formal subsumption, however, a more intensive labour process ensues, because it is controlled by the capitalist (Marx, 1976:1026). Under real subsumption to capital, the labour process undergoes qualitative change characterized by an increase in productive capacity (ibid.:1021).

The role of merchant capital is important for some categories of producers in Mallian, though its role in development and transformation of traditional economies is often retarding. Under this system the merchant advances money capital or elements of production to producers and collects the objects of their labour without supervising or intervening in the labour process.

That merchant or usurer capital does not necessarily lead to the development of the CMP has been theorized by Marx, though a tendency to wear away pre-capitalist modes is possible (Marx, 1974: 332-4; 1976: 1023). On the contrary, merchant capital can, under conditions where it dominates the source of credit in the countryside, retard the differentiation of the peasantry through the reproduction of the smallholder, which prevents productive capital from taking control of its production; and can thus impede capitalist development.

*The primacy of production*

The sphere of production has a centrality in our study of local development. Not that other spheres are unimportant; they are important including that for the 'realization' of surplus value, and I shall analyze this process in chapter 8, in relation to the introduction of systematic money-wages in the local economy. Nevertheless, the sphere of production is the primary or determining sphere and the other spheres are determined:

> Production is the real point of departure and hence also the predominant moment. Consumption as urgency,as need, is itself an intrinsic moment of productive activity. But the latter is the point of departure for realization and hence also its predominant moment (Marx: 1973: 94).

Also:

> The conclusion we reach is not that production distribution, and exchange and consumption are identical, but they all form the members of a totality, distinctions within a unity. Production dominates not only over itself, in the antithetical definition of production, but over the other elements as well. The process always returns to begin anew (ibid.:99).

Specifically, Marx divides all productive activity of an economy into departments of production which can be divided into three groups (1961/2,vol.2;part 3). Department 1 produces means of production: capital goods, machinery, chemicals, and so on. These constitute the elements of constant capital [2].

Department 2 produces wage-goods: all those consumption items and services, from food to holidays, which constitute the real wages of the workforce of any society at a point in time. These are the elements of variable capital. Department 3 produces what Marx called luxuries: goods and services which do not fit neatly into Department 2, of the above categories.

Production in Departments 1 and 2 is economically productive and performs an accumulation function. Both produce outputs which enter as inputs into further circuits of production and thus provide the material basis for future reproduction and growth in the economy. In Department 1, these are in the form of means of production; in Department 2, in the form of a reproduced worker able to perform labour.

Of course within Department 1, various branches of industry produce elements of production for other branches; in current usage, each branch or section of Department 1 performs upstream and downstream functions for each other, thereby integrating a national economy in a circuit of expanded reproduction.

In fact Department 1 production, which includes the machine tools (or machine building) industries (Dobb,196o); these are also referred to as the 'key industries'(Hirschman,1966), and are crucial to the process of development and the creation of an integrated national economy. In particular these industries perform two functions simultaneously: On the one hand these constitute the principal component of capital formation; on the other, as a final goods manufacturing industry, their development creates a demand pressure on input industries, thus generating the repercussion or integrative effects for many primary, or intermediate industries, the so-called forward and backward linkages. The backward linkages involve the input provision or derived demand, and the forward linkage has the output utilization effect.

The machine tools industry is characterized by strong backward linkages, stemming from the fact that it has a high ratio of purchased inputs to the value of its total production; these inputs include iron and steel, non-ferrous metals, rubber, glass and plastics; its expansion can stimulate the creation of new industries such as chemical fertilizers and electical equipment, petroleum, and so on.

In the absence of a capital goods and a machine tools sector, developing countries have to import these items, which structures the process of dependent development which I shall describe below.

This is the situation with regard to Pakistan, where the capital goods and machine tools sector is weak, and the national economy is thus not integrated; consequently capital equipment and production technology has to be imported; or production is based on traditional technology which is relatively inefficient; or on indigenous modern industry which is too weak and small to have a significant impact on the national economy. Such conditions contribute to a low rate of capital formation, and subordinates the national economy to the developed countries, who produce the capital goods on which national production is based.

## Capital goods technology and dependent development

In a situation where the crucial Department 1 industries are lacking or weakly developed, developing countries rely on outside sources for vital production equipment. This both absorbs surplus from the developing countries, and relocates the accumulation process in the technology and capital goods producing countries:

> [In] spite of internal economic development, countries tied to international capitalism... remain economically dependent, insofar as the production of the means of production (technology) are concentrated in advanced capitalist countries ... [The] scheme of capital reproduction - the strategic part of the reproductive scheme - is virtually non- existent in the dependent economies.Thus, from a broad perspective, the

> realization of capital accumulation *demands* a productive complementarity which does not exist within the country...Within the dependent economies capital returns to the metropole in order to complete the cycle of capitalist reproduction. That is the reason why 'technology' is so important. Its 'material'aspect is less impressive than its significance as a form of maintenance of control and as a necessary step in the process of capital accumulation ... the global process of capitalist development determines an interconnectedness between the sector of production of consumption goods and the capital goods sector, reproducing in this way the links of dependency (Cardoso,1972:90/91).

As I have indicated earlier, the heavy dependence on imported technology does not mean that no capital accumulation takes place under dependent development; rather, this form of development in developing countries establishes external links which create disjunctures between branches of the national economy such as industry and agriculture, and slows the accumulation process. In this sense, the concept of dependent development is different from that of classic dependence, which results in the underdevelopment of the Third World (Frank, op.cit).

The developing countries reliance on the developed countries for technology is indicated by the fact in the 1970s, 89 percent of developing countries imports of machinery and transport equipment come from developed countries, 6 percent from centrally planned economies, and 5 percent from other developing countries (Stewart, 1978: 122).

This dependence on external sources for technology is further illuminated with reference to South Korea, which is supposed to have transcended the dependency syndrome: in the 1980s it exported 4 percent of its machine tools, but it still had to import 65 percent of its domestic needs (Lipietz, 1984). Similar arguments would apply with regard to the capital goods sector in India and Brazil, which is fairly developed in both countries. In fact, as we shall see in the next chapter much of the capital goods production in the developing countries is by MNCs, or it is domestically produced with imported technology.

However, the capacity to produce capital goods is not a good indicator of technological capability *per se*; for example, the capacity to produce iron and steel and chemicals, cannot be translated into the capacity to produce machine tools, for example the production of tractors and other machinery (Stewart, 1978: 122). Thus in order to ascertain the capacity of an economy to produce one needs to look at both the capital goods producing capacity and the capability to produce machine tools and other technology.

It should be noted that developed countries are importers of technology too, but this is matched by equivalent exports to other developed countries, so that there is a two-way flow of technology; in contrast, developing countries are heavy net importers of technology - one way relationship countries - and become technologicallly dependent on the developed countries (Stewart, 1978:118).

I am not suggesting that the import of technology (or engagement with the international economy) in itself structures a dependent form of development; rather, it is the conditions and particular moments in developing countries' insertion into the international economy, and adoption of imported technology, which inhibits the integration of the national economy, and retards capital formation, as I indicated in the Introduction and which I shall discuss further in later chapters.

*The internationalization of capital and the international economy*

The process of dependent development that I have described can only be understood within the context of the concentration and internationalization of capital at the global level; put another way, dependent development is both a cause and consequence of the process of internationalization, which is characterized by two facets. First, centralization and concentration of capital, and secondly, an increasing, though uneven penetration of capital into various spheres of the global economy.

There are three aspects to this process of internationalization of the global economy. At an abstract level this refers to the increasing domination of the world economy by different circuits of capital: by productive capital, which has brought about a global redistribution and relocation of manufacturing, in addition to its increasing concentration and centralization, and is embodied in the operations of the MNCs; the circuit of money capital, which is characterized by growth and mobility of international financial/credit markets provided by the transnational banks; and the circuit of commodity capital reflected in a massive increase in international trade (Palloix, 1978; Aglietta, 1982; Andreff, 1984) [2].

Since the insitutional basis of these circuits of capital are located in the developed countries, the international economy is identified with, though not identical to, the developed capitalist countries.

Of particular interest to this study is that aspect of the internationalization of capital which increasingly incorporates hitherto unincorporated or partially incorporated segments of the national and local economy. Such as, for example, incorporation of Pakistan's agriculture into the international economy, as a result of increasing consumption of mechanical and biochemical inputs which are direct or indirect products of MNCs.

Of course, this incorporation has been uneven and has occured at different times: South-east Asia, Mexico, Brazil and the oil-producing countries of the Middle East have been incorporated more into the international economy than, say, some African countries south of the Sahara [2]. Generally, the greater the incorporation of a developing country into the international economy, the greater its indebtedness and dependence [3].

## Changes in the international economy

It is claimed that industrial development in the Third World, especially in the so-called Newly Industrializing Countries (NICs) such as South Korea, Taiwan, Hong Kong, Mexico and Brazil, has rendered obsolete the idea that the international economy retards, or creates a dependent form of Third

World development. On the contrary, it is claimed that integration into the international economy facilitates development and that distortions in the developing countries development is due to internal factors. Thus:

> The Asian NICs are delivering a second shock to Marxism. Not only does it remain clear that contrary to what Marx claimed, advanced capitalism can avoid disintegration, it has also been demonstrated that, contrary to the neo-Marxist's claim, new comers can rise by means of capitalism ...[and it follows that] Radical critiques employing concepts like 'periphery','dependency','exploitation' and 'delinking' have lost much of their previous attraction. The examples of the Pacific countries have demonstrated their irrelevance as analytical tools. Korea, Taiwan, Singapore and in particular Hong Kong - a colony - have played havoc with neo-Marxist views of the world; the subdued practioners of these views capture few headlines nowadays (Linder,1986:54).

With the above views in mind, in this section I shall analyze changes in the international economy as well as South Korean development as this supposedly proves that with the right policies and institutional structures, Third World countries can break out of dependent forms of development.

Whilst, undoubtedly, there have been important changes in the international economy, as well as considerable development in some Third World countries, this has not fundamentally altered the basic structure of the international economy. his restricts Third World development; and therefore an unplanned and unselective integration into the international economy generates a dependent form of development.

As I shall indicate below, South Korea's considerable development is not an exception to this general assertion about the role of the international economy. South Korea's development can be attributed to historical factors, in particular the significant investment under Japanese colonial rule, and aid from the United States, which was very similar to Marshall Aid given for post World War Two European recovery; or to put it another way, aid to Korea from the US has been very different from that given to other developing countries, with the consequence that Korea's subsequent relationship to the international economy has been different from other developing countries too.

Moreover, a significant part of what is considered to constitute and reflect Korean development, manufactured exports, including exports of capital goods and technology, is in fact produced by MNCs of developed countries, as I indicate below. In this sense, neither Korean development, nor development of any other developing country, development reflects a radical transformation the global economy, to the extent that it no longer restricts national development in the Third World. This is not to imply that the international economy affects all Third World economies in an identical fashion, or that the Third World is an homogeneous entity with a unanimity of structures and interests (Harris, 1986).

Developing countries' share of world manufacturing value added increased from 4.5 percent in 1938, to 8.1 percent in 1963, and 11 percent in 1982 (Mirza, 1986:195). According to one writer, 'by 1975 the "Third World" was responsible for about one-fifth of all the manufactured imports of the advanced capitalist countries, and in certain sectors the proportion was much higher'(Frieden, 1987: 153). Inspite of this increase in manufacturing output, however, imports of manufactures from the developing countries accounted for less than 2 percent of manufactured goods in the developed capitalist countries (UNCTAD, 1981). However, these aggregate figures hide the large differences in manufacturing output in different developing countries; with the highest rates of manufacturing output being concentrated in the NICs.

A closer look at the nature of manufacturing output in the developing countries reveals some interesting facts: a large part of many developing countries manufacturing output in fact is produced by foreign firms; that is, it is a result of foreign direct investment (FDI) by MNCs. Also, a significant portion of what comprises local 'manufacturing' is either assembly of machinery and transport equipment from kits imported from the developed countries, or local production with a high import and a low domestic content, with a value-added that varies between countries, the average being that in Mexico of between 29 to 36 percent (Jenkins, 1986:136).

This is clearly illustrated by the import into US under US tariff items 806/807, of US components sent abroad for assembly or processing. From 1966 to 1983, 806/807 imports totalled $22 billion; and grew from 4 percent of the import bill in 1966 to 10 percent in 1988. Mexico's share of 806/807 imports to the US have risen dramatically, from 8.2 percent in 1969 to 17 percent in 1983 (Muroyama and Guyford, 1988:88).

In Mexico, in 1970/4, foreign firms share of manufacturing output was 35 percent of the total output, and 50 percent of exports. Comparable figures for other countries for roughly the same period are: 30 percent and 92 percent for Singapore; Malaysia, 50 percent and 70 percent; and for Argentina, 13 and 42 percent (Jenkins, 1984:40).

Foreign control of developing countries' manufacturing output is further shown by the fact that in Mexico, foreign firms' (MNCs) share of output of the four largest firms in each industry accounted for almost 80 percent of the total output (ibid.).

Even when the ownership of manufacturing industry in the developing countries is largely domestic the producer goods of Department 1 are largely imported, so the international circuit of expanded reproduction which draws surplus into the developed economies is not circumvented, resulting in a low rate of capital accumulation, and disjuncture in the national economy. For example, as I shall indicate in the next chapter, by 1979 about 30 percent of capital goods exports from the countries of the Organization for Economic Cooperation and Development (OECD) were destined for the developing countries (OECD, 1979).

## *Korean development*

As I have mentioned earlier Korean development is considered to be the most profound among the NICs, both in terms of growth (growth rate of 7.7 percent between 1973-83) and structural transformation of the economy. According to one writer East Asian capitalism 'would produce results that make its nineteenth century performance look like that of a donkey'(Little, 1982). This considerable development, it is claimed, is due in large part to the development policies pursued by the Korean state, which included export-incentives, high rates of investment and savings, and so on (Linder 1986). The implication of this is that a large part of developing countries' problems are of their own making; they are a result of bad policies, and unproductive use of resources.

However, development policies are not adopted in a vacuum; there are national, global and institutional constraints on policies that are feasible or otherwise, for particular countries to follow. One needs to analyze Korean development within the historical context in which this has occured, as I explain below, but before this I need to outline the structure of the Korean economy in relation to the international economy.

A notable feature of Korean development is the underestimation of foreign participation in its economy. It imports 65 percent of its machine tools to meet domestic demand (Lipietz, 1984:103). Capital goods imports from the US and Japan were 14 to 20 times as much as all other forms of technology imported. On the other hand, 64 percent of South Korea's general machinery and 67 percent of its electrical machinery exports to US *came from* American MNCs in Korea (Muroyama and Guyford, 1988: 123). In 1980 exports of electronics products and components by foreign subsidiaries exceeded $1 billion and accounted for over half of the country's exports in this industry (UN/ESCAP/UNCTG 1984:54).

In the case of domestic firms' manufactures, local technology was mainly employed in the labour-intensive components of the final products. Moreover, most high-value inputs were imported to the extent that in the 1970s the domestic value-added was generally 15 percent and 20 percent of the final value of the product; in the case of electronics, this could be as low as 13 percent (Chung, 1975:21).

Korea's development, which is reflected in its export performance, has to be seen historically, in relation to the special position it occupied in US imports policy: in 1970 US imports from Korea were covered by special protection and equalled 468 billion or 21 percent of total imports (Muroyama and Guyford, 1988:123).

However, it is the historical context and nature of the relationship between the Korean economy and that of the US which is important in shaping Korean development; in particular the type of aid given to Korea, which has been along the lines of Marshall Aid to Europe, as I indicate below.

Korean development has been characterized by four phases: development under Japanese colonial rule from the early part of this century to the 1920s and 1930s; aid from the US in the 1950s and 1960s; foreign direct investments from the mid-1960s, and increasing role of the MNCs in the 1970s onwards. What follows is a brief sketch account of factors in Korean development to illustrate the qualitatively different trajectory of Korea's relationship to the international market and the developed countries, as compared to other developing countries.

For whilst most developing countries experienced distortion of their economies and even stagnation, as a result of integration into the international economy, in Korea the effect has been markedly different.

Under Japanese colonial rule manufacturing output increased from 7 percent of total commodity production in 1910/12, to 29 percent in 1939/40. Capital goods as a percentage of all manufactured goods rose from 4 percent in the early 1920s to 16 percent in the late 1930s (Burch, 1987:26). This expansive industrial capacity was inherited by the Koreans when the Japanese left; and its further utilization was made possible by subsequent relationship with the US.

In the agriculture sector, the Japanese set up chemical fertilizer plants in Korea, improved irrigation and introduced high yielding crops; in fact chemical fertilizers and high yielding seeds were in use much earlier than most currently developing countries.

Foreign assistance from the US to Korea during 1954-75 has largely been in the form of grants; which in effect amounted to a free gift. For example, during this period, out of a total of $23 billion given in assistance by the US, $16 billion were grants and $7.8 billion loans (Cathie,1989:174). This ratio of loans to grants is very different from that in Pakistan. Here grants constituted 63 percent of US aid in the First Plan; 36 percent in the Second Plan, and in 1978,0.3 percent (Government of Pakistan, 1981, *Economic Survey*). In the 1950s, US aid constituted about 20 percent of Korea's GNP, a figure far higher than in Pakistan and other developing countries.

However, it is the provision by the US of wage and producer goods as part of 'food aid' under PL480, that constitutes one of the most important contributions to Korean development. The US provided cotton and food at highly subsidized rates to Korea; cotton was the crucial raw material for the Korean textile industry which was the leading edge of Korean industrialization process in the 1960s and 1970s, and food as wage good kept wages low. In the absence of this form of aid, Korea would have had to divert valuable resources to produce more food domestically, and would have had to purchase cotton on the world market at commercial prices, since this crop is not grown in Korea.

The significance of US aid in Korean industrialization is shown by the fact that between 1945 and 1975, 40 percent of this aid was in foodstuff and raw materials, but also included machinery and manufacturing equipment, chemicals, dyes, and so forth, amounting to about $6 billion (ibid.; 104).

In this brief sketch of Korean development, I have attempted to show that the historical and structural background to Korea's development process has been different from that of most other developing countries. The basis for this development was laid under Japanese colonial rule. It was later a recipient of extensive aid from the US as one of the front line states in the cold war against communism. Since the 1970s Korean development has been impressive, but, as I have shown a significant part of manufacturing output for exports is either by MNCs and foreign firms, or manufactured with imported technology.

An important fact that emerges from this brief outline is the role of US food aid in Korea's development. This supports an important element in the theoretical framework of this study; the crucial contribution that agricultural surplus must make to Third World development.

This is not to deny the independent aspect of Korean development (insofar as one can extricate the national from the international) but this has not been as profound as made out to be, nor does it render obsolete theories of dependent capitalist development.

In this chapter I have outlined some of the basic theoretical categories that underlie this study: these have been appropriate to the three different levels and objects of our analysis: local capitalist development and the agrarian transition, the concept of dependent development of the national economy; and the international economy, which mediates the process of dependent development.

This process is concretized and reflected in the heavy reliance of developing countries on capital goods and technology manufactured by MNCs of the developed countries; though, as we have seen, the manufacturing activity may be located in the developing countries. The MNCs in turn reflect a process of concentration and centralization of capital at a global level, and as we shall see in the next chapter, increasingly control elements of production including raw materials and technology, on which Pakistan's and other Third World countries development strategy is based. As I have indicated in the Introduction and in a section in this chapter, this process creates a disjuncture in the the agricultural and industrial sectors of the national economy, which are integrated into, and dependent upon the international, rather than the national, economy. Because of this, a significant part of the valorization process takes place in the developed countries where Department I goods are produced by the MNCs.

## Notes

1. Marx defined surplus as the difference between current output and necessary product, the latter being the amount required for reproduction of labour power, but keeping in view the existing social norms. Paul Baran (1967:42) defined actual surplus as the difference between actual and current output and actual and current consumption. In this study Marx's definition is used.

2. There is a close relationship between capital goods and machine-building or machine tools industry; whilst the latter presupposes the former; the existence of capital goods does not automatically imply the existenc of a machine building industry. The major capital goods industries are iron and steel, coal and petroleum. These form the basis of the machine building and machine tools industries whose major groups comprise: *Prime movers*: hydraulic turbines, steam turbines, internal combustion engines; *machine tools and tools:* metal-cutting machine tools, measuring and cutting tools, emery wheels; *heavy-duty machinery; construction and road building*

*machinery; agricultural machinery; locomotives and vehicles; transport equipment; electrical machinery; electronics and telecommunication equipment; light industrial equipment; general machinery and tool; consumer appliances* (UNCTAD, 1964, *Some Problems of World Trade in Machinery and Equipment*, Geneva).

# 3 The international economy and national development

In discussing the main theoretical concepts of the process of capital accumulation and development, I have indicated that crucial to the whole process was the role of capital goods and technology; that is, the production of Department I goods in our theoretical scheme. It was also suggested that the absence (or weak) capital goods and technology producing capacity of developing countries made them dependent on the developed countries for these goods, which prevented a higher rate of capital accumulation and the formation of an integrated self-reliant national economy.

In this chapter I shall concretize this dependent relationship by focussing on the structure of the contemporary international economy, and in particular on the operation of the main producers of capital equipment and intermediate goods for agriculture, the multinational corporations of the developed countries. It is through the MNCs that international economic relations are mediated, as we shall see. The operation of the MNCs, however, needs to be contextualized by analyzing the evolution of the international economy of recent times and the role of the MNCs within this.

*Restructuring of the international economy: a brief outline*

As I indicated in chapter 2, the contention that the world economy has been radically transformed by the economic development of some Third World countries is not borne out by facts. In fact the trends in global economic exchange shows that developing countries share in this is relatively minor. The structure of the international economy, especially since the 1970s (I concentrate on the 1970s since this is considered to be the pivotal period which signalled the transformation of the global economy) have displayed the following characteristics: a) an increase in the imports of capital goods to the developing countries and a corresponding decline in their raw material exports; b) an increase in global trade especially between the developed countries.

The average annual increase of exports from the developed countries was 7.5 percent between 1961 and 1972, while it was 12.5 percent for technology and machine equipment, 10.4 percent for other manufactured goods, and 12.5 percent for chemicals. During approximately the same period, the trade in industrial raw materials, foodstuffs and fuel fell from 40 to 35 percent (UN, Monthly Bulletin of Statistics). This rise in the share of capital goods and a corresponding decline in the significance of raw materials in international trade is characteristic of the way the international economy has developed since the 1970s.

Underlying this trend is the rapid integration and cooperation among the developed countries, especially in the two-way flows of machinery and other capital equipment, chemicals and consumer goods. Also, the share of the developed countries in global exports has grown appreciably: from 70 percent in 1960 to 75 percent in 1965, and 80 percent in 1970. By contrast, during the same period the developing countries' share of exports has dropped to 20 percent, and the trend has continued into the 1980s.

Similar trends are reflected in the international distribution of the production of capital goods. In 1970, world production of the engineering and electrical industries was distributed as follows: 3.1 percent of these goods were produced in the developing countries, of which a small number of countries like India, China, Brazil, Korea and Taiwan, produced about 90 percent; a little over 60 percent by the OECD and 36 percent by the Eastern Bloc. In 1976 the distribution by countries of world exports of machinery and capital equipment was even more concentrated: 3.4 percent was exported by the developing countries, 9.7 by the Eastern Bloc, and almost 87 percent by the OECD (UN, Handbook for International Trade and Development Statistics, 1979).

Imports by the developing countries of machinery and transport equipment shows the magnitude of of the developing countries dependence on the developed countries. In 1976 for example, a little over 90 percent of the imports of these capital goods came from the OECD countries and only about 5 percent from the developing countries (ibid). Thus, far from radically transforming the international economy, development of the Third World has deepened their dependence on the international economy, though the extent of this differs significantly between countries.

**International agencies and national development**

The process of internationalization of the global international economy is greatly supported by international agencies other than purely economic ones like the MNCs. For example, international agencies such as the World Bank, Food and Agriculture Organization, United Nations Industrial Development Organization; and by the nationally based world-wide 'advisory' organizations such as the Harvard Institute for International Development. These have an enormous influence on the formulation of Third World countries economic and development policies, as for example the World Bank's provision of aid to developing countries in the 1980s, which was conditional on these countries privatizing their economies. Whilst the economic policies of these agencies and those of the developed countries are not identical they are closely similar, for example:

> The export promotion policies of the industrialized countries and of development funding agencies encourage mechanized farming. The World Bank is one of the development organizations that typically has supported agricultural projects with high mechanization requirements...[Joint] projects between state planners and international funding agencies often select the most expensive alternatives in terms of import costs and domestic subsidies. Tractor imports into Pakistan from the United States were promoted by Massey-ferguson, AID [Agency for International Development],the World Bank and the Harvard Institute for International Development (HIID) which found both radical and conservative regimes in Islamabad receptive to mechanized farming. The fruits of the advisors influence were a doubling of Pakistan's tractor imports between 1968 and 1972. [Advisors] from industrialized countries foster farm mechanization in Third World countries in two ways:by setting the agenda for agricultural policy (the HIID economists in Pakistan functioned as a "shadow" planning commission) and by providing financial support for investments in farm machinery...Mechanized farming is well established in all [developing] countries with the support of influential government agencies and of private and public international organizations (Schulz, 1982:34/36).

Of course, there are other alternative policies and paradigms of development, that advocate the use of small-scale, indigenous, or appropriate or intermediate technology. But these are not very influential at the level of national policy making, and offer no competition to the prevailing paradigms institutionalizeded by the powerful international agencies and commercial interests.

### The multinational corporations in the international economy

The MNCs are both an extension and a segment of the developed countries economy, which has become increasingly internationalized. They are, as I indicated in chapter 2, an aspect of this internationalization of capital which connects the economies of different countries. Therefore the MNCs penetration into developing countries economies is in effect the extension of developed countries' economies' further expansion into the economies of the developing countries, as we shall see. Whilst there are many aspects to the operation of the MNCs, I have restricted my analysis to the question of linkage or incorporation of the national and local economy into the global economy and the dependent development that this relationship engenders.

In the rest of the chapter I shall describe how the relationship of dependent development is reinforced by the operation of the MNCs, because the technology transferred to the developing countries, and the economic structures into which this enters, does not create the linkage effects with other sectors of the national economy, which remain outwardly linked to, and dependent upon, the international economy in general and the MNCs, who mediate this relationship, in particular.

For our purpose the relevant areas in which MNCs operate are in the production of capital goods and technology on which import-substitution and export-oriented industrialization of the developing countries depends. And similarly for agricultural development, the MNCs are the main producers of tractors, fertilizers, irrigation technology and seeds. That is, the use of capital equipment and intermediate goods on which the developing countries strategy of development is based.

I shall analyze each of these elements of production below, but first I need to discuss some aspects of the structure and process of the MNCs and their place in the international economy, of which they are an important constituent part. The MNCs level of operations in the global and national economy signifies the extent of internationalization of the global economy, as well as the extent of centralization and concentration of capital at the global level; their crucial role in the international economy is reflected in the fact that they concretize the expanded reproduction of capital, as suppliers of Department 1 goods.

The increased significance of MNCs activity in the world economy over the past two decades can be seen in the volume of payments for technology and technical services associated with this technology. In 1965, the receipt from sale of technology of the major developed capitalist economies of USA, UK, France, West Germany and Japan were $1.93 billion; by the early 1980s these had increased to $12 billion (US Department of Commerce, 1981; UN, 1981a) [1].

During the 1970s and 1980s the share of payments from developing countries in the total technology receipts of the major patent owning countries increased appreciably; for the USA the share of developing countries in technology payments rose from 21.2 percent in 1970 to 26.9 percent in 1983; for the UK this share increased from 21.5 percent in 1970 to 28.8 percent in 1978. For the same period for France, the share increased from 13.4 percent to 24.3 percent (OECD, 1979, 1985).

However, global distribution of patent rights are extremely uneven: in 1975, 94 percent of the worlds patent rights were owned by legal entities in the developed countries; whilst only 6 percent patent rights were registered in the developing countries. About 85 percent of these, however, were actually owned by the MNCs. So in effect, only about one percent of patent rights were owned by the developing countries (UNCTAD, 1975).

Similar concentration of MNC activity is observed in R&D: a world survey indicates that developed countries account for 97.1 percent of global R&D expenditure; within the developed capitalist countries, two-third of R&D expenditure were accounted for by about one-third of firms; and within these about 200 firms accounted for 3/4 of the research funds. Compared to this, the developing countries accounted for 2.9 percent of the R&D expenditure (OECD, 1979a).

The transfer of technology by the MNCs to the developing countries has been effected in two main ways: through direct foreign investments by MNCs and import of technology by the developing countries.

In relation to the first method, the flow of direct foreign investments from developed capitalist countries to all receiving countries increased from $4.1 billion in 1960 to $12.1 billion in 1970 and to $41.8 billion in 1980. Of these, investment in developing countries accounted for $1.8 billion in 1970 and $7.6 billion in 1980 (UN, 1983). This constitutes approximately 30 percent of total foreign investments during the last three decades.

Similarly, the total stock of foreign investments from the Organization for Economic Cooperation and Development (OECD), including reinvested earnings, in developing countries was estimated at $32.3 billion in 1967 and $89 billion in 1978 (UN, 1983). Thus, the process of internationalization or global spread of capital has increased over the years, yet its origins and control remains confined to a handful of developed countries whose multinational firms relocate in different regions of the world in search of better economic environment, which includes factors such as politically stable regimes, cheaper or more versatile and skilled labour.

Most industrial production in the developing countries, except for cottage and small-scale industries, has been based on foreign technology, which has either comprised imported machinery and equipment or this has been transferred as part of foreign investments by MNCs or their subsidiaries in the developing countries.

However, whilst the importance of technology has been increasingly recognized, few developing countries had adopted explicit policies toward industrial technology till the late 1960s. It was assumed, wrongly, as we shall see, that policies designed to achieve industrial growth based on imported technology and machinery would automatically result in domestic technological development through backward and forward linkages in the economy, that is, a form of externally induced national development.

The adoption of technology and related inputs from the MNCs into the national and local economy is the result of two broad development strategies in developing countries, though it may be argued that they have been constrained into adopting such policies by their place in the international division of labour. But this is too deterministic a view, though of course some countries have more room to manoeuvre in formulating policy, or are less constrained than others, such as the oil-producing countries, in comparison with those whose economy is dependent upon a single or very few export crops.

These strategies are, on the one hand, those that advocate import-substitution and export-oriented industrialization, and on the other, those suporting agricultural development through the adoption of modern technology such as chemical fertilizers and tractors. Of course these strategies are not mutually exclusive, and many countries follow some, or all of these, at different times, as part of their development strategy.

**Import-substitution/export oriented industrialization**

Policies for import-substitution have constituted a basic framework for industrialization in most developing countries. Often compelled by a shortage of foreign exchange and expanding local demand, there has been a growing emphasis on import-substitution, that is, the domestic production of an imported good, both to save foreign exchange and to develop the national industrial base.

These policies were largely initiated in Asian and African countries in the 1950s and 1960s (earlier in some Latin American countries such as Brazil and Argentina) and were, in some cases, extended to non-durable and intermediate goods and machinery from initial policies of import-substitution for consumer goods.

However, whether the goods produced domestically were consumer or capital goods, their production was largely based on foreign technology. This was so not only for foreign subsidiaries operating in the developing countries, but for domestically owned companies [2].

Largely as a result of import-substitution policies, the demand for various types of industrial machinery and equipment has grown rapidly, and an important aspect of import-substitution in many developing countries involves the degree to which assembly or manufacture of industrial machinery or production technology is undertaken locally, for clearly this has an important impact on all sectors of the economy, even though the machine equipment might be deployed in one specific sector.

A consequence of import-substitution policies has been that the MNCs, as major manufacturers and suppliers of industrial technology, have penetrated and have had a constraining effect on the economies of most developing countries. Of course, some developing countries such as India, have far less MNC presence than others such as Mexico and Brazil; but even in India the import content of imported technology from MNCs can be underestimated because it is more 'hidden' by the mode in which foreign capital is allowed to operate, through the so-called joint ventures undertaken by Indian and foreign firms [3].

In contrast, in Mexico, for example, MNCs increased their ownership and control in most technologically advanced sectors of the economy, and by the 1970s, the estimated market share of foreign subsidiaries was 84 percent in rubber, 80 percent in tobacco, 79 percent in electrical equipment, 67 percent in chemicals, and 62 percent in non-electrical machinery (Newfarmer and Mueller, 1980).

In Brazil in 1974, foreign subsidiaries held a major share of the assets in several sectors: 100 per cent in automobile manufacture, 85 per cent in pharmaceuticals, 61 per cent in rubber, 55 per cent in machinery and equipment, and 45 per cent in chemicals (ibid.). It follows that a significant part of what is often described as domestic manufacture of industrial goods is often MNC production, a point not recognized by Warren (1980), among others.

*Export processing free zones*

This is a relatively new form of MNCs' direct foreign investment that has emerged since the 1970s. It is characterized by the Export Processing Free Zones (EPFZ), which are enclaves in developing countries set up by MNCs almost entirely for production for the export market. The technology, management, raw materials and intermediate inputs are imported, often from their subsidiaries located elsewhere in the region or from the parent company. In the main, the only local content is labour, which is often female labour.

The EPFZs are invariably established in a locality for a short period (eg., 5 years), after which they might move on to other parts of the globe to utilize cheaper labour or to be near markets, or to politically more stable and regimes that also encourage the EPFZs ventures.

The main contribution of the EPFZs to developing countries has been the employment effect. The linkage effect has been, so far, even less profound, in the sense of deepening the national economy, than that of the traditional MNC operating in a developing country, such as Unilever in India. But evidence is begining to emerge that the local content of the EPFZ production is increasing, though this is unlikely to be very significant since the local content is often the least valuable of the final products inputs. (Cheon and Lim, 1981:136-50).

During the early 1970s most of the manufacturing was in textiles and garments. Since the mid-1970s intermediate, heavy and particularly electronics goods has expanded rapidly. For example, in the South-east Asian EPFZs, about 300,000 workers constituting about half of the total labour force employed in the zones are employed in the electronics industry (Ping, 1979) [4]. In the early 1980s, the total labour force employed in the various EPFZs of developing countries was estimated at about one million, the majority in Asia (UNIDO, 1982).

Export oriented manufacture, whether undertaken by domestically owned companies or by MNC subsidiaries, has relied heavily on foreign technology, more so than has production for the domestic market, which uses domestic or cheaper imported technology. This is because the type of technology to be utilized in export-oriented production needs to be geared to competitive factors in the external market it is seeking to serve. The case in point here is South Korea where production for export is based largely on imported technology for a higher quality product than domestically produced technology could avail; the latter was used entirely for the domestic market.

Thus, export-oriented production, particularly in the technologically advanced sectors, for complex, high-technology components and intermediate inputs, has been highly import-intensive. Moreover, the economic and technical linkages (upstream and downstream industries) with the local economy, which import-substitution was supposed to establish, have either been weak or absent in export oriented-production of the EPFZs.

## Agricultural development and MNCs

The demand for agricultural machinery and equipment as well as other inputs has also grown as a result of devlopment policies adopted in the developing countries, which have attempted to increase agricultural production through modernization, meaning primarily use of modern technology. This has resulted in greater demand for tractors and harvesters, power tillers, irrigation technology, spraying equipment, fertilizers, pesticides and increasingly, seeds.

These items have been the major inputs on which the green revolution in Pakistan and other developing countries has been based. And much of this equipment and intermediate goods are produced by the MNCs.

### *Tractors*

With agriculture continuing to be the major sector of most developing countries economies, the local production of agricultural machinery and equipment has constituted an important aspect of development planning in the developing countries. Agricultural equipment is necessary for a large variety of farm operations, ranging from irrigation, ploughing, reaping, cutting, and threshing, to drying and storage and transportation of produce to the market.

The requirements for such equipment range from hand-operated or animal-drawn equipment such as ploughs, which generally involve relatively simple hand-made technology, to agricultural machinery such as large, power-operated pumps, power-tillers, tractors, and so on, which are produced by sophisticated machine tools industry and involve rather complex production processes. And whilst the simpler technology is produced domestically, the tractors are invariably produced by large MNCs which are concentrated in a few countries notably the USA, UK, West Germany, Italy, Canada, Japan and France.

By the early 1980s these accounted for 85 percent of world tractor production (UN, 1980). It was estimated that in the late 1970s, eight MNCs accounted for 55 percent of world-wide sales of agricultural machinery (UN, 1981b). And the sales of the ten largest MNCs accounted for 75 to 80 percent of world exports of agricultural equipment (UNIDO, 1979b).

Most of the worlds production of tractors is concentrated in a few companies such as Deere and Company (USA), International Harvester (USA), Massey-Ferguson (Canada), Fiat (Italy), Ford (USA), Kubota (Japan), Renault (France), and Klockner-Humboldt-Deutz (West Germany)[5].

The tractor designs and manufacturing processes have been based on ecological and agricultural conditions in North America and Western

Europe, and are therefore, in most instances, ill-adapted to local conditions such as those of arid or tropical regions. This, however, is a mere detail compared to the far more important factor, the process of capital expansion in the economy, which the manufacture of capital equipment represents; and the loss of this capital expansion for most developing countries economies, because tractors and related equipment are manufactured outside of the national economy.

The range of tractor manufacture extends mainly to the larger units of 40 to 100 horsepower; though some smaller versions, more suited to the smaller holdings in the developing countries are also produced, mainly by Japanese manufacturers.

Unlike the heavy concentration of tractor manufacture in the MNCs of the developed countries, the production of tractors in the developing countries accounted for about 15 percent of the world output in 1980 (UN, 1981c). Most of this is concentrated in a few countries, including Argentina, Brazil, China, South Korea, and India, excluding those countries where local production consists largely of assembly operations [6].

In contrast to several other industries, the production of tractors by MNCs in the developing countries has had a very limited impact on the national economy. The generation of upstream or downstream industries (the linkage effects) has been weak or non-existent. Because for MNCs, the preferred method to serve developing country markets has remained exports, which have allowed these companies to utilize existing production facilities in their home countries and in major subsidiaries located in other developed countries, for example Massey-Ferguson, a Canadian MNC, manufactured tractors in Coventry in Britain, for export to the developing countries.

Major MNC production in the developing countries has been established in a few countries, for instance, Brazil and Mexico, where government import-substitution policies and a relatively large local market made such investments attractive. Thus, in Brazil, in the early 1980s, annual tractor production was around 55,000 to 60,000 which was accounted for by about ten foreign subsidiaries operating in the country (UN, 1980). In contrast, in Mexico, local tractor production was undertaken by Massey-Ferguson, Deere, International Harvester and Ford, and total production reached 16,000 units by 1980 (UN, 1980).

The ownership structure of foreign subsidiaries has varied among countries but they tend to operate through majority or wholly owned subsidiaries. In some countries, such as Argentina, they have been involved in joint ventures with local capital, often on a minority equity basis, which is demanded by many governments in the developing countries. Even with this arrangement, the dependent relationship continues, since production in the developing countries constitutes only a small part of the total value of the final product. For not only the production technology but also the crucial parts and components continue to be imported by the subsidiary from the parent company which allows the MNC effective control over local production.

In most developing countries, with the exception of countries such as India, Brazil and Mexico, policies aimed at indigenisation of tractor manufacture have largely failed and local content remains low. In Mexico the local content is around 50 to 60 percent, even though most of the subsidiaries have been operating in the country for two decades (UN,1979a). In Brazil, the local content has reached upto 80 percent, but most of the critical parts are still imported (UN, 1983). These figures have to be taken cautiously, however, since the local content often comprises components produced locally by other foreign firms in the country, or local firms producing these components with imported technology.

In the Middle East and Asian countries, MNCs production is limited to mainly assembly and semi-assembly operations. Ford, International Harvester, and Massey-Ferguson have such operations in Turkey, Iran (prior to the revolution) Phillipines and Pakistan. In Africa MNCs started operations in the 1970s: Ford and Klockner-Humboldt in Egypt and Fiat in Nigeria. Joint ventures with minority foreign holdings have been established by Massey-Ferguson in Kenya, Sudan, Morocco and Libya.

Two major factors have mitigated against increasing the local content of tractor production, which typifies the role of foreign capital in Third World developed: the high capital intensity and techno-economic characteristics of MNC production, and their global interests. Thus, since production of tractors with technology in use by MNCs requires large scale of production, most developing countries markets are too small for this scale of investment and production to be located in them. MNCs therefore utilize production facilities in the developed countries.

Moreover, as in other industries, only limited efforts have been undertake for R&D for adapting the design of tractors or for production techniques that are more suitable for developing countries.

*Fertilizers and pesticides*

Fertilizer is one of the major agro-chemical inputs on which the green revolution is based, and constitutes an important factor structuring links between local development and the international economy. Like tractors, fertilizers are produced by MNCs and are either imported or produced locally by MNC subsidiaries, or by domestic firms, using imported technology and intermediate inputs such as chemicals.

Fertilizers, and their necessary accompanying input, pesticides, are the product of a global pharmaceutical industry controlled by a small number of MNCs whose production has increased enormously: the value of fertilizer production increased from \$2.5 billion in 1973 to \$84 billion in 1980 (UN,1980a). Most of the production is concentrated in industrialized countries, with the USA accounting for almost 30 percent, followed by Western Europe and Japan.(ibid.).

The use of pesticides and other pharmaceuticals-derived agro-chemical products has largely been concentrated in the developed countries who consume 75 percent of world production (UN, 1980c). In the developing countries, agro-chemical production increased from about \$3.1 billion in 1973 to over \$8 billion in 1980, mainly under subsidiaries of major MNCs like Pfizer, Cyanamid, Upjohn, Hoechst and Bayer, Ciba-Geigy, Sandoz and Imperial Chemical Industries (ibid.).

Since the strategy of increasing agricultural output is based on modernizing agriculture through the use of modern technology, increase in fertilizer production is of crucial importance. And although large investments have been made in this sector, fertilizer production continues to be short of requirements in the developing countries, including that for Pakistan. For example, in 1984-85, developing countries output was projected by a UN study to be only about 19.5 percent and 18.3 percent, respectively, of global production of nitrogenous and phosphatic fertilizer (UNFAO, 1980a).

The outward-directed development of Third World countries which is structured by the combination of national development strategies and the international economy, is again exemplified by the fact that inspite of locally available raw materials, fertilizer production in the developing countries is low. This is because it requires a large capital investment and sophisticated capital intensive technology which the developing countries do not have.

Investment by MNCs has been limited inspite of policies in several developing countries to produce fertilizer through state-owned companies, though of course the technology used is imported.

*Seeds: from common heritage to private property*

The production of seeds and seed-processing technology has also, since the 1960s, increasingly come under the control of MNCs. In 1987, 70 percent of Mexico's seeds were produced by MNCs (Bhattacharjee, 1988:2089/90). Though the figure is not as high for other developing countries including Pakistan, the impact of MNC as producers and suppliers of seeds is very important as we shall see in our study of local development.

During the 1960s, 'improved' High Yielding Varieties, or pest and environmentally adaptable seeds were either obtained by farmers from international research institutes, such as the Philippines Rice Research Institute (irri varieties) operated under the aegis of UN Food and Agriculture Organization; or from national research institutes. Prior to the green revolution, the major portion of seed requirements were generally met from within the agricultural sector, as a part of the produce was kept for seed.

The internationalization of seed production under the MNCs has extended since the 1960s, to crops that are widely traded on the world market including: wheat, maize, sorghum, soyabean, oilpalms, rubber, coconut, potato, tomato, cabbage and cauliflower. Crops that constitute 'poor peoples' diet or have local or culture-specific demand do not figure large in the MNCs biotechnological development or trade (Kloppenburg, 1988).

There are four main consequences of the increased role of MNCs in global seed production and trade. First, MNCs are able to control and restrict the supply of seeds as they can patent their genetic material. Secondly, cultivators increasingly have to purchase seeds of many crops every season from seed-suppliers, as they cannot, for many crops, use seeds from the crops they have grown. Third, most of the biogenetic seeds are increasingly complex which require a package of chemical applications in order to produce. For example, a Swiss MNC, Ciba-Geigy, sells a sorghum hybrid seed to the developing countries which comes ' wrapped' in three different products: the first immunizes the plant against disease, the second against pests, and the third against a pest-control chemical which is manufactured by the MNC itself. Similarly, a US MNC, Monsanto, has genetically engineered a variety of tomato which is compatible only with one of its plant protection chemicals called 'Round up' (Kloppenburg, 1988:195; Bhattacharjee, 1988: 2089/2090).

Evidence suggests that cultivators and governments in the developing countries are increasingly being persuaded or constrained into using hybrid seed produced by MNCs. Ironically, many of the seeds re-sold to particular countries by the MNCs, have originally been obtained from these countries. It is estimated that apart from profits made from sale of seeds, the use of genetic material from plants in the developing countries has been worth several billion dollars (Mooney, 1983).

In this section of the chapter I have indicated that agriculture, as the mainstay of developing countries' economies has become increasingly dependent on large MNCs for its inputs. Like industry, agriculture now uses a package of mechanical as well as chemical and biotechnological goods for its production, which are increasingly imported, and especially with regard to HYV, these need to be constantly changed and replaced in order to produce.

This inability to re-use a part of previous years harvest as seed, means that the production process in agriculture is less and less under the control of the developing countries, and much less a product of their economies.

On the contrary, the extension of control by the MNCs over one of the main indigenously produced inputs for agriculture, seeds, has deepend their dependence on international capital, which in turn is increasingly being concentrated and centralized, with vertical and horizontal takeovers[7].

However, as I have stated earlier, MNC production and control of technology, need not have negative consequences *per se*. In fact certain positive qualities can, under specific circumstances, be attributed to the internationalization process undertaken by the MNCs. These can be efficient, and are able to provide international services. They are potentially progressive in that they can transcend nationalist, cultural and ideological particularities and view the globe as a single entity.

Under conditions of the present global economy, however, the MNCs penetrate the social and economic structures of the developing countries, which are different from those of the developed countries; therefore the MNCs impact on the developing countries is different as well, for two main reasons. Firstly, the MNCs technologies are developed for use in industrialized, capital intensive as well as energy intensive production processes, and are thus appropriate to the developing countries in a very limited sense, because of their high costs as well as the labour they displace. However, the most important impact of the MNCs and their technology is that which I have indicated above and in chapter 2: the lack of organic linkages with different sectors of the national economy; the absence of upstream and downstream industries; and the expanded reproduction which takes place outside of domestic production, since the MNCs represent Department 1 goods produced elsewhere.

The operation of the MNCs and their impact on the developing countries reflects, according to Palloix (1975:83), the 'new articulation':

> This new type of articulation characterizes the different chains of dependence in the self-expansion of capital, in particular the new type of articulation with the underdeveloped countries, which is no longer an articulation of the capitalist mode of production at the centre with other modes of production, but an articualtion within the world CMP (capitalist mode of production) itself, among differing processes of self-expansion of capital and increasingly accentuated differentiation of this expansion as between the centre and periphery. The first type of articulation between the CMP and other modes of production is pushed back into the independent circulation of underdeveloped economic and social formations; it tends to become 'marginalized' in international circulation, and hence the appearance of export industries and business transfers in the underdeveloped countries as a new characteristic of exchange relations between periphery and centre.

As a general statement the above is largely true, except the assumption of homogeneity of all developing countries and their similarity of location within the international division of labour. This is questionable. As is the extent of marginalization of developing countries economies in the international economy; this is clearly exaggerated. Because, as I have indicated above and in chapter 2, and as I shall discuss further in subsequent chapters, these economies are extremely important for the realization of value produced in the developing countries.

The import and use of imported technology and capital goods would not be a problem if there was a two-way flow of these goods between the developed and developing countries. Or if a sufficient level of capital formation had taken place in the developing countries. Under the present conditions of production in most developing countries, the MNCs penetration represents a constriction of capital accumulation in the developing countries, as well as a drain of their capital to the developed countries through the realization process which occurs through developing countries consumption of capital goods and technology from the developed countries.

**Notes**

1. The United Nations Industrial Development Organization (UNIDO)(1973), defines technology as 'sum of knowledge, experience and

skills for manufacturing a product or products and for establishing an enterprise for this purpose'.

2. Initially the import substitution had relatively little local content in manufactures, and activity was largely for assemble operations and for production of simple engineering parts and components. Over a period of time, particularly in the late 1960s and 1970s, national governments in the several developing countries began to exert pressure for increasing the local content of production. The intention was to reduce the increasing bill that had resulted from the high import intensity of production by foreign subsidiaries and domestic companies; it was also an attempt to decrease the overwhelming dependence on imported technology which had resulted from ISI through the so-called learning effect.

3. In India where import substitution has been relatively more successful than other developing countries, MNCs are still the major suppliers, directly or indirectly, of a significant portion of technology. For example, during the period 1960/69, 414 new companies were formed jointly with foreign capital, mostly in the engineering goods sector; during 1970/79, 388 new companies were formed with foreign partners.In the 1980s foreign investments increased rapidly over the previous years. In 1982, new foreign investments reached about 466 million. At the end of 1982, total cumulative foreign direct investments were about $2.2 billion. In most cases these investments were joint ventures with foreign capital. Of course, even when Indian firms'capital is entirely domestic, their activity is largely dependent on imported technology. (Government of India, 1980; 1983).

4. The role of the state in establishing and operating EPFZ is extremely important: it provides the infrastructure as well as a package of incentives. The state removes the restrictions on the import of capital and technology and raw materials, so that these can be imported duty free into the EPFZ. In addition, foreign firms can use such crucial facilities as electricity and housing at subsidized rates, tax holidays, and low interest on local borrowings. Normal industrial relations legislation in operation in the country is often suspended in the EPFZ.

5. The manufacture of tractors in the developed countries is highly capital intensive; consequently the economies of scale assume considerable importance. In the late 1960s, for instance, a study of the production costs to output revealed that in North America, unit costs of tractor production decreased by 18 percent as annual output increased from 20,000 to 90,000 units, and a further 5 percent decrease was realized as output reached 120,000 unit (Canadian Royal Commission on Farm Machinery, (1969) *Farm Machinery*, Ottawa.

6. Apart from the capital intensity of manufacturing, significant capita outlay is also required for establishing the distribution and service networks that have acted as deterrents for new entrants to the market. In the late 1970s and early 1980s, the relatively low growth rate of demand for tractors in the major developed countries, including the large excess capacity of most producers have led to further concentration in the tractor industry. In some countries there are smaller firms that manufacture specialized machinery of this type but do not compete directly with the major producers. It should be noted, that the technological features of tractor production have not undergone major changes during the 1960s when the

green revolution in the developing countries was proceeding rapidly. In other words, tractor producers did not respond specifically to conditions of agricultural production in the developing countries in terms of capital intensity or energy use of the tractors.

7. For example, a number of chemical and pharmaceutical MNCs including Shell, Monsantos, Pfizer and Ciba-Geigy, have taken over seed companies and incorporated them as their subsidiaries; and a number of MNCs producing tractors have move into manufacure of irrigation technology and other agricultural equipment (Kloppenburg, 1988).

# 4 The economic and social development of Pakistan

In the previous chapter I described some important structural changes in the global economy, in particular the rapid internationalization of capital since the 1970s, and the role of MNCs in this process. As I indicated there, the development strategies adopted in the developing countries have made the import of capital goods and technology necessary, on an increasingly large scale; and that even where these goods are produced locally, the import content of the producer and intermediate goods is high, with the negative consequences for developing countries economies that I have described briefly.

In this chapter I shall describe the causes and consequences of Pakistan's further integration into the global economy, reflected, amongst other things, in the consumption of fertilizers, tractors, seeds, pesticides, production machinery and equipment, which are produced by the MNCs, and the dependent development that accompanies this process. This chapter establishes links between the international, national and local economy; and also provides the framework and context for analyzing local development in the following chapters, and the way this is shaped by the national and international economy.

It is suggested in this chapter that the development policies adopted in Pakistan have made the country increasingly dependent on developed countries for capital and technology, with the consequence that the development process has been weak, and characterized by a low rate of capital accumulation in the national and local economy. This weakness of the economy is reflected in the poorly developed capital goods sector in general and machine tools sector in particular.

Pakistan's economic and social development intermediates the international economy and local development in Mallian and other localities in Sargodha and Sahiwal where our research was carried out. Specifically, this triangular (international, national and local) relationship creates the space for and sets limits to national and local development. Pakistan's dependent development refers not only to the need to borrow capital, but also to the root cause of this dependence, the relative absence of capital goods industries that could be the vehicle for domestic innovation in production technologies and machine tools industries, which could in turn deepen and diversify the national economy.

The development policies followed in Pakistan have necessitated the use of imported technology in manufacturing and in agriculture, and this has been crucial in shaping its structure of dependent capitalist development as I shall indicate below.

After describing the main features of Pakistan's economy and society I shall analyze the development of industry and agriculture in Pakistan and their relationship to the international economy in general and MNCs in particular.

*The state and development policy: the five year plans*

The state in Pakistan assumes varied roles including representing and regulating interests and demands of various social groups and classes, which need not concern us here. For our purpose the two most important state functions are regulation of the inflow of foreign capital and direction of development policies embodied in the five year plans. The country is now in its seventh five year plan (1988/93) which has been preceded by the sixth five year plan (1983/88), fifth plan (1978/83),fourth plan (1970/75) third plan (1965/70), second plan (1960/65), first plan (1955/60), which were preceded by the so-called pre-plan period begining in about 1949.

The empirical study in the following chapters is located within the third, fourth, fifth and sixth plans. Data from the local areas was updated in 1987 after the original fieldwork in 1978. Each of these plans emphasized different aspects and objectives including accelerating industrial growth, (first plan), impetus to agricultural development, (third plan); these plans also emphasized different strategies at various times, from import-substitution to export promotion, and so on.

## The structure of Pakistan's economy

There have been two important moments in the development of Pakistan,s economy: import-substitution industrialization and the rapid agricultural change referred to as the 'green revolution' (GR) both of which had the effect of making the country's development process increasingly more dependent on the international economy, even though high rates of growth were registered in both sectors of the economy (the attempt at export-oriented development, particularly in manufactures has not been successful, and as we shall see, exports depend to a large extent on agricultural produce and goods that have a large agricultural component).

In broad outline, Pakistan has been transformed from a mainly primary goods producing country exporting jute and raw cotton (mainly to Britain), and an importer of manufactured consumer goods in the 1950s, to a more complex and diversified economy but one which is increasingly dependent economy on the economies of the developed countries.

Table 4.1: Structure of Pakistan's Economy 1949-1988

Sectoral origin of GDP (at 1959/60 factor cost) in %.

| | 1949/50 | 1959/60 | 1964/5 | 1970/1 | 1974/5 | 1977/8 | 1987/8 |
|---|---|---|---|---|---|---|---|
| Agriculture | 60.0 | 53.1 | 49.1 | 35.0 | 36.3 | 32.0 | 26.2 |
| Manufacturing | 5.9 | 9.3 | 11.0 | 16.3 | 15.7 | 13.4 | 16.9 |
| Large scale | 1.4 | 5.0 | 7.1 | | | | |
| Small scale | 4.4 | 4.3 | 3.8 | | | | |
| Other activities | 34.2 | 37.7 | 40.0 | | | | 53.0 |

Source: Lewis (1970:9) and Government of Pakistan 1979, 1981/82, 1988/89.

Table 4.1 shows changes in the relative share of the Gross Domestic Product (GDP) over time. Immediately after independence, during the pre-plan period in 1949/50, manufacturing accounted for 5.9 percent of the GDP; it was 16.3 percent of the GDP in 1970/71, and 13.4 percent in 1977/78.

Agriculture's share of the GDP declined from 60 percent in 1949/50 to 35 percent in 1970/71; and form 32 percent in 1978/79, to 30 percent in 1981/2 (Government of Pakistan, 1979;1982). In 1988 agriculture accounted for 26.2 percent of the GDP; and manufacturing 16.9 percent. Wholesale and retail (16.7), public adminstration and defence (9.6), transport, storage and communications (8.2), services (7.2) and others (15.2) percent respectively, shared the rest (Government of Pakistan, 1988/89). Manufacturing's share of the GDP has thus increased from 6 percent in 1949/50 to 13.4 percent in 1977/78, to 17 percent in 1981/82.

In manufacturing, cotton textiles account for approximately 27 percent of total manufactures, followed by sugar (7.4) and cigarettes (4.5) and light machine and surgical instruments (Government of Pakistan, 1978).

Agriculture is still the most important sector of the economy, employing a little over half the labour force. Its importance outweighs even its large share in the GDP since agriculture provides the raw materials for a large portion of the manufactures. These consist of cotton cloth, cotton yarn, leather, carpets and rugs, clothing and hosiery. In 1987/88 these accounted for over 60 percent of manufactured exports (Government of Pakistan, 1988/89).

*Pakistan's trade*

For exports, however, the economy relies heavily on two commodities, rice and cotton. The production of these agricultural, and other, manufactured, exports, is dependent on import and use of foreign technology which is generally manufactured by MNCs, as we have seen in the last chapter. This is inevitable, as I have said, given the relative lack of a capital goods industry, in particular Department I goods which provide the elements of production for agriculture and industry.

In fact capital goods comprise a large part of imports. For example, about one-third of Pakistan's imports consisted of capital goods in the 1970s. In 1987/88, capital goods comprising petroleum and products, non-electrical machinery, transport equipment, iron and steel and chemicals formed almost 60 percent of total imports (Government of Pakistan, 1988/89). The Karachi Steel Mill which began production in the early 1980s with a capacity of 1 million tonnes, should undoubtedly produce a downstream effect, though this has still to be realized.

Cotton yarn and cloth which accounted for 28 percent of imports in 1951/52, declined to less than 0.5 percent in 1964/5 (Lewis, 1970:11). On the other hand, imports of iron and steel and related products increased from 7.4 percent to 8.7 percent between 1951/52 and 1958/59, to 16.6 percent in 1964/65 (Ibid.) Similar trends were also observed in the import of machinery, transport, and electrical equipment. These were 9.2 percent of total imports in 1951/52, 25.4 percent in 1959/60, and 33.4 percent in 1964/65 (ibid.).

*Import-substitution industrialization*

The high rate of industrial growth in the 1950s were due largely to the import-substitution of consumer goods; that is, the domestic production of cloth and other consumer durables.

This was made possible by the strategy of import-substitution industrialization (ISI), from the mid-1950s, which was financed largely through external borrowing, whose magnitude we shall see shortly.

The process of ISI for consumer goods had a negative effect on the country's economy in that it diverted resources away from, and left unprotected, potential development of the domestic capital goods sector. Moreover, there was no clear planning as to how the import of capital goods for the production of consumer goods was to be paid for.

There was no significant increase in manufacturing output for export or curtailment of consumption, so that savings remained low. Agricultural growth began to decline and food had to be imported, an ironic situation for a predominantly agricultural country, which had exported food in the past.

Pakistan began to rely increasingly on external sources to finance its development. The structure of deepening financial and technological dependence that emerged during this period was a logical outcome of a complex configuration of Pakistan's place in the international division of labour established during the colonial period, and its development policies which are in part a reflection of dominant class interests and historically specific national culture.

I shall come back to discuss issues of financial and technological dependence after I have analyzed the development of agriculture and its place in the national economy.

**The development of agriculture**

As we have seen agriculture is still the dominant sector of the economy. Over half the workforce is employed in this sector and 70 percent of the population lives in the rural areas. During the mid-1950s and 1960s, when industry experienced high growth rates, agriculture was relatively stagnant. Upto 1960 growth rate of crop production was estimated to be 2.3 per annum; between 1960/69 it increased to 5.4 percent (Stevens, et al., 1976:291). Public investment in agriculture declined from 2.5 percent in 1959 whilst that of private investment rose from 2.9 percent in 1960 to 3.5 percent in 1969 (Ibid.:291).

Between 1965 and 1974 some of the more spectacular growth rates were confined to wheat and rice which experienced increases of upto 70 per cent or more. For the country as a whole, agricultural production increased by 52.3 percent between 1960/61 and 1971/72, and 24.3 percent between 1971/72 and 1979/80 (Government of Pakistan, 1981, *Agricultural Statistics*).

*The green revolution*

The green revolution (GR) is understood by some to have radically transformed agriculture in Pakistan and other developing countries. One of the aims of the GR according to its advocates, which includes the World Bank, is to achieve self-sufficiency in food, which had to be imported to make up for deficits in domestic production, and to produce a surplus to earn foreign exchange to pay for manufactured imports, as well as for investment. Pakistan has only partly achieved this objective at a high cost and also by deepening its dependence on the world market, as we shall see.

To define the green revolution is problematical, even more so to quantify this; but a growth rate of 5 percent per annum is acceptable in that it is sufficient to meet the population increase of about 2-3 percent per annum of most developing countries, and thus contribute to capital formation (Byres, 1972:101).

What are the causes and and consequences of the GR in Pakistan and what have been its effects at a local level? The GR, which partly accentuated and accelerated the tendency of capitalist development in Pakistan's agriculture, is premissed on the increased use of mechanical and bio-petrochemical inputs: irrigation technology, tractors and power tillers, chemical fertilizers, High Yielding Varieties (HYV) seeds, and pesticides.

These inputs were made accessible to cultivators by subsidized loans provided by the state, mainly to the larger owners of land.

The state in turn received loans from the World Bank and other agencies and governments of the developed and rich countries, to finance agricultural development. In Pakistan these loans were disbursed through the Agricultural Development Bank of Pakistan (ADBP) and by commercial banks such as the Habib Bank and Muslim Commercial Bank.

*Agricultural credit*

The magnitude of the increase in loans to agriculture is shown by the following figures: loans provided by all institutional credit agencies rose from rupees (Rs) Rs 149.83 million in 1960/61 (index=100), to Rs 150.34 million, (index=100.3), in 1965/66; Rs 209.3 million (index=139.7) in 1966/67; Rs 256.58 million, (index=171.2) in 1967/68; to Rs 293.98 million, (index=196.2), in 1968/69 (Stevens, et al. 1976:373). At 1978 prices £1 was worth about 25 Rupees.

This was an increase of 100 percent in loans advanced by institutional credit agencies during the years 1967 to 1969. (It should be stressed, however, that institutional loans form a small portion of the total agricultural credit in Pakistan - as we shall see in our local study - most loans are obtained through informal sources, mainly relatives, money-lenders and merchants). The objective behind the strategy was to increase output by increasing inputs for agriculture; that these would break the cycle of low productivity in agriculture, which was due to low fertilizer input, inadequate and untimely water resources, as well as inadequate provision and use of plant protection chemicals. Mechanization of agriculture, through increased use of tractors was supposed to make cultivation more efficient, but this claim is disputed, as we shall see.

Similar to industrial development the role of the state has been crucial in the developmet of agriculture in Pakistan. In addition to providing loans to cultivators it has subsidized equipment such as tractors, tubewells and fertilizers and HYV, sometimes upto 50 percent or more of the market price (Griffin, 1974: 53).

*Fertilizer consumption*

There has been a large increase in the consumption of fertilizers of various types (nitrogenous, urea, phosphates). From 1964 to 1970 fertilizer consumption in Pakistan increased five times (Stevens, et al., 1976:232). Between 1972/73 and 1981/82, fertilizer consumption in the country increased almost three-fold, from 407.4 thousand tons to 1134.85 thousand tons (Government of Pakistan, 1983, *Agricultural statistics*). Per acre fertilizer consumption increased by about 134 percent between 1972/73 and 1981/82, that is from 22.5 lbs to 50 lbs per acre (ibid.). Inspite of this increase, as we shall see in our local study, fertilizer consumption remains extremely low, often much below the optimal quantity required.

*Irrigation technology*

Large parts of Pakistan are semi-arid and water resources are a major factor influencing both the types of crops grown and cropping intensity. This is true for Punjab, where our empirical study is conducted, as for other regions of the country. The importance of water resources can be assessed by the fact that classification of land depends on type of water availability. As we shall see in chapter 5, the two major classifications of land are *barani* (rainfed) and irrigated land. The former describes areas which, for one reason or another, lack adequate irrigation facilities and are therefore dependent on seasonal rainfall to water the land; this is an unreliable and uncontrolled source of water for agricultural development to take place, and the least developed agricultural districts in the country are *barani*.

The irrigated areas have a variety of sources of water: canal, tubewells, water-pumps, as well as rain. Though both areas use a variety and combination of watering techniques, there is a clear demarcation between the areas in that the main sources of water availability is either rain or tubewell and canal irrigation with supplemental water from other sources. Roughly, the northern part of the Pakistani Punjab is *barani* and the south, south-western and central districts are irrigated. The green revolution on the whole has been confined to the irrigated districts. The following passage shows the importance of water resources in Pakistan, and also great optimism about the possibilities of achieving economic change entirely through a technical approach to economic development. An approach which ignores questions of political economy at both international and national levels:

> One of the most significant phenomena in agricultural development in Pakistan has been the installation of private tubewells by farmers of West Pakistan at an exceedingly fast rate during the second plan period (1960-65). Installation of these tubewells has enabled the farmers to intensify irrigation and make important changes in cropping patterns in order to maximize the income from their crop production...[The result of the surveys] indicate that West Pakistan is likely to attain a rate of increase of agricultural production unparalleled in the history of agriculture. (Mohammad, 1965: 1).

Tubewells were the precusors of the green revolution's package comprising the new technology and were installed prior to the systematic introduction of the seed-fertilizer-tractor inputs of the late sixties. Tubewells in Pakistan increased from 31,600 at the end of 1964 to 75,700 in 1968, a two and a half times increase (Stevens, et al.,1976:85). By the early to mid 1980s, almost 200,000 tubewells had been installed (Government of Pakistan, 1985, *Economic Survey*). Since the mid-1960s, canals and tubewells increased farm gate water availability from nearly 64 million acre feet to 98 million acre feet in the 1980s (ibid.). This made an important contribution towards overcoming constraints imposed on agricultural development by lack of water, though water shortage (sometimes acute) still remains.

The crucial importance of modern technology such as tubewells in increasing water availability, and its impact on agricultural output, is shown by a study which attributed the 26 percent increase in agricultural output in Pakistan from 1960 to 1965 to the following factors: groundwater (tubewells), 9 percent; additional surface water, 4 percent; fertilizer, 5 percent; plant protection, 4 percent; new seed, 3 percent; other factors, one percent (cited in Stevens, et al., 1976:331).

The technology content of tubewells is now mainly domestic though some of the crucial parts are still imported. Dams, the other source of irrigation as well as hydroelectric power are constructed mainly with imported technology and materials or technology produced locally under licence.

*The ecological impact of irrigation*

The potential for large increases in agricultural output still remains to be realized, though the possibility for this is significantly reduced by the fact that water-logging and salinity and other ecological damage due to seepage from irrigation systems and lack of adequate drainage, has rendered large tracts of land uncultivable. For instance, during the first five year plan period, about 6 million acres were affected by water-logging and salinity, with a yearly increase of about 50,000 affected acres per year. In the second plan period it was estimated that about 50 percent of irrigated land or 12 million acres was affected; and during the third plan period it was estimated that between 70,000 to 100,000 acres were being lost annually (Ahmed and Amjad, 1984:137). However, under various reclamation schemes, including Salinity Control and Reclamation Project (SCARP), the problem has somewhat abated and during 1979-80, about 15 percent of damaged land had been reclaimed (ibid.:137). As we shall see, this ecological damage in the country as a whole, which severely curtails agricultural development, is present at the local level in our areas of research, and this is an important factor in that impedes local development.

*Pesticides and plant protection*

The HYV seeds are prone to infestation due to the highly nutritious contents of fertilizers, but also because the naturally occurring landraces that protect the seeds are rearanged or destroyed by chemical fertilizer. Thus pesticides are an important element in the green revolution package. And as I indicated in chapter 3, many pharmaceutical companies are producing seeds which can only be protected by their own make of pesticides.

Pesticide use while on the increase, is much below the optimum required in Pakistan mainly because of its high cost, but also because of negligent cultural practices.

Sprayed area increased from about 417,000 acres in 1978 to 750,000 acres in 1982, but this represents only about 5 percent of total cropped area of the country (Government of Pakistan, *Agricultural statistics of Pakistan*, 1983). Spoliage of produce both due to infestation and to ineffective storage practices could well be upto 25 percent of the total agricultural produce in Pakistan.

*High yielding varieties of seeds*

As I indicated in chapter 3, the production of HYV seeds for wheat, rice, vegetables and hybrid maize are increasingly being produced outside of agriculture: at one extreme the petro-chemical and pharmaceutical MNCs are taking over seed production. At the other, peasant producers use part of their current or previous year's crop as seed, though this practice is decreasing, because the HYVs do not seed well, and new strains have to be introduced regularly, or else the tendency is for the yields to decline. Thus, increasingly seeds have to be obtained on the market, which are produced by national and international research institutes in addition to those produced by the MNCs.

In Pakistan many varieties of grain and other plant seeds are imported, this is especially so for vegetable crops such as potatoes and tobacco, which are obtained from Holland and Belgium. In our areas of research, particularly in Sahiwal, the larger commercial growers, and sometimes the peasant producers as well, who cultivate potatoes, use seeds which are produced in these countries.

The spread of HYV in Pakistan has been rapid: in 1972/73 about 41 percent of area sown with rice was under HYV seeds, which were initially provided by the International Rice Research Institute (IRRI) in the Philippines. For wheat, the so-called Mexi-Pak varieties covered about 57 percent of the area under wheat in 1971/72, and 85 percent of the area in 1981/82 (ibid.) As I have mentioned previously, the HYV give high yields if used in combination with optimal amount of water and chemical fertilizer; without this combination the yields are very poor.

*Tractors and related machinery*

There has been a large increase in tractors in the country. In 1959 there were about two thousand, by the mid-1980s these had increased to over 200,000 (Government of Pakistan, 1987, *Economic Survey,)*. The tractors are either imported or assembled in Pakistan in about seven assembly plants. More than 50 percent of the total loans disbursed by the ADBP between 1976 and 1982 were for the purchase of tractors which the government encouraged:

> The Government of Pakistan...has encouraged the use of large tractors and wheat combine harvesters through its policy of subsidising interest rates and the price of foreign exchange for inputs of agricultural equipment. Even as early as 1964/5, over a third of all loans granted by the Agricultural Development Bank were for the purchase of tractors and other mechanical equipment (Griffin,1974:53).

The major supplier of tractors to Pakistan is Massey-Ferguson, one of the large MNCs that I have discussed in chapter 3, but Fiat, Ford, International Harvester and Kubota, among others, are imported as well. Generally, the tractors are of the large to medium size, with horsepower of between 40 to 60, though smaller makes of around 15 horsepower are increasing. The two-wheeled power-tillers, much in use in South-east Asia are still relatively rare in Pakistan.

Tractors have only in part displaced the traditional ox-drawn plough for tilling and furrowing the soil. These still comprise the dominant mode of cultivation and are often used in combination with tractors.

The contribution of tractors to productivity is disputed but their labour displacement effects have been confirmed by a number of reliable studies. The report of a survey conducted by the International Bank for Reconstruction and Development (IBRD) concluded that:

> The labour used per farm increased overall for every size group [of cultivator] ...the labour used per cultivated acre decreased by some 40 %. This was exacerbated by tenant displacement which averaged 2.25 per farm. Using different assumptions as to the amounts of labour provided by tenant families it is estimated that the full-time jobs replaced by each tractor is 11.8, 9.7, or 7.5 respectively. (1975:11).

Another study, cited by Griffin, came to similar conclusions:

> Contrary to expectation, or hope, that mechanization would increase the demand for labour, the widespread introduction of tractors in the Punjab and Sind has led to the eviction of tenants, a decline in employment on large farms and an attempt by big landlords to increase further the size of their holdings. In one study, in fact, it was estimated that increased use of tractors on large farms led to a reduction in the utilization of labour by as much as 50% per acre (1974:53/4).

A more recent study found that deployment of a 24 horsepower tractor had the effect of net labour displacement: the use of this type of tractor will create one job in manufacturing for three years, one job for reparing and servicing, and one job for an operator/driver. The tractor displaces eleven jobs, giving a net loss of eight jobs (Kardar, 1986:158). If this is the case, then net labour displacement by 200,000 tractors of 40-60 horsepower has been enormous. But the enormity of this problem would not be so great if displced labour were to be re-employed in the manufacture of these tractors or in any other sector of industry; on the contrary, this structural change in the employment of the labour force would both reflect and contribute to an expansion in the productive capacity of the national economy, in the way it has done for the economy of the developed countries.

Though the labour displacing effects of tractors is evident, their use has enabled a more regular, timely and intensive cultivation. This is especially so where soils are hard or need to be furrowed deeper, and in wet-farming in rice cultivation where wet and muddy conditions are rather more easily negotiated by tractors than by the animal-drawn plough.

Also, because of their versatility, and labour-saving ability, tractors are particularly useful during periods of peak labour demands, where proper timing can contribute to a better cultivation and higher output. But this is only marginally beneficial, and may not be so at all in relation to the cost incurred by the use of tractors in the economy.

The IBRD study referred to earlier focuses on the effects of tractors. It shows an increase in the average size of farms when tractors have been introduced. Of the 202 farms surveyed by the study, only 23 did not increase their acreage. For the survey as a whole, however, there was an increase of 45 to 109 acres per farm (IBRD, 1975). The sources of additional land were:

| | percent |
|---|---|
| land previously cultivated | 22 |
| land previously rented out | 42 |
| land newly rented-in | 24 |
| land newly purchased | 12 |

The introduction of tractors has had important consequences for agriculture in both economic and social terms. As the above figures indicate, apart from 'land previously uncultivated,' all other sources of additional land would have affected tenancy relations because of resumption. 'Land previously uncultivated,' which accounted for 22 percent of additional sources of land, is most probably land which could not be cultivated using traditional technology (because of hard soil). It can be surmised that this was beneficial, at least for the owner. However, in terms of area affected by tractor use, the 42 percent of 'land previously rented out' and now resumed would have had a negative employment effect, since it would have been based on the eviction of tenants.

### The development of indigenous agriculture related industries

The weak development of a capital goods industry in Pakistan, especially of industry providing inputs for agriculture, is reflected in the limited extent and scale of industrial development generated by the green revolution since the mid-1960s. Evidence from two rather informative studies (one is an empirical study based on a survey) affirms this; these also affirm one of the main assertions of our study: that industrial development in Pakistan has been wholly inadequate to meet the input requirements for a self-reliant, autonomous and integrated (with industry) development of agriculture.

In one of the studies, by Child and Kaneda (1975), that I have mentioned, which is based on a survey carried out in 1970, indicates the emergence of two types of small-scale engineering industry especially in the Punjab, as a direct result of the green revolution. One type of firm produces diesel engines (whose prototype is the one-cylinder, horizontal slow-speed 1924 model English Rustin engine) for tubewells and related equipment. This type of firm is located mainly in the Lahore and Sialkot districts; the second type of firm is located in the Lyallpur (renamed Faisalabad) district and produces standard farm equipment such as fodder choppers and cane crushers (ibid.: 250/251). There were a total of about 533 firms in both type of industries, and almost 70 percent of them employed less than 10 workers each. The total number of workers employed by the firms was 7,556 of which tubewell firms employed 6,032, and non-tubewell firms employed 1,525 workers (ibid.:267). This constituted a negligible proportion (0.3 percent) of the total industrial labour force of Pakistan in 1970 of about 2.28 million (Ahmed and Amjad, 1987:203).

A crucial factor from our theoretical perspective is the extent to which these small-scale indigenous firms are externally dependent for their production. In fact the firms in question imported both raw materials such as pig iron, sheet metal and copper tubing; as well as crucial components of capital equipment like forged steel crank shafts, which are purchased from large-scale firms or commercial importers located in Lahore (ibid.:257).

The extent of this dependence on imported equipment, even by technologically the least sophisticated firms is illustrated by the following:

> There were complaints [by the managers of small-scale technologically less sophisticated firms] about the quality of equipment and materials from socialist, that is, East European, countries. On the other hand, there was high and unanimous praise for imports, such as cutting tools, from the People's Republic of China. The firm managers admired U.S. or Western European equipment but said that it is terribly overpriced...[However] capital equipment *is* imported into Pakistan by the country's *large-scale* enterprises, which benefit from the heavy subsidies implicit in tied-aid programs...(ibid.:257/58).

The second study (Aftab and Rahim, 1986) that I have mentioned uses secondary data to analyze the development of a small-scale agriculturally related engineering sector. They cite data to describe the emergence of 419 iron casting units and 2,141 light engineering units, employing a total of 13,000 workers; which is an average of about 5 workers per unit.

Apart from the almost insignificant size of the workforce employed (as a proportion of the total industrial labour force in 1978 of about 2.82 million), and the extremely small scale of production, these units were still dependent on imported components to complete the manufacture of their equipment (ibid.:68). Thus:

> The prior establishment of large enterprises that imported the technology of tubewell production into the country was another condition necessary for the emergence of the small-scale sector. Small firms obtained necessary skills and physical inputs such as simple machine tools, iron castings, diesel engine components, etc., from large firms in the industry (ibid.:73).

The two main suppliers of technology and production equipment to the small-scale manufacturing sector are a domestic firm, BECO (Batala Enigineering Company) and a subsidiary of a multinational corporation. The latter: 'expanded in the most sophisticated product areas such as large capacity turbine tubewells, submersible pumps and, along with BECO became a major supplier of these and similar products to the public sector'(Aftab and Rahim, 1986:69). Since the operation of the multinational subsidiary is rather clear, in so far as it provides foreign manufactured technology, one need not discuss its role in the development of an indigenous capital goods sector in any detail.

The situation is somewhat different for BECO, for its operation reflects the extent to which a relatively autonomous capital goods sector has developed in Pakistan. To produce agricultural technology and related equipment such as diesel engines and centrifugal pumps, BECO:

> [O]btained designs of slow-speed diesel engines from a British firm and at the same time imported equipment for their production...it set up a joint company with KSB-AG, a West German firm specialising in pumps and turbines...BECO [also] established technical collaboration with overseas - American (turbines), British (electric motors) and German (high speed diesel engines) - firms. Thus ...all or much of the technical know how required for the production of various types of diesel engines, water pumps, etc., was imported into the Punjab through the medium of BECO (ibid.:65).

The passages cited above support one of the main assertions of this study, that Pakistan (and other developing countries) lack a significant domestic capital goods and technology generating sectors. As I have indicated, and as I shall discuss further in this work, where these sectors exist they still depend, in many important ways, on the import of foreign manufactured components which are often the most critical elements of the total product.

## Foreign loans and debt

The development and transformation of industry and agriculture that I have described in this chapter, has depended on imported technology, such as tractors, and textile machinery, or on the domestic production of the elements of production, such as fertilizers and irrigation technology, produced with imported capital goods. Acquisition of these capital goods and technologies in turn has depended heavily on foreign loans, so that a financial dependence has been accompanied by the technological dependence that I have discussed.

Pakistan's debt burden has increased over time: by the end of fiscal year 1988 total accumulated debt reached us$18.3 billion, or around 50 percent of the GDP. Debt servicing requirements have risen rapidly from $1.1 billion in 1983 (30 percent of export receipts), to more than $2 billion, or 37 percent of the export receipts in 1988; though this is lower than the 45 percent of exports in 1986 and 1987 (IMF,1989).

The sharp rise in debt becomes more clear if aid flows are looked at over a longer time period. This rose from one percent of the GNP in 1955 to 2.75 percent in 1961 and 9 percent in 1964 (Ahmed and Amjad, 1984:291); indicating that under the development policies pursued in Pakistan so far increased development is accompanied by, if not premissed on increased indebtedness.

In terms of capital formation too, the significance of loans has increased over time: In 1964, 32 percent of gross domestic capital formation was financed by aid; this figure declined to 28 percent in 1980 as a result of large foreign remittances by Pakistani workers in the Middle East (ibid.). In 1980 these remittances amounted to Rs 18,187 million and to a large degree compensated for low domestic savings and balanced a persistent trade deficit (ibid.:8). Domestic savings, however, remain low; for example in 1980, gross foreign aid as percentage of GNP was 4.85, gross investment was 15.25 percent of GNP, and domestic savings 6.16 of GNP which is almost half India's (ibid.:291).

Apart from the fact that foreign loans have been obtained or tied-in for the purchase of capital goods and consumption goods from abroad, there is a considerable outflow of capital for debt servicing. For example, between 1974/5 and 1980/81 US$ 6,963 million were disbursed as aid of which US$ 4,102 million were repatriated as debt servicing charges (ibid.:293). The magnitude of capital outflow from the country is further shown by the following figures: during the late 1960s, total private remittances (profits, dividends, royalties, trade marks and technical fees) averaged about 135 million rupees a year, whereas the average yearly inflow of private foreign investment average about 85 million rupees (Chaudhry, 1970:102). Thus, total outflow of capital during this period *was 150 percent of inflows of investment*. This pattern of capital flows has not changed, and outflows may have increasd during the late 1980s, though there no reliable data on this.

Unlike other developing countries in Latin America and South-east Asia, Pakistan is not the recipient of very large direct private foreign investment; and in the late 1960s, only about 15 percent of the total corporate business was foreign owned (ibid.:101). The major part of this investment, about 40 percent, was in manufacturing. Most likely this figure is an underestimate, as the number of joint ventures with Middle Eastern states has increased since 1973.

However, an Export Processing Zone is being located in Karachi which could herald a new departure in the relationship between Pakistan and the international economy with large inflows of capital and technology, but with limited, if not negative, consequences of an enclave economy that I have described briefly in chapters 2 and 3.

The sources of loans have changed over time reflecting changes in the global economy as well as Pakistan's policy of not relying on a single or small group of countries for aid; or alternatively, the inability of one source to meet the country's demand for loans.

During the First Plan period (1955-60) almost 100 percent of foreign aid loans were obtained from aid-Pakistan Consortium under the overall regulation of the World Bank. By 1978/79, loans from the Consortium declined to 69 percent, whilst that from non-Consortium countries (mainly the Eastern Bloc countries and China) increased to 15 percent of the total. Aid from Islamic countries constituted 10 percent of the total, though this varied from 46 percent of the total in 1973/74 to 16 percent in 1975/76 (Ahmed and Amjad, 1984:301). The role of the International Monetary Fund (IMF) has increased also: in 1978/79 its contribution constituted 5 percent of Pakistan's loans (ibid).

However diversified Pakistan's sources of aid may become, it nevertheless relies heavily on external sources for financing its development. The debt burden has increased in proportion to its integration into the international economy which is a consequence of the complex configuration of development strategies Pakistan has adopted since independence and the working of the international economy. This indebtedness would not be so damaging in the long run if the national economy was being deepend and a sound basis was being laid for its future integration and development. As for instance, in the creation of capital goods and technology generating sectors which create upstream and downstream linkages and an expansion in the domestic productive capacity. In the absence of this trajectory of development, the loans incurred by Pakistan have had highly contradictory, if not negative, consequences for the country's development.

### *The social and economic context of Pakistan's development*

In the previous sections of this chapter I have described briefly Pakistan's social and economic transformation as a result of its further integration into the international economy, of which it is a part. The aim was to show Pakistan's integration into the international economy which has been facilitated, the import of production equipment for development, and the loans on which this development has depended. The specifically national context of this process has largely been taken as given. In this section I shall contextualize Pakistan's economic and social development and provide some indicators that reflect this process. This includes income distribution and distribution of the country's resources, in particular land, as this is of direct relevance for our local study.

Pakistan is one of the poorest countries in the world though it has ostensibly (in per capita terms though not in life expectancy) the highest standard of living in South Asia. With a per capita GNP of US$380 in 1982 it is supposedly on the verge of becoming a middle income country, a category which includes countries with a per capita income of about US$500 (World Bank, 1984). Be that as it may, Pakistan lags behind many other developing countries with similar or lower income levels in welfare, education, health and sanitation, and other amenities that determine the quality of life of a nation.

According to the World Bank's Review of Pakistan's Sixth Plan report, the highest quintile of population received 42.7 percent of the national income, whilst the lowest quintile received 8.2 percent of the income only (World Bank, 1984).

Similarly, a study by the Household Income and Expenditure Survey of 1979 showed that income inequalities were increasing: the share of national income of the poorest 30 percent fell from 18 percent in 1968/69 to 13.4 percent in 1979; during the same period income of the top 20 percent rose from 42.6 percent to 44.1 percent (Mahmood, 1984). An International Labour Office study reported that almost 40 percent of the rural population were living below the 'poverty line' measured in terms of a minimum requirment of 2550 calories per day. The same study concluded that approximately 28 and 35 pecent of the population would be regarded as 'very poor' and 'poor' (ILO, 1983).

With a population of about 100 million, the population is increasing at about 3 percent per annum, one of the highest rates of growth in the world. In 1979 there was one physician per 5000 persons and one hospital bed for 1600 persons. Adult literacy in 1978 was 24 percent and has risen to about 30 percent in the mid-1980s. Only about 27 percent of the population had access to potable water in 1978 (World Bank, 1984). Clearly, Pakistan's dependent development and economic policies have not brought benefits to the mass of the Pakistani people; and as I have mentioned, in terms of education, health and sanitation, Pakistan lags behind countries with comparable development and resources.

### *Dependent agricultural development*

As I have indicated, the green revolution, as a particular moment in Pakistan's agrarian development has been crucially dependent on international capital. Specifically, on the use of directly or indirectly imported intermediate and capital equipment produced by MNCs, for raising production in agriculture. In the previous sections our analysis was mainly confined to two integrated macro structures, the international and the national economy; though as I have acknowledged, the national economy is the outcome of the complex configuration of these two structures and relationships.

The specific economic, social and institutional context of Pakistan's agriculture into which the international economy enters and takes shape has been alluded to in passing. It is now necessary to look at the effects of this process more concretely. This will also provided a more specific context which will connect the local and the international economic processes, which determine local development.

The net effect of the green revolution (GR) has been further development of capitalist agrarian relations (Cleaver, 1972; Byres, 1972); and an increase in regional and class disparity in output and income. The latter is clearly illustrated by the disparity in the use of fertilizer, the main determinant of increased output, by different classes of cultivators.

The 1972 Agricultural Census shows a markedly higher proportion of farms applying fertilizer (52 percent as compared to 33 percent in 1960); as well as a higher share of cropped land receiving fertilizer (43 percent as against 12 percent in 1960). However, the disparity in the use of fertilizer by different classes of cultivators has increased, as the following figures show: The 1960 Agricultural Census showed the use of both chemical and organic fertilizer to be much higher on smaller farms. For example, the share of net sown area manured fell from 58 percent on farms of less than one acre to 5 percent on farms of 50 acres or more.

According to the 1972 Census however, 49 percent of the cropped area of farms of 150 acres or more reported use of fertilizer, compared to 35 percent of farms under one acre. These figures of course hide the quality (combination of different compounds) and quantity of fertilizer consumption, which, as we shall see in our local study, is higher on larger farms.

Other aspects of agrarian transformation in Pakistan are reflected in changes in cropping intensity. Figures compiled from the 1972 and 1960 Census show that in 1960 cropping intensity was 103; in 1972 it increased to 111, though it differed between different class of cultivators. For instance in 1972, farms below 5 acres had a cropping intensity of 133 compared to 116 in 1960; farms of 150 acres and over had a cropping intensity of 88 in 1972, compared to 57 in 1960; and so on for other classes of cultivators, reflecting trends and patterns similar to those in the local areas where our research was conducted.

Of course the consequences of the GR have been different to those intended: it was anticipated that food production could be increased within the existing production relations in agriculture, by adopting a technicist approach of increasing production inputs (which were often not adequate in quantity); and without prior institutional changes such as land distribution. It was expected that agricultural development would save foreign exchange by creating food self-sufficiency, mobilize capital in the form of transferred savings or extraction of surplus through manipulation of intersectoral terms of trade with industry; that agricultural development would re-absorb labour released through mechanization; or that this labour would be usefully absorbed into off-farm activities and social overhead construction; and that it would reduce seasonal unemployment and underemployment through year-round multiple cropping and intensity of cultivation. It was also anticpated that agricultural development would raise incomes of small farmers and the rural population in general, thus restoring balanced growth and enlarging the home market and creating opportunities for domestic manufacturing industry.

However, as we shall see these intentions have been realized to a very limited extent; if they have been realized even partially, this has been at considerable cost, and have not overcome the basic structural deficiences in the national economy which lie at root of the country's development problems - the weakly developed key industries produced by Department 1.

*Land distribution in Pakistan*

The three main determinants of Pakistan's agrarian structure are land distribution, land tenure patterns, and ecological conditions which I have discussed already. The ceiling on the amount of land that can be owned by one individual is effectively that provisioned under the 1972 Land Reforms: 150 acres of irrigated and 300 acres of unirrigated land, excluding orchards and mechanized farms and other categories which need not concern us here.

Table 4.2 outlines the structure of agrarian relations in Pakistan. The table shows that in 1972 small farms with holdings of less than 5 acres acres constituted 28 percent of total farms but accounted for only 5 percent of the farm area and about 6 percent of the cultivated area.

In contrast large farms operating 50 acres or more and comprising about 3 percent of total farms, constitute 24 percent of the farm area and 18 percent of the cultivated acreage. In between the extremes, farms of middling categories operating 12.5 to less than 50 acres, and constituting 29 percent of total farms, account for about 45 percent of farm and 48 percent of the acreage under cultivation. This clearly shows the unequal distribution of land and the unequal control over resources that this implies. As we shall see, the unequal distribution of land, land tenures and ecological conditions are crucial in conditioning local development.

However, whilst the distribution of land in Pakistan is skewed and unequal, it does not depict a simple two-tier model with very large landowners with extensive holdings juxtaposed with numerous smallholders and the landless. The scenario is one of a land of numerous peasant proprietors with large landowners at the top and substantial smallholders and landless at the bottom. In other words the distribution of land is unequal and hierarchical, rather than two-tier or binary.

One observable trend between 1960 and 1972 is the increase in the number of peasants holding the least amount of land. According to the 1972 Census there were 9,159,038 farms in the under five acre category. It is not possible to deduce from the 'macro' data the number/percentage increase in the six million 0-5 acre category, those peasants who have fallen in this category because of fragmentation of land or because of sale of land under economic compulsion such as indebtedness.

*The social organization of Pakistan's agriculture*

The social organization of production in Pakistan's agriculture is constitutive of three broad categories of farms: peasant proprietors, tenants, and landowning - and of course gradations and sub-categories within these. The first category includes those who own and self-cultivate their land; tenant farms are worked by occupancy or tenants-at-will who rent in land for a proportion of the product or money-rent. Landowner farms for the present will simply be taken taken to mean those which are worked by tenants for rent in cash or kind, or by wage labourers.

## Table 4.2: Distribution of land in Pakistan

| SIZE OF FARM | FARMS | | FARM AREA | | CULTIVATED AREA | | CULTIVATED AREA AS % OF FARM AREA | AVERAGE SIZE OF | |
|---|---|---|---|---|---|---|---|---|---|
| | NUMBER | PERCENT | TOTAL | PERCENT | TOTAL | PERCENT | | FARM AREA | CULTIVATED AREA |
| 1 | 2 | 3 | 4 | 5 | 6 | 7 | 8 | 9 | 10 |
| All farms | 37,61,940 | x | 4,92,06,552 | x | 4,07,50,255 | x | 83 | x | x |
| Government farms | 252 | x | 1,46,010 | x | 53,840 | x | 37 | x | x |
| Private farms - Total | 37,61,688 | 100 | 4,90,60,542 | 100 | 4,06,96,415 | 100 | 83 | 13.0 | 10.8 |
| 150 acres and above | 16,163 | | 44,81,803 | 9 | 20,68,780 | 5 | 46 | 277.3 | 128.0 |
| 150 " to 50.0 acres | 1,02,641 | 3 | 74,02,094 | 15 | 52,40,157 | 13 | 71 | 72.1 | 51.1 |
| 50 " " 25.0 " | 2,69,146 | 8 | 92,15,260 | 19 | 77,36,099 | 19 | 84 | 31.9 | 26.8 |
| 25.0 " " 12.5 " | 7,93,928 | 21 | 1,30,61,022 | 27 | 1,17,84,083 | 29 | 90 | 16.5 | 14.0 |
| 12.5 " " 7.5 " | 9,20,848 | 24 | 89,08,584 | 18 | 83,22,859 | 20 | 93 | 9.7 | 9.0 |
| 7.5 " " 5.0 " | 5,79,924 | 15 | 34,29,045 | 7 | 31,97,170 | 8 | 93 | 5.9 | 5.5 |
| 5.0 " " 2.5 " | 5,38,421 | 14 | 19,01,342 | 4 | 17,44,991 | 4 | 92 | 3.5 | 3.2 |
| 2.5 " " 1.0 " | 3,64,155 | 10 | 5,84,253 | 1 | 5,31,158 | 1 | 91 | 1.6 | 1.5 |
| under 1.0 acre | 1,56,462 | 4 | 77,129 | | 71,118 | | 92 | 0.5 | 0.5 |

Source: Pakistan Census of Agriculture, 1972, Government of Pakistan, Lahore.

Table 4.3: Number and area of owner-cum-tenant farms

| SIZE OF FARM | ALL FARMS | | OWNER-CUM-TENANT FARMS | | OWNER-CUM-TENANT FARMS AREA | | | | | |
|---|---|---|---|---|---|---|---|---|---|---|
| | NUMBER | AREA | NUMBER | PERCENT | OWNED SELF OPERATED | SHARE-CROPPED | LEASED | OTHER | TOTAL | PERCENT |
| 1 | 2 | 3 | 4 | 5 | 6 | 7 | 8 | 9 | 10 | 11 |
| Private farms - Total | 37,61,688 | 4,90,60,542 | 8,96,602 | 100 | 69,87,650 | 63,50,966 | 15,84,223 | 2,37,292 | 1,51,60,131 | 100 |
| 150 acres and above | 16,163 | 44,81,803 | 4,593 | 1 | 7,58,032 | 3,14,323 | 1,95,425 | 56,745 | 13,24,525 | 9 |
| 150 " to 50.0 acres | 1,02,641 | 74,02,094 | 36,164 | 4 | 13,47,573 | 9,25,655 | 3,43,871 | 47,689 | 26,64,788 | 18 |
| 50 " " 25.0 " | 2,89,146 | 92,15,260 | 99,368 | 11 | 15,08,358 | 13,73,510 | 3,73,923 | 43,648 | 32,99,439 | 22 |
| 25 " " 12.5 " | 7,93,928 | 1,30,61,022 | 2,50,461 | 28 | 18,18,543 | 20,13,381 | 3,90,526 | 45,998 | 42,68,488 | 28 |
| 12.5 " " 7.5 " | 9,20,848 | 89,08,584 | 2,43,439 | 27 | 10,07,991 | 11,53,812 | 1,78,330 | 22,803 | 23,62,936 | 16 |
| 7.5 " " 5.0 " | 5,79,924 | 34,29,045 | 1,37,634 | 15 | 3,63,861 | 3,99,275 | 66,195 | 10,962 | 8,40,293 | 6 |
| 5.0 " " 2.5 " | 5,38,421 | 19,01,342 | 94,115 | 10 | 1,60,167 | 1,51,648 | 30,482 | 7,362 | 3,49,659 | 2 |
| 2.5 " " 1.0 " | 3,64,155 | 5,84,253 | 27,108 | 3 | 21,882 | 18,411 | 5,212 | 1,962 | 47,467 | |
| under 1.0 acre | 1,56,462 | 77,139 | 3,750 | | 1,243 | 951 | 259 | 123 | 2,576 | |

Source: *ibid.*

Apart from a few districts in the Punjab, the majority of tenancies are held under sharecropping contract; in many, but not all, instances these can be constitutive of non-capitalist production relations, as we shall see.

Table 4.3 shows the number and area of owner-cum-tenant farms. The high proportion of sharecropped farms especially in the 7.5 to 12.5 acre category, who number 600,000 out of about 2 million sharecropped, is surprising; equally surprising is the number of sharecropped farms in the 25-100 acre category, which is supposed to have spearheaded the GR. It appears that the 'middle class' farmer or 'kulak' has proceeded to develop capitalism whilst retaining significant pockets of sharetenancy which may be constitutive of non-capitalist production relations. Sharetenancy has figured greatly in the various debates on the modes of production in agriculture in south Asia, and has generally been identified with pre-capitalist relations, an assertion which is questionable as we shall see in the following chapters.

It also needs to be mentioned that agricultural incomes remain untaxed in Pakistan, though *ushr* has been introduced since the early 1980s. This is a social welfare tax on 75 percent of the gross value of agricultural produce (to make allowances for costs of production); it is self-assessd but is collected compulsarily from landowners and tenants at the rate of about 5 percent of the produce. Cultivators with low production levels of wheat plus some other indigent categories are exempt from *ushr*.

The exemption of agricultural incomes from tax deprives Pakistan's economy of a valuable source of capital formation - whose consequences for local development I shall discuss in chapters 8 and 9.

In this chapter I have described the transformation of Pakistan's economy in relation to its further integration into the global economy. I have described how the development policies adopted by successive governments in Pakistan have made the economy increasingly dependent on foreign capital, equipment and technology, including the external financing of this development process. Two processes in particular have deepend the country's dependence on the global economy, import-substitution industrialization for consumption goods, and the green revolution strategy which has depended crucially for its elements of production on directly or indirectly imported capital and intermediate goods.

I have related this process to the internationalization of capital reflected in the operation of the MNCs who produce and control, irrespective of their geographical location, capital and intermediate goods on which developing countries, including Pakistan's, development strategy is based. This chapter also provides the context for, and links the constraining effects of the global economy on the extent and quality of local development process, as it is incorporated into and shaped by the larger economy.

# 5 Production relations in the local economy

The increasing integration of the national into the international economy that I have described has a local dimension: the penetration of capital into and transformation of the local economy and its incorporation into the national and international economy. This is premissed on a dual process of import and use of machinery and other elements of production and articles of consumption, into the village economy, and an increase in the export of local produce into the national and international markets.

The local economy into which capital penetrates comprises heterogeneous structures some of which facilitate and others impede development and transformation. Larger landholdings and access to adequate quantities of capital facilitate development; whilst small-scale agricultural and artisan production impedes this process. Moreover, these structures establish the modality or possibilities of some type of development, whilst precluding others. That is, whether agricultural development is landlord or peasant led, an issue which I raised briefly in chapter 2.

In the following chapters I shall concretize the process of national and international development discussed at a more general level in the previous chapters. I do this by analyzing local development, and the way this is shaped by the complex configuration of local, national and international processes. As I shall indicate, local development has been predicated on increasing internationalization of the local economy, though there are specifically local factors, such as the local political economy and ecology, that have an important impact on development as well. In other words whilst international capital transforms the local economy, the latter in turn shapes and transforms this capital, and gives it its operative quality.

In the analyses that follow, particular emphasis is placed on the process of production in Mallian, as this concretizes the extent of local development and shapes the agrarian transition. Of course local development is an uneven process, with different branches of production coming under the control of capital at different times, and in different ways, as we shall see.

The process of production in Mallian is conditioned by a number of social, economic, political and ecological processes, of which ownership of land is the main determinant, and constitutes the main element of the local political economy.

Moreover, an understanding of the local economy and its incorporation into the larger national and international structures is essential as this forms the matrix of capitalist development in Mallian. Thus the aim of this chapter is to provide a descriptive analyses of Mallian's socio-economic structure in its local, national and international setting; that is, the structure into which international and national capital penetrates.

### *The region: Sheikhupura district*

Sheikhupura district, which constitutes Mallian's immediate spatial, economic and social environment, has an area of 2,312 square miles and a population of nearly two million; giving a population density of 804 persons per square mile. The district is composed of the Sharaqpur, Shahdara and Sheikhupura *tehsils* or sub-districts. Tehsils, rather than districts, reflect more accurately the socio-economic structure of a locality; therefore I shall describe some salient features of Sheikhupura tehsil, based on information I obtained from the Agricultural Development Bank of Pakistan (ADBP), Sheikhupura tehsil branch, and from the the District Revenue Offices.

There are 291 villages in the tehsil with a population of 812,876 giving an average of about 2,793 persons per village. The total acreage of the tehsil is 593,166 acres, an average of 2,038 acres per village. The main crops grown in the tehsil are: wheat, rice, barley, grain, sugar cane, cotton, fodder and maize.

In 1977 there were 1,318 tractors in the tehsil (1738 in 1987) an average of 4.5 tractors per village; put another way, there is one tractor for every 450 acres in the tehsil. There are 2,580 tubewells in the tehsil, an average of 9 per village; in addition there are 32 wells operated by draught animals.

### *Mallian: location and setting*

The village is located about three miles off the Lahore-Sheikhupura road, a strip of metalled road connecting Lahore city and Sheikhupura town. The village lies at about 20 miles distance from Lahore and six miles from Sheikhupura. Access to Mallian from the main road is by a tertiary (*kacha*) road which is a distance of about three miles. There is also a railway track about 1.5 miles from Mallian and the nearest railway station is two miles away.

Mallian households can be classified according to their productive activity and relationship to land; these are, broadly, agricutural and non-agricutural households. The agricultural households are further classified into landowning and non-landowning households; the latter are comprised mainly of sharetenants and leaseholding tenants. Agricultural households are defined as those which derive the major portion of their income from agriculture, irrespective of whether land is owned or rented. Where necessary all categories of agricultural households are referred to as 'landholders'. Of course there is overlap among some of these households, though the broad classification is appropriate, as we shall see.

Non-agricultural households are those which derive the major portion of their income from non-agricultural work: included in this category are artisan and service castes households, and households dependent upon work outside of Mallian economy, in nearby industry. An important dimension of the households classification is that according to socio-economic status. By socio-economic status I mean the esteem or recognition accorded to members of households with a particular place in the village hierarchy which is largely, but not exclusively, derived from relationship to land.

There are 408 holds in Mallian with a population of about 3000. The village and its cultivated area is relatively large by Pakistani standards (typical village in the Punjab has about 1200 acres) and is also larger than the typical village in the tehsil.

Out of a total of 408 households in Mallian 221 (54 percent) are agricultural and of these 91 (41 percent) own land; these constitute 22 percent of all village households. Put another way, about 60 percent of agricultural households do not own any land and these are 32 percent of the total village households. The 197 non-agricultural households constitute 45.8 percent of village housholds. These also include households which had previously owned some land.

In a way, artisan households may also be considered 'agricultural' since, *prima facie*, they represent the unity of agriculture and industry, a relationship that characterizes non-capitalist production embodied in *sep* that I have described briefly in the Introduction and which I shall discuss further below. The majority of other non-agricultural households are employed outside of Mallian economy, mainly in modern industry located nearby, which I shall discuss in detail in chapter 8.

**Classes in Mallian**

The households in Mallian can be categorized into various classes according to their relationship to the means of production and their position in the local social division of labour - in the present context this means principally the relationship to land and to instruments of production in the case of artisans. The term 'rural classes' rather than peasant classes is used (the former subsumes the latter) since there exists a substantial landlord class in Mallian (and in the Punjab) and a class of artisans as well.

The identification of rural classes, and in particular, peasant classes, has been an area of some dispute in studies of rural social formations [1]. Our definition of classes in the rural Punjab are, with some modification, similar to those of Haider and Kuhnen (1974:52-67). These are:

1) Landless agricultural labourers: these do not own any land but work as labourers for wage, or are tied to landlords and rich peasants on a hereditary basis.

2) Poor peasants: includes those owning upto 5 acres of irrigated land or 12 acres of unirrigated land. They are termed poor as they are generally unable to subsist on this land and have to supplement their income by hiring out their labour or renting in additional land.

3) Small peasants own 6 to 10 acres. They are able, under normal conditions, to reproduce themselves with a small margin over the subsistence level, depending on the size of the household.

4) Middle peasants own 11 to 25 acres. The range of resources subsumed under this category vary considerably, but their essential characteristic is that they are relatively self-sufficient, and under normal consitions they do not need to hire in or hire out land or labour.

5) Rich peasants own 25 to 50 acres: a considerable surplus can be produced on this land; which is in excess of what they can cultivate themselves; so hiring in labour and renting out land is common to this category of owners.

6) Small and large landlords. The former own 50 to 150 acres; the latter over 150 acres. The landlords differ from rich peasants in that they normally do not physically cultivate their land, though they may supervise or manage their cultivation. Within this category of owners a varied set of production relations can be found based on: sharetenancy, wage-labourers, and 'tied' labour. The landlords relatively large size of holdings enable them to appropriate considerable surpluses, which are sold on the market, and reinvested or consumed, or both.

There are other classes in Mallian which I need to consider briefly: the tenants and artisans. There are different types of tenants, classified according to the tenancy arrangements and share of the product (normally half, as we shall see in this chapter), but generally those who cultivate more than 12 acres are above the subsistence level. Some are able to accumulate considerable surpluses, particularly in Sahiwal district.

Artisans cannot be considered peasants, though their work is tied to peasant production: they produce ploughs, harrows, and other traditional technology, as means of production for peasant cultivation. The artisans own their own means of production and in this sense are not strictly members of the rural proletariat, though some have been proletarianized, and most are poor. The artisans under *sep* represent the unity of agriculture and handicraft industry which in its pure form is the linchpin of a feudalistic rural economy.

**Household structure, income and consumption**

There are approximately 3000 persons who live in the 408 households in Mallian, an average of about seven persons per household. The typical household consists of husband, wife and four or five children (generally male children and unmarried females live with their parents); though joint and extended households are also found. The extended household generally consists of married brothers or sometimes patrilineal cousins and their wives and children. The joint household normally consists of brothers, their sons and their sons' children. In general, the size of agricultural households is somewhat larger (an average of almost nine persons) than the non-agricultural households (with an average of about five to six persons); reflecting lack of work for, and also greater geographical mobility of, the non-landowning households.

The range of household incomes in Mallian varies enormously, from below rupees (Rs) 2,400 (at 1980 prices £1 equalled about rupees 25) per annum, considered to be the minimum subsistence income for an average household, to over several *lakhs* (one lakh is 100,000) of Rupees. Since there is such a wide range of income distribution, average household income of the village would be a meaningless abstraction. A more meaningful way of assessing income levels in the village is to give average income for the different socio-economic strata or producer groups in the village.

Households in Mallian have the following average annual income: those owning over 50 acres, Rs 102,250; those owning between 25 to 50 acres, Rs 38,500; between 11 to 25 acres, Rs 19,000; those owning 6 to 10 acres the income is about Rs 8000; upto 5 acres, Rs 8000. The figures given are for farm income rather than total household income, which in some cases could be higher as this is often supplemented by off-farm employment and commercial activities.

The incomes of landless sharetenants is generally less than half of those owning an equivalent amount of land (as this involves half-share of the product); income is also supplemented by off-farm work, or casual work in the locality. The average household income for this category averages at about Rs 5,200 per annum. For landless agricultural labourers, annual household income is about Rs 5000, and for artisan/service castes, Rs 6000.

Clearly some households can meet all their subsistence needs and still have a large surplus, whilst others have to borrow money to cover their subsistence needs and are perpetually indebted to landowners or merchants, as we shall see. The basis of this unequal distribution of income is directly related to the unequal distribution of land in Mallian and the differential access to resources (and to power, influence and authority).

On average a typical household of seven members consumes from about 35 to 50 *maunds* (1 maund=82 lbs) of wheat, and 24 to 50 maunds of rice per year. The better-off households consume more wheat made into local bread while the poorer households consume more rice. The latter eat the bread and rice with lentils, yoghourt, vegetables and pickles, and eat meat once a fortnight. The 'middling' households (e.g. small peasants to middle peasants) in addition to food consumed by the poorer households, eat meat once a week. Among the larger owners meat is eaten at least three times a week and more butter and other dairy produce is consumed. About two or three meals a day are eaten by all households.

Consumption of other, non-productive items varies too: from coarse cotton clothes and minimal consumption of consumer durables to expensive clothes and televisions, radios, refrigerators, scooters, bicycles, horse-drawn carriages and cars. As we shall see in chapters 8 and 9, the consumption of these items is important for the realization of surplus value and represents the appropriation of the local surplus by national and international capital, which is a drain on investible surplus.

## Resources in Mallian

### *Land*

Land is the most important means of production in Mallian with the majority of households dependent on it for their livelihood either directly (landholders) or indirectly (artisans). Table 5.1 shows the classification of land and water resources in the village.

Table 5.1: Type of land and water resources in Mallian

| | acres | percent |
|---|---|---|
| Uncultivable waste | 262 | 7.55 |
| Canal and well irrigated | 165 | 4.75 |
| Canal irrigated | 1619 | 46.69 |
| Well irrigated | 12 | 0.34 |
| Well and canal irrigated | 30 | 0.86 |
| Rainfed | 3 | 0.09 |
| Culturable waste | 1476 | 42.57 |
| Total | 3467 | 100.00 |

Revenue assessed
at Rs 32,645 per season
Source: Mallian Records Book

The reliability, however, of some figures in Table 5.1 are questionable; the amount of land designated as waste is exaggerated according to both our survey and informants in the village; consequently land under crop is underestimated too. A more reliable figure based on the survey is included wherever this is relevant.

*Water resources*

There were 27 tubewells in Mallian in 1978 (which had increased to 33 in 1987). In addition there are 6 wells operated by animals. Canal water, which provides irrigation for most of the cultivted land in Mallian, is provided by channels fed from the Upper Chenab Canal.

*Climate*

Annual rainfall in the Mallian region (which is part of the central Punjab) is about 20 inches per year of which 15 inches or 76 percent falls between June and September; the rest falls intermittently during the winter months (Spate, 1957:42-55).

*Temperature*

Daytime temperature in the area ranges from 50-55 degrees fahrenheit in the winter though night time temperature can be much lower. The summer mean temperatures range from 85-95 degrees fahrenheit with daytime temperatures ranging from 100-120 degrees fahrenheit.

*Soil*

This is substantially the same as the rest of the central Punjab: deep, sandy alluvial with an upper soil which is loam of light to medium quality and is, on the whole, fertile, having most minerals for bacterial activity of the soil (Calvert, 1936:149).

*Tractors and other technology*

In 1978 there were 17 tractors operating in Mallian (increased to 26 in 1987) mainly Massey-Ferguson and Fiat of 40 to 60 horsepower. Almost 60 percent of cultivators had manual wheat threshers, though only four households owned electric-powered ones. There is also one modern wheat flour mill and one rice-husking mill, which operate mainly during the harvesting periods.

*Cattle and other animals*

Almost all households in Mallian own livestock: these are either draught animals or milch cows and buffaloes; the former are needed for ploughing and pulling carts; the latter for the milk and milk products which are either consumed or sold on the market. Also, there are about 40 households in the village that own sizeable number of animals, generally about 12 or more; these include cows, buffaloes, donkeys, horses, goats, sheep and sometimes camels; the largest landowner in the village has some 300 milch cows and buffaloes as well as horses, goats and donkeys. However, ownership of assets in the form of livestock is not analyzed in detail since the focus is on the process of production, and not ownership of assets, though as we shall see animals are an extremely important source of power for ploughing and irrigation from wells; moreover, possession of draught animals is often a precondition for obtaining a tenancy contract.

## Landowning agricultural households

### *Land distribution*

The most important factor in Mallian's economy is the unequal distribution of land. If the 3,258.5 cultivable acres in Mallian were equally distributed among the 91 households, each household would get about 35.5 acres each. If the land were distributed among all the village households, each would have about 8 acres. This is more than the subsistence unit of 5 irrigated acres per household. In fact, land is distributed as shown in Table 5.2.

Table 5.2: Distribution of land in Mallian 1978

| Land owned (acres) | Households No. | % | Land Amount | % |
|---|---|---|---|---|
| 150 + | 3 | 3.2 | 1097.5 | 33.7 |
| 150 -100 | 2 | 2.0 | 240.5 | 07.5 |
| 100 - 50 | 3 | 3.2 | 211.0 | 06.5 |
| 50 - 25 | 31 | 34. | 1207.5 | 37.0 |
| 25 - 10 | 19 | 21.0 | 308.5 | 09.5 |
| 10 - 5 | 15 | 16.5 | 135. | 54.5 |
| 5 - 1 | 18 | 19.8 | 58.0 | 01.8 |
| | 91 | 100.0 | 3258.5 | 100.0 |

Of course, if all households in Mallian were included in the table .the land distribution would be even more skewed.

Table 5.2 shows that 39 housholds, constituting 42.4 percent of the households, own 84.6 percent of land in Mallian. Three households, owning 150 acres or more, and constituting 3.2 percent of households, own 33.7 percent of the land. At the other end, 33 households, or 36 percent of the total, own a total of 193.5 acres, or 5.9 percent of the land. However, the bulk of the land with 1207.5 acres (37 percent) is owned within the 25 to 50 acre range, i.e. by the rich peasant category.

The unequal distribution of land is the basis of agrarian production relations in Mallian; those households which do not have enough land to subsist on have to rent additional land to farm; and those households that own more land than they can cultivate, hire in labour for cultivation, or rent out surplus land.

This unequal distribution of land not only differentiates Mallian households into particular classes; it is also related to caste and *biraderi* (local patrilineal groups which are roughly equivalent to the Hindu *jati*) in the village [1].

Table 5.3 shows that *dogars* with 51 percent of households own 53 percent of the land. The *virk jats* with 12 percent of households own nearly 11 percent of the land. One *syed* household owns 10 percent of the land, and so on for the other biraderis.

Whilst the economic and political power which landownership bestows on castes and biraderis is important, equally important is the internal differentiation of landownership within biraderis; for example amongst the dogars' 51 households and 1,735 acres, there is a variation of 2 to 500 acres: 22 households own 20 to 37.5 acres; one household owns 40 acres and 7 households own 50 acres; 2 households own 60 and 500 acres each.

Table 5.3: Households owning land in Mallian by caste/biraderi

| Caste/biraderi | Households No. | Households % | Land Amount (acres) | % |
|---|---|---|---|---|
| Dogar | 51 | 56 | 1735 | 53.2 |
| Virk(Jat) | 11 | 12 | 352.5 | 10.8 |
| Syed | 1 | 1 | 338.5 | 10.3 |
| Pathan | 1 | 1 | 259 | 4.9 |
| Grahya | 1 | 1 | 103 | 3.1 |
| STM Ltd | 1 | 1 | 100 | 3.0 |
| Baloch | 1 | 1 | 51 | 1.6 |
| Varaich | 1 | 1 | 50 | 1.5 |
| Bhatti (Rajput) | 1 | 1 | 50 | 1.5 |
| Gujar | 1 | 1 | 50 | 1.5 |
| Cheema (Jat) | 1 | 1 | 28 | 0.8 |
| Waqf | 1 | 1 | 27 | 0.8 |
| Arain | 8 | 8.8 | 26 | 0.8 |
| Bajwa (Jat) | 1 | 1.0 | 12.5 | 0.4 |
| Chauhan | 1 | 1.0 | 8.0 | 0.2 |
| Bhatti (Jat) | 1 | 1.0 | 10.5 | 0.3 |
| Kumhar (Potters) | 5.5 | 5.5 | 17.0 | 0.5 |
| Nai (Barber) | 1 | 1.0 | 12.5 | 0.4 |
| Tarkhan (Carpenter) | 1 | 1.0 | 3.0 | 0.1 |
| | 91 | 100.0 | 3258.5 | 100.0 |

Intra-biraderi inequalities in land distribution is further shown by the virk households: 4 households own 10 acres each; 2 own 12.5 acres each; one household owns 137.5 acres. Households of other biraderis are too few and own too little land to show the marked internal inequalities in land distribution.

The significance of this intra-biraderi differentiation is that whilst caste-biraderi links households vertically, class (property) links the households horizontally [3]. This fact often causes a disjuncture between 'loyalty' to biraderi and class interests where these do not overlap. This internal differentiation reflects the developing class relations in Mallian and in the countryside as a whole. However, this disjuncture between biraderi and class affects mainly the landowning households and much less the artisans, landless labourers and other traditionally lower status groups, though they may, and sometimes do, act as corporate bodies in minor disputes. This shows that there is no *a priori* separation between biraderi and class, and the relationship between the two has to be empirically verified.

**Non-landowning agricultural households**

Table 5.4: Non-landowning agricultural households in Mallian

| Caste/biraderi | Households No. | % |
|---|---|---|
| Dogar | 29 | 22.3 |
| Arain | 9 | 7.0 |
| Bajwa (Jat) | 5 | 3.8 |
| Kumhar (Potter) | 1 | 0.8 |
| Asai (Christian) | 60 | 46.0 |
| Rajput (Minhas) | 8 | 6.0 |
| Weaver (Bhatti) | 3 | 2.3 |
| Weaver (Julaha) | 4 | 3.0 |
| Changar | 8 | 6.0 |
| Mendicant (faqir) | 3 | 2.3 |
| | 130 | 100.0 |

Non-landowning agricultural households constitute 32 percent of the village total and provide the bulk of agricultural labourers, sharecroppers and other types of tenants. The diversity of caste and biraderi among these households reflects both a flux in and specialization of the local social division of labour. So that whilst some households are employed in general agricultural work requiring little skill and specialization, others do highly specialized work. For example, christians (converts from the former untouchables) invariably comprise the hereditary sharetenants in the village. It is from these households that the bulk of 'tied' or bonded agricultural labourers are drawn. As we shall see in chapter 8, this groups' class disabilities are compounded by factors such as ethnicity and religion, for they are generally descendents of aboriginal groups or former untouchables converted to Islam or Christianity.

Specialized work or occupational specialization in the local division of labour is exemplified by the *changar* households who provide most of the labour for rice transplanting. The whole household, men, women and children participate in this work, which requires great expertise in transplanting nursery rice (paddy), and is carried out in difficult conditions of summer heat and rains.

In Sheikhupura district at least, rice transplanting has been the specialization of the changars as far back as the latter part of the nineteenth century (Sheikhupura District Gazetteer, 1935). Evidence from the fieldwork suggests that the changars are heavily concentrated in rice transplanting partly because they are debarred from other higher status and less strenous occupations within the local social division of labour: they are aboriginal people of a low staus and often itinerant, working and moving from village to village.

Other households in Mallian reflect a process of proletarianization and diverisification of economic activity. The former is illustrated by the 29 dogar households who for various reasons have alienated their land to other dogars and in many cases have become their tenants. The way that class conflict between tenant and landlord can be muted or exacerbated within the biraderi is thus apparent.

Diversification of economic activity is reflected in households which are engaged in agricultural work but in addition derive some of their income from work in modern industry in the locality.

*Tenancy in Mallian*

There are three major types of tenancies in the village: hereditary tenants, tenants at will, and fixed rent tenants. Hereditary (also called occupancy) tenants are usually sharecroppers who rent in land from the same landlord and can be considered 'tied' to these owners mainly through the debt mechanism. Theoretically they cannot be evicted from the land; in practice however, this can happen easily. As I have said, in Mallian hereditary sharetenants are usually converts from the former untouchables. They are also *de facto* tied to their contracting landowners because they lack alternative job opportunities, including restrictions in employment in nearby industry, as we shall see in chapter 8.

Tenants-at-will are generally of a higher socio-economic standing than hereditary tenants: many of them own land (or had once owned land) and rent-in additional land, as the land they own is not enough to provide an adequate livelihood.

Contracts are usually on a seasonal or yearly basis and the agreement is verbal, without written legal binding.

In both types of tenancies, rent is paid in kind, usually a share of the gross output of 50:50, 60:40, and so on, depending on the quality of the soil, costs of production, labour productivity, availability of alternative employment, power relations between the owner and tenant and so on.

Over the last twenty years or so, fixed-rent tenancy has also developed, though this is still not the dominant form. Under this arrangement, a tenant rents in land for a specified period and pays a fixed money-rent to the owner. In 1978, rent per acre in Mallian varied from Rs 300 to 3,200 per year. This large variation is due to various factors including differing quality of the soil, water availability, and amount of land rented.

A theoretical discussion of sharetenancy is essential because it is a very important feature of the agrarian economy, and there exists an extensive body of literature most of which attempts to construct a general theory of sharecropping (or sharetenancy - these are synonymous terms) on the causes and consequences of this phenomena; but I shall argue that a general theory of sharetenancy is not possible.

Cheung (1968:1107/22), bases his arguments on certain assumptions derived from empirical conditions in Taiwan. He asserts that sharecropping is an efficient arrangement for agricultural production. For Cheung the two main elements in sharecropping are transaction costs and risk. The former involves costs which involve an indeterminate set of sub-elements such as negotiating rentals, overseeing, and so on; whilst the latter means the risk (in terms of success or failure) involved in the cultivation of crops.

Earlier, Marshall (1956), had pointed to the disincentives inherent in the structure of sharetenancy, and therefore this was conceived as an obstacle to agricultural improvement; because unstable tenancies offered the sharetenant little incentive for investment in land.

Marx's views (1974:794-96), are that sharecropping is a transitional form between the feudal and capitalist mode of agricultural production. Whilst this is true in the sense that the highly developed agricultures of the developed countries have witnessed the disappearence of sharetenancy, this abstract theorizing cannot (and is not intended to) account for the existence of sharecropping in the many different empirical conditions in which it exists.

There have been a number of attempts to analyze sharetenancy within a Marxist framework. These have generally, often inadvertently, provided a definitive theory of sharetenancy, which I shall argue, is not possible. For example, Bhaduri (1973; 1983), has attempted to show that sharetenancy is incompatible with the development of productive forces because the landlord will not make technological improvements as this will increase the incomes of tenants, and hence free them from the semi-feudal agrestic servitude which allows them multiple modes of surplus appropriation: including usury and surplus labour. For Bhaduri, this multiple appropriation is also the main reason why sharetenancy precludes incentives for improving agriculture. I shall have more to say on Bhaduri's thesis in chapter 9, but suffice it to say here that if this theses is correct, then why has agricultural improvement taken place?

As I shall indicate, our empirical evidence from Mallian, Sahiwal and Sargodha, does not corroborate Bhaduri's assertions on the conditions of reproduction of sharetenancy.

Gupta (1980), concludes that sharetenancy signals the formal subjection of labour to capital and is thus compatible with the earlier stages of capitalist development. In such a view all types of sharetenancies are considered alike; which, I shall point out below, is fallacious. Gupta's unproblematical view of sharetenancy, as a mere expression of an early phase of capitalist development, goes contrary to the theoretical framework within which his analysis located, since the role of sharetenancy as an obstacle in the development of capitalism has been an important part of Marxist discourse on this issue.

In an interesting article Pearce (1983:63), suggests that 'sharecropping is conjuncturally a consistent form of appropriation where supervision costs are high or where the labour process is characterized by uncertainty'. This attempt at constructing a general theory is untenable. As I have suggested, the conditions of existence for sharetenancy are too diverse and varied that no general theory is possible. As we shall see in our areas of research, the reasons for the existence of sharetenancy include: quality and fertility of land, where owners find renting out their land can be more profitable than self-cultivation, as a mode of labour mobilization, because of particular types of crops grown which require greater labour inputs, and desire by landowners to have an entourage of followers from among their tenants.

**Non-agricultural households**

There are 187 households in this category, almost 46 percent of the village total. These are engaged in a wide variety of occupations: from the traditional artisan/service castes' working under sep to trade and commerce and work in nearby modern industry. Many households in this category are employed in temporary seasonal work in agriculture (during harvesting) whilst others have subsidiary occupations in agriculture. In addition many such households have a traditional occupation though they might not be employed in this; most notably for example in Mallian, the potters have taken up shopkeeping and the carrying trade; others include barbers as cooks, and fisherman as water-carriers.

Under the traditional economy, artisans/service castes fitted rather neatly into the hierarchy of occupation and status circumbscribed by sep. They now have a much wider occupational structure, as we shall see below. Some of these households have accumulated wealth but their status within the village remains ambiguous, because they are not accorded the esteem bestowed on landowners. Of course, the lack of fitness between the traditional and the present occupation, and accumulation of wealth among non-agricultural households, reflects important changes in the local economy.

*The production cycle in agricultural*

The agricultural cycle in Mallian consists of two seasons in the year: *kharif*, which are summer crops, sown in June-July and harvested in November-December; and the *rabi* or winter crops, sown in October-November and harvested in April-May.

The intensity and pace of economic and social activity in the village is related to this seasonal progression, though compared to earlier periods cultivation is becoming 'freer' and more intense and relatively less constrained by natural and climatic variations such as rain and temperatures.

Social activity also was formerly controlled by these conditions but this too is becoming increasingly independent. For example, tubewell irrigation can now provide water almost all the year round; previously a great deal depended on rains and availability of water from the canals. This often fluctuated and/or was unreliable. This clearly demarcated slack and busy periods. Whilst this demarcation is now somewhat blurred, the agricultural cycle still conditions the intensity of economic and social activity in Mallian which can be outlined as follows: From about mid-April to mid-June: much work, employment of additional labour to tide over peak period, harvesting of rabi crops (wheat, vegetables, fodder); preparation of the seed beds and sowing of kharif crops (rice, cotton, vegetables, fodder).

From about mid-June to mid-September: little work, except for weeding and irrigation. During the second half of this period work is often impeded by rains and high temperatures (this however is becoming less of a constraint with the introduction of modern technology such as tractors).

From mid-September to mid-January: much work, employment of additional labour including that of women, harvesting of kharif crops. preparation of seed beds and sowing of rabi crops.

Mid-January to mid-April: little work; land is irrigated, and by the end of this period certain vegetable crops and sugar cane is sown.

*Agricultural landscape* Running parallel on the north side of the village is a secondary canal which is fed from the Upper Chenab Canal which flows about five miles away. This canal has several channels which distribute water to Mallian. These in turn feed water to smaller channels (*khal*) which distribute water to the fields. These are usually two to three feet wide and one to two feet deep. They are constructed parallel to elevated edges (*vat*), that run rectangular around the fields. The fields are divided into portions by clods of earth five to nine inches high: this is not only to measure land but also for watering each portion in a controlled way. Water is allowed to flow or is dammed, from the channels by blocking (or removing) terminals with clods of earth (*band*).

Not all classes of cultivators have access to canal water: often they do not have the distributary channels around their fields as these are costly to construct. The water from tubewells is distributed on the same principles, though as we shall see, this irrigates the fields quicker but also tends to wash away and overflow the *bands* in the fields because of its greater velocity. Generally, the best constructed and maintained channels are on the larger owners lands.

A notable feature in Mallian as in Pakistan as a whole, is that land very rarely exists in one contiguous piece. Holdings are fragmented and scattered all over the village. Even the very largest holdings are intersected by other fields. For example, in Mallian even the largest owner only has 100 of his 500 acres in one piece. The rest are scattered around the village in smaller portions. Whilst 100 acres in one piece is large for Mallian and for the country as a whole, it highlights the fragmentation which delimits the economies of scale from modern technology.

### *The economy under sep*

As I mentioned in the Introduction sep is the Pakistani equivalent of the Indian *jajmani* system which is: 'A feudalistic system of prescribed, hereditary obligations of payments and of occupational and ceremonial duties between two or more families of different castes in the same locality' (Beidelman 1959:6). Sep is arranged between the artisan/service and agricultural households; the former include occupations such as carpenters, blacksmiths, shoemakers, bards, washers/dyers. Under sep these households provide services and products such as iron and metal implements, hoes, tips for ploughs, repair work, barber sevice, and shoes, for agricultural households in return for agricultural produce mainly grain.

In Mallian the rate of remuneration between sepi households fluctuate within definite parameters, according to the volume of work discharged. The carpenters and smiths are generally paid 2.5 maunds each of rice and wheat per season for every plough that a household operates. In general the service castes' households receive less payments than the artisans.

There are three blacksmith and 5 carpenter households in Mallian. The blacksmiths have sep with 20 to 30 households each, the carpenters with 30 households each. The shoemaker has sep with 6 households. Of course, these households have transactions outside of sep as well, on an *ad hoc* basis, usually in cash or the equivalent in grain. In other words, whilst most of the transactions consist of barter, transactions on the market in cash are increasing thereby widening and further monetizing the local economy.

*Land revenue in Mallian*

There are two main types of revenue: water rates and land revenue. The amount payable depends on the quantity of water used and crops grown. In 1978, for irrigated HYV wheat, water rate was Rs 10.40 per acre and land revenue Rs 9.12 per acre. For irrigated HYV rice the water rate was Rs 16.86 and for land revenue Rs 12.15 per acre.

The revenue demand set by the state for Mallian is Rs 32,645 per season. However, according to both the *patwari* (revenue official) and the *numberdar* (headman of the village and revenue collector), only about 3 percent of revenue is collected. And this mainly from the smaller owners, the larger owners rarely pay their dues. As I indicated in chapter 4, there is no tax on agricultural incomes though *ushr* a 5 percent agricultural tax is collected by the state. Revenue is assessed every 20 or 30 years; this means that current assessment does not reflect changes in production over the years. Revenue was last assessed in Mallian in 1950. Clearly, non-taxing of agricultural incomes and low rate of revenue collection means that a very valuable source of investible surplus and potential capital formation is lost to non-productive consumption of the larger owners.

*The local political economy*

There are other aspects of Mallian that need to be discussed in order to establish the matrix into which international and national capital penetrates, namely power authority and status in the locality. This is largely but not exclusively conditioned by the amount of land owned. Landlords and peasants who hire labour or rent land have considerable power over the people they employ, especially since alternative job opportunities are scarce. By having control over land (e.g., by threatening not to renew tenancies), the larger landowners are able to coerce unpaid labour out of their tenants or labourers, or induce them to join their factions.

Authority in Mallian is directly or indirectly derived from relationship with the state apparatus [2]. People with authority are mainly the 'influentials' and 'notables' who in Mallian are the larger owners. They have informal connections with the banks, revenue officials, police, magistrates, officials of the provincial and district adminstrative structures, owners and managers of local industry, and so on.

Often local landowners also hold political or bureaucratic office. For example, the largest owner in Mallian was a member of the so-called Basic Democracies Scheme in 1960-67 (Tinker, 1968). This gave him authority over important decision-making processes such as building of schools, roads, health and family planning, as well as access to influential individuals in bureaucratic and political structures.

The status system in Mallian is more complex. Whilst not wholly dependent on land, this is still the most important determinant of status. For instance, traditional landowning biraderis have higher prestige though they may no longer own land; and *vice versa*: some non-landowning biraderis have low status in the village even though they own land. Marriages for instance are invariably intra-biraderi.

The domination of Mallian's social economy by landowners does not go unquestioned by the subordinate classes. But neither can one detect a situation of a simple class struggle between landlords on the one hand, and those with little or no land, on the other.

Apart from formal politics which are a part of, and configure with national political processes, there are politics of the village itself, which though not unrelated to the outside, have their own specificity. In Mallian these are articulated by the two main factions, one led by the largest owner in the village, a dogar, and the other by the second largest, a virk jat. Both these factions are, on the whole, vertical alignments based not on socio-economic class but on the perceived identity of interest which one faction or the other represents. The factions are composed of individuals who are related to, or are dependent upon, the heads of either of the two factions, for example, members of the same biraderi, tenants and labourers (cf. Alavi, 1973). It is not necessary to go into details on the object of local politics, except that this involves questions of power, authority and influence with officialdom outside, and numerical support in Mallian, a process which uses up local resources which could be used more productively as we shall see in the following chapters.

**Mallian and the larger market**

Mallian is the largest village within a 6 mile radius and its economy is linked in important ways to the regional and national and international economy. As I point out below, this relationship is mediated primarily by the market in Sheikhupura town and in Lahore City.

The village is part of the local social division of labour comprised of a number of villages; its economy is larger and more dynamic and it draws labour from local villages which have smaller or less dynamic economies that cannot absorb their own labour force. Also, for historical reasons, some occupational specializations are found in some villages and not in others. An example of the local social division of labour is provided by one village about three miles northwest of Mallian. The village is small, with about 500 acres, most of which are owned by a single *rajput* lineage of owner-cultivators. About 40 changar households have settled there, but whose labour is not fully employed in that village. Therefore a large number of changars work in Mallian in rice-transplanting, as I have described in a previous section.

Another example of Mallian's linkage with the local and regional economy is provided by specialized artisan production. Mallian has no artisans making earthen pots, though there is a resident biraderi of potters who are no longer engaged in this occupation. Residents of Mallian buy their earthen pots from a nearby village, or from itinerant sellers, and their metal pots from Sheikhupura which is the regional market.

By virtue of its location (near to Sheikhupura and access to a main road and railway) Mallian is a market for the local economy, as well as an intermediary between the local and the larger regional economy. Smaller producers or sellers from within the locality carry out transactions in Mallian. Commodities are often sold in Mallian, rather than in the larger market in Sheikhupura, either because the quantities sold are small or to avoid transportation costs.

### *The market in Sheikhupura*

There are four Mallian landowners who have an *ahrth* (commission agency). Their transactions are conducted in their office-godowns located in the grain market in Sheikhupura. Here their own produce and that of other producers in Mallian and other villages from the locality, is sold to buyers from all over Pakistan, but mainly from the large cities of Lahore and Karachi. From here the produce is sold on the national and international market.

Put simply, the ahrthis (who are sometimes landowners) usually charge 2 to 3 percent of the value of the produce for buying and selling grain. Conversely, the buyers also have to pay 2 to 3 percent of the value of the produce as agents fee. Adjacent to the grain market is the vegetable market. Here too, transactions are carried out on the same principles as the grain market, except that the commission for selling is much higher, between 6 to 12 percent, and for buying 2 to 3 percent.

Many commission agents double up as money-lenders and provide loans, in particular to smaller producers to grow vegetables; for this they are willing to lend money rather more freely than for grain production. Profits from vegetables are higher than from grain; though in the latter case they tend to buy during harvest when prices are on a par with the governments procurement price, and sell throughout the year when the market prices are well above the procurement price.

The commission agents also exercise control over the production process in the local economy through the sale of fertilizer and seed. They buy up stocks from government depots or from cultivators throughout the year and sell during the sowing season when prices are higher. In particular they can control the production and labour processes of the small producers by giving fertilizer in exchange for produce; or sell fertilizer on credit on condition that the produce is marketed through them.

The size of the grain market and the number of commission agents has increased enormously since the 1960s; this has not only enlarged the market in terms of the volume of transactions, but it has also internationalized it by linking it to the national and global markets, through sale and consumption of goods.

The relationship between the local and national and international market is mediated mainly by the larger landowners in Mallian who market large surpluses of agricultural produce; they also import great bulk of the commodities into the locality, comprised both of consumption goods and elements of production manufactured mainly by MNCs and linked to the national and local economy by the international circuits of capital which I have discussed in previous chapters. These goods include: articles of clothing, food, beverages, tractors, tubewells, cold storage and refrigeration plants, and pesticides.

Of course not all sectors of Mallian economy are incorporated into the international economy equally or at the same time, nor subject to an even and equal development of capitalist production; for as we have seen Mallian's economy is heterogeneous, comprising sectors and processes which may, as we shall see in the following chapters, facilitate or impede capitalist development and the agrarian transition that accompanies the global incorporation of the local economy.

**Notes**

1. The vertical linkages of biraderis have mainly a social and ideological relevance; economic links retain their significance to a limited extent only. It should be noted that the various laws of pre-emption, e.g., the 1913 Pre-emption of Land Act, restricts land being alienated outside of a lineage, without land first being offered for sale within the lineage.

2. Authority derived from office at the local level in the rural areas of Pakistan has taken different forms, varying with the changing political and economic structures of the country. Under the Ayub Khan regime (1958-1969), there was a hierarchical system of elected and appointed representation called 'basic democracies'. The system was suspended during the Z.A.Bhutto regime (1972-77), when elected provincial assemblies were setup.

# 6 Economic and social development of the local economy

Certain historical periods are distinguished from others by the relative speed of change and development. The 'green revolution' in Mallian represents one such period. The period is the late 1960s to 1978, the high tide of the green revolution, though as I have stated earlier, Mallian has undergone gradual change over a long period including that under British colonial rule.

The rapid change is most discernible in the following areas: increased area under crop; increased availability of credit; increased use of HYV seeds, fertilizers, tractors, tubewells and other modern technology. These changes increased output and brought about a significant transformation in the production relations and the labour process in the local economy. For example, there was greater impetus towards converting tenants into wage labourers and resumption by owners of land previously worked by tenants.

This process of change was premissed on greater use of elements of production from an increasingly internationalized capital, which further integrated Mallian into the national and international economy; a process which has both facilitated and impeded local development as we shall see.

Another source of change, which I shall analyze in chapter 8, was the location of modern industry in the locality which had a important effect on capitalist development and the agrarian transition.

*Crops grown and land under cultivation*

Table 6.1: Kharif crops grown in Mallian in 1977 in acres

| Crop | Area cultivated |
| --- | --- |
| Rice | 2,071 |
| Millet | 7 |
| Maize | 4 |
| Sesame | 1 |
| Fodder (gowara) | 10 |
| Fodder (chari) | 92 |
| Other fodder | 170 |
| Vegetables | 30 |
| Cotton | 1 |
| Lugan | 2 |
| Sugar cane | 18 |
| Orchards | 5 |
| Pepper | 3 |
| | 2,416 |

Source: Mallian Records Book [1].

Table 6.2: Rabi crops grown in Mallian in 1977

| Crop | Area cultivated (acres) |
|---|---|
| Wheat | 1,808 |
| Other grains | 8 |
| Lentils | 23 |
| Vegetables | 33 |
| Rape | 6 |
| Fodder (shaftal) | 612 |
| Fruit | 8 |
| | 2,498 |

Source: Mallian Records Book

The total cultivable area in Mallian increased from 1,729 acres in 1967 to 3,258.5 acres in 1977. In 1977 the total area under crop for rabi and kharif was 4,914 out of a possible 6,517 acres per year; that is 45 percent of the land for two seasons in the year [2]. In terms of two crops per year of total cultivable land, 150 percent of the land was cultivated [3]. This cropping intensity of 150 in Mallian is somewhat higher than the cropping intensity of 137 found by Khan (1975:16) in Gujranwala, a rice growing district adjacent to Sheikhupura.

Kharif crops in Mallian take up 2,416 acres (74 percent) of cultivable area; 26 percent of the area is left fallow. Rabi crops take up 2,498 acres (76 percent), of the cultivable area, with 24 percent left fallow.

Rice is the major crop in kharif, this takes up 85.7 percent of land under cultivation, that is, 2,071 acres. In rabi 1,808 acres, 72.3 percent of the land, was under wheat and 612 acres or 24 percent of the land was under fodder, and 33 acres (1.32 percent) under vegetables.

The relatively large area under fodder is related to a number of factors. First, the village has a relatively large cultivable area which requires draught animals for ploughing and transporting goods and for the upkeep of milch cows and buffaloes; second, there is a large dairy farm in the village, with some 300 cows and buffaloes for whom fodder is required as feed; apart from growing his own, the owner of the dairy buys up fodder from smaller cultivators; third, there is demand for fodder in Sheikhupura town for *tongas* (horse drawn carriages), dairy farms and other households that keep animals; fourth, the *shaftal* variety of fodder is grown for seeding, and fetches a high price on the market; fifth, there is evidence that acreage under fodder is exaggerated to evade revenue as this is low for fodder compared to other crops because it requires relatively less water compared to other crops.

**Changes in acreage and cropping patterns**

1967, as a base year for comparison with subsequent years is useful in that the green revolution package had not been introduced into Mallian to any large extent; this enables one to measure the magnitude of subsequent changes.

Table 6.3 shows that cultivated area from kharif 1967 to kharif 1977 increased by 76.6 percent, that is from 1,368 to 2,416 acres. Area under cultivation increased by 87.4 percent; under fodder by 94.6 percent, whilst area under sugar cane decreased by 58 percent. In 1977, 30 acres were under vegetable crops, whilst in 1967 the figure was negligible.

Similar changes are observable from table 6.4 for rabi crops over the same decade. Cultivated area between 1967 and 1977 increased by 1,423 acres, an increase of 132 percent. The area under wheat increased by 1,390 acres or 332.5 percent. Fodder crops increased in absolute acreage by 26 acres but in relative terms it declined from 54 percent of rabi area in 1967 to 24.5 percent in 1977.

Cropping intensity in 1967 was 141.2, increasing to 150 in 1978 [4]. *Prima facie* these increases in cropping intensity do not seem significant enough; but in fact, they show some important changes, especially the increase of vegetables under crop. This increase I think is considerably understated, possibly because land revenue and water rates payable for vegetables are higher in comparison to fodder and grain. The understatement could be as much as 100 percent. Also, since these (official) statistics are based on returns at the end of each season, the double or multiple cropping between the periods is generally not calculated: for example, there can be three crops of potatoes between September and May.

The cultivation of vegetables of course is very important for the development of the scale of production based on socialized labour processes, such as that of the *juts* which I shall discuss later in this chapter. The increase in cultivation of vegetables is the direct result of increased availabilty of water by tubewells, and other inputs such as fertilizers and pesticides, and of course development of the national and international market especially in the middle east.

Of course cropping intensity had changed in the early 1960s; this was due to increase in the number of tubewells operating in the area. According to a survey by the Pakistan Institute of Development Economics of an area that included Sheikhupura District, cropping intensity increased from 84 in the early 1960s to 134 in the mid-1960s. This increase was imputed to be entirely due to greater availability of water. On the basis of information obtained in Mallian, cropping intensity in Mallian was low too, probably near 100. However, as I have said, changes during 1967-77 were of a qualitative sort, as I indicate below.

*Adoption of high yielding varieties of seeds* (HYVs)

In Mallian both the relative and absolute acreage is greater for rice than for any other crop. This is due in part to an ecological condition, salinity in the area, and rice is less affected by this. The increase in area under rice after 1967 is also due to adoption of HYV (irri-6 and related sub-varieties) that I have discussed in previous chapters. Prior to this, local varieties including *basmati*, a superior variety, were cultivated. Gradually, the HYVs, which give substantially higher yields, supplanted the traditional varieties.

The adoption of HYV wheat occurred a little later. As table 6.4 shows, in rabi 1967, 418 acres were under wheat; of this only 8 acres were under HYV. In rabi of 1969 there was a marked shift in the adoption of HYV: out of a total acreage of 616 acres under wheat, 563 acres were under HYV, and only about 50 acres under the traditional varieties. Put another way, in 1967 only about 2 percent of wheat acreage was under HYV; in 1969 it was about 90 percent.

Table 6.3: Comparison of main kharif crops grown in Mallian - 1967 and 1977

| 1967 | | | | 1977 | | | |
|---|---|---|---|---|---|---|---|
| Crops Grown (acres) | | | As % of total cultivated kharif (adjusted) | Crops Grown (acres) | | | As % of total cultivated kharif (adjusted) |
| Rice | 1,105 | (various HYVs including traditional) | 80.7 | Rice | 2,071 | (new varieties and Basmati) | 85.7 |
| Fodder | 150 | | 10.9 | Fodder | 271 | | 11.2 |
| Sugar cane | 43 | | 3.1 | Vegetables | 30 | | 1.2 |
| Other | 70 | | | Sugar cane | 18 | | 0.74 |
| | | | | Other | 35 | | 1.5 |
| | 1,368 | | 100.0 | | 2,416 | | 100.00 |

Source: Mallian Records Book

Table 6.4: Comparison of main rabi crops grown in Mallian - 1967 and 1977

| | Crops Grown (acres) | As % of total cultivated kharif (adjusted) | | Crops Grown (acres) | As % of total cultivated kharif |
|---|---|---|---|---|---|
| Wheat | 418 (410 traditional varieties) | 38.8 | Wheat | 1,808 | 72.3 |
| Fodder | 586 | 54.5 | Vegetables | 35 | 1.4 |
| Other | 71 | 6.7 | Fodder | 612 | 24.5 |
| | | | Other | 43 | 1.7 |
| | 1,075 | 100.0 | | 2,498 | 100.0 |

Source: Mallian Records Book

*Increase in output*

The average yields per acre increased significantly during this period. In 1967 per acre yield of traditional varieties of rice was between 20 to 25 *maunds* (1 maund=82 lbs); in 1977 the average yield had increased to between 35 to 45 maunds per acre[5]. Generally, the yields are higher on the larger holdings, and the 'inverse' relationship between size of land and yield no longer holds true in Mallian or in other areas (Khan, 1975; Berry and Cline, 1979; Hill, 1983).

There have also been increases in per acre yields of wheat: before 1967 these were in the range of 12 to 15 maunds though higher yields were sometimes possible. In 1977 average yields had increased to between 20 to 25 maunds, the average or typical yield being 25 maunds per acre [5]. Here too, the highest yields per acre are obtained on larger farms, as we shall see in the next chapter, and the inverse relationship no longer holds for wheat either.

However, in Mallian there has not been any significant increase in yields since the mid-1970s, and there is evidence that these might even have declined (Alavi, 1976). This might be due to the fact that marginal land has been brought under cultivation, and the negative effects of chemical fertilizer which is an important issue that I shall discuss in chapter 9.

*Credit in Mallian*

The green revolution inputs have been adopted largely on the basis of loans provided by the state and obtained from international sources; these represent the financial circuit of international capital that links the local to the international economy. These loans have been of crucial importance in the development of agriculture in Mallian for two main reasons: The use of modern inputs which are part of the green revolution package had to be purchased on the market with loans obtained from the ADBP and other commercial banks, and cultivators had initially to be induced to use these on a large enough scale.

Despite the rapid increase in the provision of credit facilities, the volume of loans from institutional sources (state, commercial banks) was estimated at 47 percent of the total disbursed in Pakistan (Malik, 1977). That is, in Pakistan, 53 percent of the total credit came from non-institutional sources such as family, friends, money-lenders, and *ahrthis*.

Under the aegis of the state the Agricultural Development Bank (ADBP) provides credit for short, medium and long term periods. The short term loans are normally given on a seasonal or yearly basis for items such as seeds, fertilizers, labour charges, marketing of crops, hire of ploughs and oxen, preparation of seed-beds, and so on. Medium term loans are given for 5 years and are intended for levelling land, bush clearance, purchase of oxen, indigenous tools and implements, sinking of wells, poultry farms, tractors and tubewells [6].

The long term loans are given for 10 years for animal husbandry, dairy farming, combine harvesters, construction of buildings for storage, cold storage plants, fisheries and other large investment.

Upto 1977 the total long term credit disbursed by the ADBP in Mallian was Rs 348,586; loans for purchase of tractors was Rs 436,574 and short term loans amounted to Rs 87,948 [7]. Whilst these figures are compounded from the ADBP (Sheikhupura tehsil branch) since 1964, there is no reason to assume (given the number of tubewells, tractors, and other equipment are above average for the typical Punjab village), that the yearly rate of credit disbursement and its use does not follow the national trends. These are shown in table 6.5 (the Rupees are in *lakhs*, 1 lakh=100,000).

Table 6.5: Loans disbursed by ADBP

| Year | Total disbursed |
|---|---|
| 1964-65 | 40,469 |
| 1965-66 | 67,975 |
| 1966-67 | 100,481 |
| 1976-77 | 638,770 |

Source: Malik (1977)

The 940 percent increase in the provision of credit from Rs 670 lakh to Rs 6387.70 lakhs between 1965-66 and 1976-77 reflects the general trend in agrarian change outlined above, which was so crucially dependent on credit to purchase elements of production.

The larger landowners receive most of the state-provided loans, particularly the medium and long term loans and the smaller owners are recipients of short term loans. According to Khan (1975:106): 'The amount of debt generally increases with the size of the farm. The highest amounts are for farms over 50 acres. In most districts the lowest amounts of debt are reported by farmers holding under 12.5 acres'. This is corroborated by our research in Mallian: The incidence of debt is highest among larger owners and the size of debt increases with the size of the holding. Smaller owners, such as middle, small and poor peasants and tenants tend to borrow from non-institutional sources.

Of course owners of larger holdings borrow more because they need a greater outlay for their production, and they can borrow more because they own larger amounts of land, which is used as collateral. Thus state policies are clearly biased in favour of the larger owners, and this has led to a polarizition in the quality of cultivation between larger and smaller owners. As we shall see in detail in the next chapter, the increase in the influx of money-capital into Mallian has been of great significance; it has changed the technical conditions of the labour and production processes, and contributed to the agrarian transition. Capital now controls the labour and production processes to a far greater extent than hitherto. This development, of course, has proceeded simultaneously with greater integration and dependence on the international economy.

## Changes in production technology

The increased inflow of money-capital into Mallian has been the basis on which the new technology of the green revolution has been adopted. This new technology can be bio-chemical, such as in fertilizers, pesticides, and HYVs, or mechanical, which include tubewells, tractors and other equipment, (Byres, 1972).

During the period under consideration, that is 1967-78, tractors in Mallian increased from 3 to 17; operating at first alongside and complementing the traditional animal drawn ploughs, then supplanting them, especially on large farms.

Tractors are generally bought with bank loans and infrequently from private sources, and during this period they were subsidized by upto about 50 percent of the market price by the state. In 1977/78 the major condition to receive loans to purchase tractors was ownership of a minimum of 25 acres of land. As these cost from Rs 40,000 to Rs 60,000 or more at the time, they are beyond the means of most landowners in Mallian. Hence the role of the state in technological innovation has been extremely important.

Tractors contribute towards a more efficient agriculture in Mallian's ecological conditions: deeper furrowing and turning of the soil, timely ploughing, sowing and harvesting. This efficiency is both direct and indirect: direct because the tractor is technologically more efficient than the traditional plough; indirectly, because tractors can relieve the heavy demand for labour during peak periods of activity.

However, as I have indicated in previous chapters, whilst a more efficient cultivation is possible with tractors, their costs in terms of labour displacement and appropriation of surplus and loss of foreign exchange, tends to outweigh their benefits, at least under the current economic and employment conditions in Pakistan.

A tractor takes about 3 man-hours to plough and prepare one acre of land for sowing, and generally, about 4 ploughings are needed for preparation of the soil. Under the traditional method, the land is ploughed by means of a hook which does not invert but cuts the soil. The plough is drawn by oxen and in general 13 to 20 ploughings are necessary to prepare the soil. After ploughing, the clods of earth are broken by means of a wooden beam. This also levels the earth so that the fields can be irrigated evenly. It takes about 6 man-hours to prepare one acre of land for ploughing under the traditional method. Moreover, this application of a non-furrowing-turning plough (which is technically not a plough), requires that all crop residues be pulled out of the ground beforehand.

The importance of tubewells in the national context has been described in chapter 4 where, of the 26 percent increase in agricultural output during the second five year plan (1960-65), 9 percent of the increase was attributed to tubewells and 4 percent to surface water. I also showed that the number of tubewells in Pakistan had increased several fold during this period. There has been a similar increase in tubewells in Mallian. These increased almost 5 times from 6 in 1960 to 15 in 1967 to 27 in 1978. This rate of increase follows the trend for Sheikhupura District as a whole: in 1959/60 there were

85 tubewells, in 1960/61 there were 74, in 1962/63, 323, and in 1963/64 there were 455 (Mohammad 1965:49).

It takes about 2 to 2.8 hours to irrigate one acre of land by a 1.5 cusec (cubic foot per second) tubewell; this is the standard tubewell in use in Mallian. The traditional method of irrigation by Persian wells is, in comparison, inefficient. By this the well is put into motion by capstains which are driven by oxen, and it takes about 12 hours to irrigate one acre. The land is irrigated by under-the bed method: by this, fields are divided by small *bands* (clods of earth used to construct embankments) into square or rectangular beds which are then consecutively submerged. The frequency of irrigation differs from crops. Wheat is submerged 4 to 5 times, while sugar cane is submerged 15 times and rice 20 times or more. Vegetables on the other hand require very frequent but controlled water application (too much or too little can damage them easily). Tubewells provide this. And in addition, the almost constant availabilty of water allows for multiple cropping throughout the year.

Modern technology is also used for harvesting crops: this is either electric or diesel operated, or manually. In Mallian in 1977/78, there were 4 electric wheat threshers; and about 60 percent of the agricultural households owned a manual wheat thresher. Rice husking and wheat grinding is done in small, modern mills in Mallian.

The main traditional implement used for harvesting is the small handled sickle. Traditionally for rice, following the after-ripening the grain is threshed in the field. For this purpose a small hollow is made in the ground and is trampled down. Then a wooden beam is laid in front of the hollow; the workers beat bundles of rice stalks with the ears against the beam until all grains have been separated. For wheat, threshing begins by driving an ox-drawn plank over the ears until all grains have fallen out. After this, the chaff is separated from the grain by 'fanning', that is, by throwing it into the air. The use of modern means of threshing wheat and rice and then grinding and husking them represent important changes in the labour and production process as compared to the slow and often wasteful traditional methods.

*Fertilizer consumption*

The changes indicated above, especially the increased water availability, have enabled a much larger fertilizer input, which in turn has increased per acre output; though an optimal amount of fertilizer is used mainly, though not exclusively, by the larger cultivators.

Poor peasants and sharetenants generally use less than the optimal amount; for example, use of one bag of urea where 1.5 bags is optimal; and no DAP (di ammonium phosphate) is used where 0.5 bag is required for optimal combination of fertilizers. None except the larger owners or the capitalistic smaller owners use triple or single super phosphates, an expensive and particularly potent fertilizer supplement.

Leaving aside the controversy over the long term effects of chemical fertilizers on the soil, these have overcome a severe constraint on agriculture imposed by a shortage of farmyard manure, the traditional source of fertilizer. The valuable dung from animals is dried and used as fuel so that timely and adequate supplies were always lacking. Also, the manure was left gathered in the open in the village dung heaps, so that it lost its moisture in the hot season or was washed away during the rains.

Prior to availability of chemical fertilizers, an insignificant amount of (natural) fertilizers were used in Mallian. Now the use of chemical fertilizers is about 10 times that of manure. This as well as an increased water supply has facilitated multiple cropping and timely cultivation of crops such as vegetables. These can now be grown in much larger quantities all the year round since they have a shorter production time.

*Changes in rent and tenancy*

The structure of rent and tenancy arrangements has already been described in chapter 4. It was shown that these vary according to factors such as soil fertility, power relations between landowners and tenants, water resources, and so on.

In fact one of the most important factors that destabilized rents and tenancy arrangements in Mallian has been increased water availabilty, but other factors that I shall describe below, impinged on this process too.

After the installation of private and government owned tubewells (1964-69) rents simply increased by 30 to 200 percent to the 1978 level of Rs 300 to Rs 3,200 per acre a year; but this development mainly affected tenants on fixed rent contracts.

A more interesting development took place in the share tenancy (rather than fixed rent) contracts: Prior to installation of tubewells, the landowners' share was usually either 1/3 of the gross produce with costs shared in the same proportions, or 1/2 of the gross produce and half-share of the costs of production. After the installation of tubewells some landowners began to appropriate 2/3 or 60 percent of gross produce on irrigated portions of their land.

However, this arrangement never became dominant in Mallian for a number of reasons. First, not all land in Mallian had access to tubewell water and was thus excluded from the new arrangemants; second, some of the land was of below average fertility; third, modern industry in the locality provided an alternative means of livelihood to prospective tenants; fourth, the land policies of the Peoples Party of Pakistan under the Z.A. Bhutto regime (1972-77) were seemingly in favour of the tenants, and this staved off possible imposition of rents in favour of the landowners.

These variations in tenancy arrangements and in the share of the product in Mallian have parallels in the Indian context (Bardhan and Rudra 1980; Bardhan 1976; Rudra 1975).

Sharecropping has also declined in Mallian due to resumption by owners. According to information obtained from Mallian, before 1960 the landlord-peasant sharecropping system was almost universal, where almost 70 percent of the land was sharecropped; the rest was worked by agricultural labourers on sep. This proportion has now changed to 40 percent of land under sharetenancy.

Table 6.6: Changes in the profitability of cultivating one acre of wheat with and without tubewell irrigation in Mallian - 1978

| | Rate per Maund (Rs ) | Acre-Yield | Gross Return per acre | Cost of Production per acre | | Net Return per acre | | Cost of Production per Maund | |
|---|---|---|---|---|---|---|---|---|---|
| | | | | Excluding Land Rent | Including Land Rent | Excluding Rent | Including Rent | Excluding Land Rent | Including Land Rent |
| <u>Tubewell irrigated</u> | | | | | | | | | |
| Wheat | 37 | 25 | 1,000 | 602 | 852 | 398 | 148 | 24.0 | 34.0 |
| <u>Without Tubewell</u> | | | | | | | | | |
| Wheat | 37.0 | 12 | 450 | 236 | 386 | 214 | 64 | 23.62 | 38.62 |

Source: Sample Survey

*Changes in profitability of cultivation*

The changes described in the previous sections are reflected in changes in profitability of cultivation under tubewell irrigation which made possible the use of accompanying inputs such as chemical fertilizers and HYV seed.

Table 6.6 shows that net return (including rent) on an acre of irrigated HYV wheat is Rs 148; profitability of traditional varieties without irrigation is Rs 64 per acre, i.e. Rs 84 or 131 percent lower than under HYV. This clearly shows the role of the new technology in development of productive forces and its contribution to the agrarian transition.

*Changes in the social organization of labour*

*Wage labour* The emergence of wage labour is important in that this reflects changes in production relations and is the basis of capital accumulation, and hence the agrarian transition. The emergence of wage labour and rural proletariat can best be analyzed within the context of other landless agricultural households in Mallian in 1978:

| | | |
|---|---|---|
| 1. | Landless agricultural households | 130 households |
| 2. | Agricultural workers on sep | 75 persons |
| 3. | Agricultural workers on cash wage | 36 persons |
| 4. | Seasonal/migratory workers | Indefinite number |

All categories of workers, with the exception of juts are from Mallian's 130 landless agricultural households. Agricultural workers on sep are not a new development, as they have long been part of the traditional rural economy. However, their status is ambiguous: on the one hand they can be considered proletarians who are paid in kind; on the other they are 'tied' to the landlords through the debt mechanism and therefore are not free. And since they are not strictly a new development they need not be considered here in any detail. In contrast the emergence of agricultural labourers on cash and the juts are reflective of important developments in the social organization of production in Mallian.

In 1978 there were 36 agricultural wage labourers on cash wages, having increased from 6 in about 1969, and these can be considered rural proletarians in a proper sense. Sixteen of these wage labourers are employed by MD, the largest landowner in Mallian. Initially he employed 6 workers in 1972 which were increased to 16 in 1978. Another 20 workers are employed in the village by other larger landowners, as we shall see in the next chapter. This category of workers are an increasing group, their increase being an expression of general change in Mallian's economy along capitalistic lines.

*Emergence of the juts*

The juts are a new development in the local economy [8]. These are groups of 'free' individuals who have joined together as labourers in a group. They work in a number of ways: on a per job basis for weeding fields, sowing and harvesting vegetables and fruit and generally meeting short term demands for labour. They also work on a daily basis, where the job needs to be completed in a day; or they work on a seasonal basis, mainly cultivating vegetables for half-share of the product, where they provide all the labour but do not contribute towards any other costs of production.

Juts are not permanently employed by cultivators - but they are able to find work for about 20 days in the month, working and moving from one farm to another, for most of the year.

The formation of juts is a response to and part of a developing capitalist production process in Mallian which has increased the demand for intensive but periodic labour input throughout the year, mainly for cultivation of market garden produce.

The juts differ from earlier forms of collective labour in that they can be and usually are, an extra-biraderi and village grouping. They also differ from previous forms of collective labour in that the latter operated only during peak periods in the agricultural cycle (cotton picking, cane-cutting, bundling), were generally paid in kind, and were involved in some form of reciprocal labour exchange.

The juts around Mallian are usually composed of 5-20 persons; most though not all are from outside the village. They work in a circle of villages as a roving band of rural proletarians. But these are not permanent groupings and individuals can belong to more than one jut. In Mallian in 1978, there were about 12 juts comprising 60 individuals, all from landless agricultural households. During fieldwork in 1978 no smallholder was reported to have been working in a jut; for supplementary work they tend to work outside of agriculture, mainly in nearby modern industry.

As I have said, the emergence of juts is reflective of capitalist production in agriculture in its early stages: a number of individuals who previously worked in isolation, now bring themselves together to engage in socialized labour. Note that the juts bring themselves together in response to the needs of the local economy which is in the initial stage of capitalist development. A higher stage would be signalled by capital bringing individual workers together into juts and taking control over the labour process. As indicated in chapter 2, this would signify the real subsumption of labour to capital.

The fact that the jut is employed for most, but not for all the year, shows the extent to which agriculture has become an 'industry' and much less determined by climate and ecology. However, unlike workers in nearby industry, the juts are not unionized and they do not take part in any collective bargaining; though their wage of Rs 20 to Rs 30 per day is similar to the wage rate for casual work in industry (Guisinger and Irfan, 1980). Perhaps the comparability of wages in the area is responsible for the lack of militancy among agricultural workers demanding higher wages and better work conditions, a militancy which has been observed in the Indian Punjab (Bhalla 1976:A28)[9].

The process of drawing labour into Mallian from the local economy reflects a number of important characteristics of local development: Firstly, there is a process of centralization and concentration of capital mainly on the larger holdings, and involves the production of crops that not only require a high capital outlay and modern inputs but are produced for the market. Secondly, capitalist development even within the same region is unevenly developed and developing unevenly.

Uneven development relieves labour from one locality to another, usually from less developed to more developed localities such as Mallian. So that the labour released in thc villages around Mallian, and in Mallian itself is to some extent reabsorbed in the village. But this reabsorption does not always occur, or is limited in scope so that landlessness can increase in both relative and absolute terms (Byres, 1977).

*Changars* The work of changars, a caste of hereditary rice (paddy or nursery rice) transplanters is constitutive of the sort of qualitative changes in the labour process reflected so clearly in the formation of juts. The changars work is based on household labour, as I have described in the previous chapter. However, since household labour still underlies rice transplantation, it can appear as if the labour process has not changed. But this would be erroneous as the changars work has become increasingly a part of capitalist production.

It is the nature of rice production which calls forth the sort of seasonal household labour that changars provide: this follows from the assertion I made in chapter 2, that the object of the labour process (rice transplanting) conditions the labour process itself. Hence the 'masking' of real change by the appearance of labour as household labour.

The changars, unlike the juts, have been part of the local economy for a long time. In the early part of this century they worked in the production of cotton in the district which declined due to increased salinity and was superseded by rice cultivation (Gujranwala District Gazetteer, 1935:92). The changars now 'monopolize' cultivation of rice and in particular transplanting.

The process of rice production in Mallian now is different from the earlier period: especially since the late 1960s it has become more 'active' and intensive, and output has increased. Because of this increased work in Mallian, about 8 changar households have migrated to Mallian from other villages, and from one village in particular that I mentioned in chapter 5. More do not move as there is lack of housing space in Mallian, and because they do not wish to come under the tutelage of any one landowning biraderi, which could easily be the case even though the changars have apparently accumulated considerable financial resources [10].

**Changes in sep**

As we have seen, sep underlies the traditional local social division of labour in which the products of artisan/service households are exchanged for products of agricultural households. One aim of this research is to see the extent to which sep relations have been transformed or dissolved. This dissolution is both a precondition for, and in turn reflects, capitalist development in the countryside. Specifically, our analysis focusses on the extent to which artisan/service castes' households in Mallian follow their traditional occupations; and conversely the extent to which these have disappeared or been transformed.

Of course not all sep production is of equal importance in the reproduction of non-capitalist production. Some, like that of the bard or barber is relatively dispensable. On the other hand, the production of the blacksmith and carpenter households is crucial for Mallian economy. In some ways, these households have gained in importance as agriculture has intensified, now based on an increase in the use of modern technology, including increased deployment of tractors, threshers, and tubewells.

In order to analyze the reproduction or dissolution of sep, the artisan/service housholds were categorized as follows:

a) households that continue their traditional occupation as their main occupation;

b) households whose traditional occupation is now their subsidiary occupation;

c) households that have changed or severed links.

Table 6.7: Caste/biraderi and occupation of non-agricultural households in Mallian - 1978

| Caste/biraderi | Households No. | Households % | Traditional occupation | Present occupation |
|---|---|---|---|---|
| Arain | 8 | 4.27 | cultivation | industry,misc. |
| Sheikh | 9 | 4.81 | trade (misc.) | casual,industry |
| Chauhan | 1 | 0.53 | cultivation | industry |
| Bhatti (Jat) | 2 | 1.06 | cultivation | shopkeeping |
| Kumhar | 14 | 7.48 | pottery | 4(carrying trade & shopkg) 10 (industry) |
| Barber (nai) | 4 | 2.13 | barber,cook | barber |
| Carpenter (tarkhan) | 5 | 2.67 | carpenter | carpenter |
| Shoemaker (mochi) | 10 | 5.34 | shoemaking | 4 shoemkg, 16 industry |
| Rajput Minhas | 72 | 38.50 | nondescript | mainly industry |
| Weaver (julaha & Bhatti) (change of biraderi name but not occupation) | 2 | 1.06 | weaver | industry |
| Oil presser (teli) | 14 | 7.48 | oil-presser | oilpress.secondary occup.trade.industry |
| Butter (Jat) | 1 | 0.53 | cultivation | |
| Zirger | 1 | 0.53 | nondescript | industry |
| Weaver (different type) | 16 | 8.55 | weaving | industry |
| Fishermen (machi) | 8 | 4.27 | fishermen | industry |
| Chowkidar | 1 | 0.53 | guard | guard |
| Butcher (nasai) | 4 | 2.13 | butcher | 1(butcher) 3 industry |
| Dyer/washer (rangrez) | 5 | 2.67 | dyer | dyer, washer |
| Blacksmith (lohar) | 3 | 1.60 | blacksmith | blacksmith |
| Mendicant (sanyasi) | 3 | 1.60 | mendicant | non-descript. |
| Goldsmiths (sunyara) | 3 | 1.60 | goldsmith | jewellery trade; rent in lands |
| Bard (mirasi) | 1 | 0.53 | bard | messengers & hanger-on to landlords |

Source: Sample Survey

It was found that 29 (15.5 percent), artisan/service households continue their traditional occupation (potter 5, shoemaker 4, blacksmith 3, butcher 1, bard 1, goldsmith 3, barber 2, dyer/tailor 5, and carpenter 5). For 22 (11.6 percent) of households the traditional occupation has been transformed into subsidiary or secondary occupation (weaver 12, oil-presser 9, barber 2, chauhan 1, sheikh 9, arain 8).

Sixty-five (34.7 percent), households do not follow their traditional occupation (weaver 4, potter 9, bhatti jat 2, bhutter jat 1, oil-presser 9, barber 2, chauhan 1, sheikh 9, arain 8).

Seventy-six (40 percent), households could not be placed in any definite traditional occupation and can be left out of the reckoning.

Table 6.7 shows the biraderi/caste, traditional and current occupation of non-agricultural households in Mallian. The two weaver households are employed in industry; similarly the zirger and bhutter households. The 8 fisherman/water carrier households are all employed in industry. Only 2 barber households are employed in this their traditional occupation. Of the 4 butcher households, 3 work in industry, and one sets up a butcher's stall twice a week in Mallian. The 14 oilpresser households still have this as their subsidiary occupation. The 5 dyer households still carry out a number of jobs such as dyeing and washing clothes which is within their traditional vocation. The mendicant households are employed in nearby industry but also do casual work in the village or in the local town market. The bard households are engaged mainly in one aspect of their multifunctional occupation, as hangers-on, messengers and experts on the geneology of the leading families in the village.

The goldsmith households traditional occupation of making jewellery and trading in gold and silver is still their main work, though there has been some diversification in their work. Some individuals from these households have gone to Saudi Arabia and are reputedly working there as jewellers. These households have accumulated significant money-capital and invested in a number of areas, including local transport and agriculture.

Table 6.7 indicates that weavers have been affected most by the breakup of sep and development of modern textile industry, which has gradually displaced household production. The weavers work, however, has not disappeared, because the cloth they produce, a heavy duty coarse country cloth, is still used for making hard-wearing clothes.

### *The reproduction of sep*

I have indicated that the carpenter and the blacksmith are more important for sep than other artisan/service households, as they are crucial to the process of peasant production. In Mallian these households are working with a greater intensity than before, which shows a quantitative change and therefore a partial transformation of sep relations. For example, one of the carpenter households reported an increase in sep from 30 to 40 households since 1972.

Payments in cash and/or grain on a job basis have increased for work such as repairing doors, locks, hinges and also for agricultural implements. This co-existence of hereditary form of payments and payments in cash for work outside of sep is similar to the situation described in India by Epstein (1962:208; 1973:124).

The artisans also increasingly purchase their raw materials from outside of the village: pre-packed and processed oil (not from the oilpresser), more sophisticated tools and implements of production, seasoned wood (formerly from the carpenter) and so on. These items and others are now bought in Sheikhupura town or even Lahore, thus breaking the relative self-sufficiency which underlies the reproduction of sep.

It should be added that there is remarkably little research on artisans in South Asia; this has generally been on their socio-economic conditions, and has rarely been located within the problematic of capitalist development and the extension of the home market [Rajaraman, 1975:284-86; Bhalla, 1976:A28; Saghir Ahmad, 1972; 1976). The conclusions of one such research in the Indian Punjab differ from our conclusions with regard to the artisans:

> The artisan cannot find remunerative work because of the household industry or lack of demand for their traditional skills. A case study of two villages in Patiala district with differing degrees of economic development shows that most of the artisans are joining the class of agricultural labourers result of mechanisation and introduction of new farm machinery in agriculture... It is quite obvious that the benefits of development have gone least to this class, and it stands on the verge of extinction (Singh, M., 1979:594).

Our analysis of this phenomena in Mallian suggests that these conclusions are one-sided, and that decline in artisan work is but one tendency among others which are reinforcing and even expanding artisans work. This conclusion is supported by Epstein (1962:208-9), who described changes among blacksmiths and carpenters in two villages in South India. Epstein found that both these occupations were still in existence in 1970, 10 ten years after her original research in the same area, though on a different more 'market' basis (Epstein 1973:124).

In this chapter I have described economic and social development in Mallian, especially since 1967. I have indicated that agricultural output was raised by overcoming constraints in water availabilty through expansion of tubewell irrigation, and increased use of chemical fertilizers, HYV and other inputs. I analyzed the partial transformation (since non-capitalist production is extant) of agriculture which became more mechanized and increasingly premissed on capital and wage labour. I also described the development of new forms of labour processes such as that of the juts and the relative demise of sep. Of course these developments have been premissed on greater integration of Mallian into the national and international economy, and the dominant moment of the circuit of international capital that links the local to the larger economy - the part that valorizes during expanded reproduction, takes place in the developed countries and thus delimits the extent of local developmemt.

## Notes

1. As I have said in the methodology section, the Mallian records book (*Lal kitab*) is the official register of seasonal agricultural statistics compiled by the *patwari* (revenue official); this is kept in the district adminstrative offices in Sheikhupura.

2. There are several ways of calculating cropping intensity, but generally it can be defined as the percentage of the area cropped in either kharif and rabi season. For example, if in Mallian 45 percent of the land is cultivated in kharif and 60 percent in rabi then the cropping intensity is 105. If all the land is sown in both seasons, then cropping intensity is 200 percent. Thus the total cultivable land in Mallian is 3258.5 acres per season; two seasons in the year would give 6517 acres; actual amount of land cultivated in Mallian is 4914 acres so that cropping intensity is 4914/6517 x 100 = 75 percent x 2 = 151 percent.

3. If one calculates on the basis of land available per season, that is 3258.5 acres, and area given to crops per year, then cropping intensity would be 4914/3258.5 x 100 = 151.

4. Cropping intensity in 1967 was 141.2; total cultivable area was 1729 acres; *rabi* 1075 and *kharif* 1368; therefore cropping intensity = 2443/1729 100 = 141.2.

5. The yield per acre of rice in Mallian compares very favourable with that found in India (Frankel, 1971; and Djurfeldt and Lindberg, 1975).

6. In 1978 those owning 25 acres or more were eligible for medium term loans from the state; these were for the purchase of capital equipment such as tubewells, tractors, threshers and other items.

7. These figures were obtained from the ADBP, Sheikupura tehsil branch.

8. The jut as a form of organization of labour is not mentioned in a detailed description of labour in Gujranwala Ditrict written in 1895; Sheikhupura was a part of this district till 1919, when the latter became a separate district. In this gazetteer, the following types of workers are mentioned: *lachains*, getting Rs 21 per annum cash and 1/4 of the produce of the land they cultivated; *kamans*, paid Rs 2 per month with food daily and clothing on ceremonial occasions. *Sepis* and *athris*, who get a daily wage or a share of the crop reaped. Harvest labourers including women employed in cotton picking receive from 1/6 to 1/8 of the cotton, among other receipts. The gazetteer does mention that changars have been known to receive as much as 1/4 of the cotton fibre (Gujranwala District Gazetteer, 1935:82).

9. In the Indian Punjab, Bhalla (1976:128) writes '[the increase in casual employment in agriculture] has not led to collecting bargaining...Individually, the casual agricultural labourer can, and does, say on occasions to one of the cultivators who regularly hires him:"I will not work today"...Collectively, in action - far removed still from collective wage bargaining - labourers in a village may arrive at some sort of consensus that for the coming harvest each should stick to a demand for Rs'Y' per day

instead of the lesser sum of Rs'X', which was paid last year. But this is a consensus which is implemented by individuals'.

10. The changars are very reluctant to divulge information about their incomes and gave figures for their incomes which were apparently much lower than that suggested by informants in Mallian.

# 7 The production process in the local economy

In this chapter I shall concretize further some of the processes of social and economic development by focussing on the process of production and labour process of a representative sample of producer households in Mallian since the international circuit of capital links household production in Mallian to the international economy through the local, national and international market for producer and consumer goods.

As I shall indicate this process is complex and contradictory in that the increased ouput of productive units is dependent on increased inputs which are directly or indirectly produced in the developed countries by the multinational corporations; a process whose expanded reproduction or valorization takes place outside of the national economy. This not only precludes a higher rate of capital accumulation, but also makes the most productive households in the local economy more dependent on the international economy for inputs that increase output; conversely, the less productive households are least dependent on the international economy and remain integrated into sep and the local economy.

The analysis in this chapter is conducted with reference to intensive type data collected by a sample of households as described in the methodology section in Appendix 3. This data consists of a representative sample of 75 households of landowning, non-landowning agricultural, and non-agricultural households. These categories are further classified into subcategories of landlord, peasant, wage-labour, sharetenant, artisan/service, and other households.

*Method for analyzing the production and labour process in Mallian*

The method for analyzing the process of production, and the labour process underlying this, follows from our theoretical discussion of capitalist production in chapter 2. The criteria for determining capitalist/non-capitalist production is:

The form and intensity of labour use: whether production is premissed on wage-labour, sharetenancy, number of workers employed per acre.

Capital: constant and variable capital consisting of modern technology such as tractors, tubewells, fertilizers, and wages.

Market relations: buying and selling of means of subsistence, amount of surplus generated, commodity production, and indebtedness.

Irrigation and water availability: this is important as water shortage is a major constraint on agrarian production in Mallian.

Of course, most of these factors are interrelated, for example the amount of land owned determines market relations, the ability to purchase tubewells and tractors and access to state-provided credit.

*Profitability of crop production*

In order to analyze the labour processes that underlie the major productive activities of Mallian households, I shall describe the production of some major crops. This is based on an optimal cultivation on land of average fertility as reflected in the rental of Rs 500 an acre per year which is typical for Mallian. Some of the costs of production such as revenue are fixed, others such as fertilizers or labour vary.

However, whilst the costs of production vary, these do so within the range of the average costs of inputs in the area. Of course, the returns vary also, mainly due to the quanitity and quality of inputs, the fertility of soil and the crops grown.

The labour and production process described in tables 7.1, 7.2, 7.3 and 7.4 are applicable to all categories of agricultural households, with the difference that production can be based on hired or household labour, or both. The processes and costs of production described in the tables is based on observation of a number of holdings in Mallian and other areas then reconstituted into a 'model.'

A major difference that is apparent between the processes described in tables 7.1, 7.2, 7.3, and those of table 7.4, is that land in table 7.4 is cultivated with suboptimal water (which is very similar to rainfed conditions) and fewer processes are involved. In addition there is a significant difference in the profits from cultivation described in table 7.4 and 7.1. In table 7.4 the gross returns to one acre of traditional wheat is Rs 450, compared to HYV wheat described in table 7.1 where returns are Rs 1000 per acre.

The highest returns are observed in table 7.3 where a vegetable crop (potato), gives a net return of Rs 6,277 per acre, excluding rent. The costs of production are high too, at Rs 3,172, excluding rent. The profitability of vegetables is thus obvious and I have described in chapter 6 the increase of area under vegetables in Mallian.

## Landowning agricultural households

### *Large landowning households*

These are defined as households owning over 100 acres. There are three households in this subcategory and each is analyzed in succession.

*Case study* 1 MD belongs to the dogar biraderi and owns 500 acres of land in Mallian. In addition he owns another 300 acres in three other villages in the locality. In Mallian, 450 of the 500 acres are cultivated; the other 50 acres are taken up by a dairy farm, veterinary clinic, housing compounds, and infertile land.

MDs holdings are irrigated by 8 private electric tubewells and water from the Upper Chenab Canal. He deploys 4 tractors having bought his first in 1967. In addition he owns 2 rice and 2 wheat electric-powered threshers. Once his holdings are consolidated, he aims to invest in a combine harvester.

MDs 450 cultivable acres are organized for cultivation as follows:

| | acres | % |
|---|---|---|
| Self-cultivation | 200 | 44 |
| Rented out on fixed money rent | 50 | 11 |
| Parcelled out to sharetenants | 125 | 28 |
| Land not cultivated in 1977/78 | 75 | 17 |

Table 7.1: The production of one irrigated acre of HYV (Mexi-Pak) wheat in Mallian - 1978

| | Process/Input | Cost (Rupees) | Total Costs (Rupees) | Remarks |
|---|---|---|---|---|
| 1. | Preparatory tillage: | | | |
| | 4 ploughings and plankings (15-20 by traditional methods @ Rs.5) | 20.00 per ploughing and planking | 80.00 | |
| 2. | Seed Bed Preparation: | | | |
| | 2 ploughings and plankings | 20.00 per ploughing and planking | 40.00 | |
| 3. | Sowing | 6.00 per acre | 6.00 | One Rabi drill can sow 4 acres in a day |
| 4. | Seed | 50.00 per maund | 50.00 | Seed rate: one maund per acre |
| 5. | Bund (embankment) making | 9.00 per man-day | 4.50 | 2 men for 1/4 day |
| 6. | Fertilizer: | | | |
| | (i) 1.1/2 bags of urea | 68.00 per bag | 102.00 | |
| | 1/2 bag of DAP | 72.00 per bag | 36.00 | |
| | (ii) transportation | 1.00 per bag | 2.00 | |
| | (iii) 2 applications | 9.00 per man-day | 4.50 | 1/4 man-day per application |
| 7. | Irrigation: | | | |
| | (i) cleaning of water courses | 9.00 per man-day | 4.50 | 1/2 man-day |
| | (ii) labour charges for 5 irrigations | 9.00 per man-day | 11.25 | 1/4 man-day per irrigation |
| | (iii) tubewell irrigation (1 suppl. irrgn) | 10.00 per hour | 20.00 | 2 hours per acre |
| 8. | Interculture with bar harrow | 6.00 per acre | 6.00 | One bar harrow can cover 4 acres in a day |
| 9. | Harvesting: | | | |
| | (i) harvesting | 37.00 per maund | 74.00 | 2.00 maunds of grain |
| | (ii) threshing: 3 man-days | 9.00 per man-day | 27.00 | |
| | 2 pairs of bullocks | 12.00 per pair of bullock | 24.00 | |
| | (iii) winnowing | 37.00 per maund | 46.25 | 2 years of grain per maund of wheat |
| 10. | Artisans | 37.00 per maund | 9.25 | 10 seers of grain per acre |
| 11. | Land Revenue and other taxes | 9.12 per acre | 9.12 | |

| | Process/Input | Cost | Total Costs | Remarks |
|---|---|---|---|---|
| | | (Rupees) | (Rupees) | |
| 12. | Water rate (canal water charges) | 10.40 per acre | 10.40 | Fixed rate |
| 13. | Interest on investment of 12% per annum for 6 months on variable cost (items 1-4 & 6 & 8) | | 21.37 | |
| 14. | Management charges (Rakha) | 28.00 per acre per year | 14.00 | One Manager for 150 acres and 140% cropping intensity at Rs.400.00 per month |
| 15. | Rend of land | 500.00 per acre | 250.00 | For six months |
| | Cost of production per acre | | | |
| | (i) excluding land rent | | 602.14 | |
| | (ii) including land rent | | 852.14 | |
| | Gross return per acre | | 1000.00 | 25 maunds of grain @ Rs.37.00 per maund and 25 maunds of Bhusa @ Rs 5.00 per maund minus transport etc. charges @ Rs 2.00 per maund of grain |
| | Net return per acre | | | |
| | (i) excluding land rent | | 397.86 | |
| | (ii) including land rent | | 147.86 | |
| | Cost of production per maund | | | |
| | (i) excluding land rent | | 24.08 | |
| | (ii) including land rent | | 34.08 | |

Table 7.2: The production of one irrigated acre of HYV (Irri-6) paddy in Mallian - 1978

| | Process/Input | Cost (Rupees) | Total Costs (Rupees) | Remarks |
|---|---|---|---|---|
| 1. | Preparatory tillage and seed bed preparation: | | | |
| | (i) 4 ploughings & plankings (15-20 by traditional method @ Rs.5) | 20.00 per ploughing & planking | 80.00 | |
| | (ii) 2 puddlings & plankings | 30.00 per puddling & planking | 60.00 | |
| 2. | Raising of Nursery: | | | |
| | (i) Cost of seed (paddy) | 35.00 per maund | 6.13 | Seed rate: 7 seer/acre |
| | (ii) Preparation of nursery bed and sowing | 9.00 per man-day | 9.00 | 1 man-day |
| | (iii) Farm Yard manure | 20.00 per cart load | 10.00 | 1/2 cart load |
| 3. | Transplanting: | | | |
| | (i) Uprooting of Nursery | 9.00 per man-day | 4.50 | 1/2 man-day |
| | (ii) Transportation of Nursery | 9.00 per man-day | 2.25 | 1/4 man-day |
| | (iii) Transplanting charges | 9.00 per man-day | 40.50 | 4.1/2 man-day |
| 4. | Fertilizer: | | | |
| | (i) 1 bag of urea | 68.00 per bag | 68.00 | |
| | 1 bag of DAP | 72.00 per bag | 72.00 | |
| | (ii) Transportation cost | 1.00 per bag | 2.00 | |
| | (iii) 2 Applications | 9.00 per man-day | 4.50 | 1/4 man-day per application |
| 5. | Irrigation: | | | |
| | (i) Cleaning of water courses | 9.00 per man-day | 9.00 | 1 man-day |
| | (ii) Labour charges for 16 irrigations | 9.00 per man-day | 36.00 | 1/4 man-day per irrigation |
| | (iii) Tubewell irrigation (2 suppl. irrgns) | 10.00 per hour | 40.00 | 2 hours per acre per irrigation |
| 6. | Weeding | 9.00 per man-day | 36.00 | 4 man-day |
| 7. | Plant protection charges | | | |
| | (i) 4 Nursery sprays | 25.00 per acre per spray | 6.25 | 1/16 of an acre |
| | (ii) 2 crops sprays | 25.00 per acre per spray | 50.00 | |

| | Process/Input | Cost (Rupees) | Total Costs (Rupees) | Remarks |
|---|---|---|---|---|
| 8. | Harvesting:<br>(i) Harvesting)<br>(ii) Threshing )<br>(iii) Winnowing ) | 20.00 per maund of paddy | 168.75 | 5 seer per maund of paddy |
| 9. | Artisans | 30.00 per maund | 3.00 | 4 seers of paddy |
| 10. | Water rate | 16.86 per acre | 16.86 | |
| 11. | Land revenue and other taxes | 12.15 per acre | 12.15 | |
| 12. | Interest on investment @ 12% per annum for 6 months (items 1-5 & 7) | | 30.00 | |
| 13. | Management charges (Rakha) | 28.00 per acre per year | 11.00 | 1 Manager for 150 acres and 140% cropping intensity at Rs.400/- per month |
| 14. | Rent of land | 500.00 per acre | 250.00 | For 6 months |
| | Coat of production per acre | | | |
| | (i) excluding land rent | | 780.89 | |
| | (ii) including land rent | | 1030.89 | |
| | Gross return per acre | | 1320.00 | 45 mds of paddy @ Rs.30.00 per md. & 30 mds of straw @ Rs.2.00 per md. minus transportation charges @ Rs.2.00 per md. of grain |
| Net return per acre | | | | |
| | (i) excluding land rent | | 539.11 | |
| | (ii) including land rent | | 289.11 | |
| Cost of production per maund | | | | |
| | (i) excluding land rent | | 17.35 | |
| | (ii) including land rent | | 22.91 | |

## Table 7.3: The production of one irrigated acre of potato in Mallian - 1978

| | Process/Input | Cost (Rupees) | Total Costs (Rupees) | Remarks |
|---|---|---|---|---|
| 1. | Preparatory tillage: | | | |
| | 4 ploughings & plankings (15-20 by traditional method @ Rs.5) | 20.00 per ploughing & planking | 80.00 | |
| 2. | Seed bed preparation: | | | |
| | 4 ploughings & plankings | 20.00 per ploughing & planking | 80.00 | |
| 3. | Cost of: | | | |
| | (i) seed | 100.00 per maund | 1500.00 | Seed rate: 15 mds/acre |
| | (ii) seed treatment | | 10.00 | |
| | (iii) seed cutting | 9.00 per man-day | 27.00 | 3 man-days |
| 4. | Sowing | | | |
| | (i) ridge making | 9.00 per man-day | 72.00 | 8 man-day |
| | (ii) planting of seed | 9.00 per man-day | 36.00 | 4 man-day |
| 5. | Farm Yard Manure | | | |
| | (i) 20 cart loads | 20.00 per cart load | 400.00 | |
| | (ii) loading, unloading and spreading | 9.00 per man-day | 27.00 | 3 man-day |
| | (iii) two pairs of bullocks | 12.00 per pair of bullock | 24.00 | |
| 6. | Fertilizer | | | |
| | (i) urea 1.1/2 bags | 68.00 per bag | 102.00 | |
| | DAP 1.1/2 bags | 72.00 per bag | 108.00 | |
| | (ii) transportation cost | 1.00 per bag | 3.00 | |
| | (iii) 2 applications | 9.00 per man-day | 2.25 | 1/8 man-day per application |
| 7. | Plant protection (3 crop sprays) | 25.00 per acre | 75.00 | |
| 8. | Irrigation | | | |
| | (i) cleaning of water courses | 9.00 per man-day | 4.50 | 1/2 man-day |
| | (ii) labour charges for 12 irrigations | 9.00 per man-day | 27.00 | 1/4 man-day per irrigation |
| 9. | Inter-culture (2 hoeings/earthing-up) | 9.00 per man-day | 216.00 | 12 man-day per hoeing |

| | Process/Input | Cost (Rupees) | Total Costs (Rupees) | Remarks |
|---|---|---|---|---|
| 10. | Harvesting: | | | |
| | (i) harvesting (digging) | 9.00 per man-day | 144.00 | 16 man-days |
| | (ii) sorting of potato | 9.00 per man-day | 36.00 | 4 man-days |
| 11. | Land revenue and other taxes | 12.15 per acre | 12.15 | |
| 12. | Water rate (canal water) | 20.00 per acre | 20.00 | |
| 13. | Interest on investment @ 12% per annum for 6 months (items 1-7) | | 152.78 | |
| 14. | Management charges (Rakha) | 28.00 per acre per year | 14.00 | For 6 months |
| 15. | Land rent | 500.00 per acre per year | 250.00 | For 6 months |
| | Cost of production per acre: | | | |
| | (i) excluding land rent | | 3172.68 | |
| | (ii) including land rent | | 3422.68 | |
| | Gross return per acre | | 9450.00 | 150 mds of potato @ Rs 65.00 per md. minus transportation etc. charges @ Rs 2.00 per maund |
| | Net return per acre: | | | |
| | (i) excluding land rent | | 6277.32 | |
| | (ii) including land rent | | 6027.32 | |
| | Cost of production per maund | | | |
| | (i) excluding land rent | | 21.15 | |
| | (ii) including land rent | | 22.82 | |

Table 7.4: The production of one acre of wheat (traditional variety) with suboptimal irrigation in Mallian - 1978

| | Process/Input | Cost (Rupees) | Total Costs (Rupees) | Remarks |
|---|---|---|---|---|
| 1. | Preparatory tillage: | | | |
| | 2 ploughings and plankings (10-15 by traditional method @ Rs.5) | 20.00 per ploughing & planking | 40.00 | |
| 2. | Seed bed preparation: | | | |
| | 1 ploughing and planking | 20.00 per ploughing & planking | 20.00 | |
| 3. | Sowing by pore method | 20.00 per pair of bullocks | 20.00 | |
| 4. | Seed | 40.00 per maund | 40.00 | Seed rate: one maund per acre |
| 5. | Fertilizer: | | | |
| | (i) 1/2 bag of urea | 68.00 per bag | 34.00 | |
| | (ii) transportation charges | 1.00 per bag | 0.50 | |
| | (iii) one application | 9.00 per man-day | 2.25 | 1/4 man-day per application |
| 6. | Harvesting | | | |
| | (i) cutting | 9.00 per man-day | 27.00 | 3 man-day |
| | (ii) threshing and winnowing | 9.00 per man-day & | 18.00 | 2 mna-day and |
| | | 20.00 per pair of bullocks | 10.00 | 1 pair of bullocks for half a day |
| 7. | Artisans | 37.00 per maund | 9.25 | 10 seers of grain per acre |
| 8. | Interest on investment @ 12% per annum for 6 months (items 1-2 and 4-5) | | 8.20 | |
| 9. | Management charges | | 7.00 | |

| | Process/Input | Cost (Rupees) | Total Costs (Rupees) | Remarks |
|---|---|---|---|---|
| 10. | Rent of land | | 150.00 | |
| | Cost of production per acre | | | |
| | (i) excluding land rent | | 236.20 | |
| | (ii) including land rent | | 386.00 | |
| | Gross return per acre | | 450.00 | 10 maunds of grain @ Rs 37 per maund and 10 maunds of straw (bhusa) @ Rs 10 per maund minus transportation etc. charges @ Rs 2 per maund of grain |
| | Net return per acre | | | |
| | (i) excluding land rent | | 214 | |
| | (ii) including land rent | | 64 | |
| | Cost of production per maund | | | |
| | (i) excluding land rent | | 23.62 | |
| | (ii) including land rent | | 38.62 | |

Table 7.5: Crops grown on MD's self-cultivated holding - kharif 1977

| Crop | Land Cultivated (acres) | Average Yield per Acre (maunds) | Total Yield (maunds) | Market Price per Maund (Rs ) | Average Gross Income/ Acre (Rs ) | Total Gross Income (Rs ) | Average Cost per Acre (Rs ) | Total Costs (Rs ) | Net Income per Acre (Rs ) | Total Net Income (Rs ) | Amount Marketed (maunds) | Per cent Marketed |
|---|---|---|---|---|---|---|---|---|---|---|---|---|
| | (1) | (2) | (3) | (4) | (5) | (6) | (7) | (8) | (9) | (10) | (11) | (12) |
| Paddy (basmati) | 100 | 24 | 2400 | 52 | 1248 | 124,800 | 500 | 50,000 | 748 | 74,800 | 2350 | 98 |
| Paddy (Irri-6) | 25 | 50 | 1250 | 30 | 1500 | 37,500 | 500 | 12,500 | 1000 | 25,000 | 1150 | 92 |
| Fodder | 25 | 132 | 3300 | 6 | 792 | 19,800 | 200 | 5,000 | 592 | 14,800 | 3300* | 100 |
| Grand Total | 150 | | | | | 182,100 | | 67,500 | | 114,600 | | |

*Considered as selling on the market though he sells to himself, i.e. for his dairy farm

Table 7.6: Crops grown on MD's self-cultivated holding - rabi 1977

| Crop | Land Cultivated (acres) | Average Yield per Acre (maunds) | Total Yield (maunds) | Market Price per Maund (Rs ) | Average Gross Income/ Acre (Rs ) | Total Gross Income (Rs ) | Average Cost per Acre (Rs ) | Total Costs (Rs ) | Net Income per Acre (Rs ) | Total Net Income (Rs ) | Amount Marketed (maunds) | Per cent Marketed |
|---|---|---|---|---|---|---|---|---|---|---|---|---|
| | (1) | (2) | (3) | (4) | (5) | (6) | (7) | (8) | (9) | (10) | (11) | (12) |
| Wheat (Maxi-Pak) | 125 | 40 | 5000 | 37 | 1480 | 185,000 | 450 | 56,250 | 1030 | 128,750 | 4800 | 96 |
| Fodder seeds (shaffal) | 75 | 6 | 450 | 300 | 1800 | 135,000 | 300 | 22,500 | 1500 | 112,500 | 150 | 33 |
| Grand Total | 200 | | | | | | | 78,750 | | 241,250 | | |

Cropping intensity = 175

Table 7.7: Fertilizer used on MD's self-cultivated holding - 1977

| | | | |
|---|---|---|---|
| 1. | Rice (Basmati and Irri-6) | 1 Bag urea | Rs 68 |
| | | 1 Bag DAP (Di ammonium phosphate) | Rs 72 |
| | | | Rs 140 |
| 2. | Wheat (Mexi-Pak) | 1.1/2 Bags urea | Rs 102 |
| | | 1/2 Bag DAP | Rs 36 |
| | | | Rs 138 |
| 3. | Fodder | 1/2 Bag urea | Rs 34 |
| | | 1/2 Bag DAP | Rs 36 |
| | | | Rs 70 |

Table 7.8: Costs of production and returns on MD's self-cultivated holding - 1977

| | Cost of Production (Rs ) | Net Income (Rs ) |
|---|---|---|
| Kharif Crop | 67,500 | 114,600 |
| Rabi Crop | 78,750 | 241,250 |
| Total for the Year | 146,250 | 355,850 Yearly |

Average net income per acre of kharif crops = Rs 764

Average net income per acre rabi crop = Rs 1206.25

Table 7.9: Crops grown on CB's self-cultivated holding: kharif 1977

| Crop | Land Cultivated (acres) | Average Yield per Acre (maunds) | Total Yield (maunds) | Market Price per Maund (Rs ) | Average Gross Income/ Acre (Rs ) | Total Gross Income (Rs ) | Average Cost per Acre (Rs ) | Total Costs (Rs ) | Net Income per Acre (Rs ) | Total Net Income (Rs ) | Amount Marketed (maunds) | Per cent Marketed |
|---|---|---|---|---|---|---|---|---|---|---|---|---|
| | (1) | (2) | (3) | (4) | (5) | (6) | (7) | (8) | (9) | (10) | (11) | (12) |
| Paddy (Irri-6) | 36 | 30 | 1080 | 30 | 900 | 32,400 | 400 | 14,400 | 500 | 18,000 | 1030 | 95 |
| Paddy (Basmati) | 5 | 20 | 100 | 52 | 1040 | 5,200 | 400 | 2,000 | 640 | 3,200 | 50 | 50 |
| Fodder | 25 | 70 | 1750 | 6 | 420 | 10,500 | 200 | 5,000 | 220 | 5,500 | 500 | 28.5 |
| Total | 66 | | | | | | | 21,400 | | 26,700 | | |

Table 7.10: Crops grown on CB's self-cultivated holding: rabi 1977

| | | | | | | | | | | | | |
|---|---|---|---|---|---|---|---|---|---|---|---|---|
| Wheat (Mexi-Pak) | 62 | 25 | 1550 | 37 | 925 | 5,735 | 400 | 24,800 | 525 | 32,550 | 1250 | 80.6 |
| Fodder (shaftal) | 11 | 5 | 55 | 300 | 1500 | 16,500 | 300 | 3,300 | 1200 | 13,200 | 44 | 88 |
| Total | 73 | | | | | | | 28,100 | | 45,750 | | |

Fifty acres are rented to tenants for between Rs 500 to Rs 2000 (average Rs 800), an acre per year. Included in this category are 2 households that rent in 12 acres each from MD. In turn each household cultivates 6 acres of vegetables on half share with juts, who provide the labour but do not contribute towards the cost of production; in some seasons and for certain crops, the juts are paid in cash. MD does not cultivate vegetables because of high production and supervision costs. Moreover, given his large holdings he is not compelled to intensive cultivation.

The 125 acres are given to 10 sharetenants (12.5 acres each) on half share including the production costs. Previously MD had more of his land sharecropped but he evicted two households from the land in 1971/72 and brought this under self-cultivation [1]. MDs tenants display a whole range of relationships to land: some are landless, others are smallholders, some middle and rich peasants.

The 200 acre self-cultivated holding is worked by 16 full-time permanently employed labourers; of these 15 are from landless households and one from a household with 2 acres. During periods of peak labour demand additional workers are employed for both general work such as cutting, bundling, and stacking grain, and more specialized work such as rice transplanting.

MDs cultivation is shown in tables 7.5 and 7.6. The costs of production are below those shown in table 7.1 and 7.2 which could be due to the economies of scale, to the unpaid work of sharetenants on his self-cultivated holdings, and to better quality of land [2].

As shown in table 7.7, fertilizer use on MDs holdings are optimal for the crops grown; 1 bag each of urea and DAP for rice and 1.5 bags urea and 0.5 bag DAP for wheat. MDs cultivation shows that most of the crops grown are generally those that require extensive cultivation: rice, wheat and fodder [3] rather than those requiring intensive cultivation such as vegetables.

The average net income per acre of rabi crops at Rs 1,206 is higher than the average net income per acre of kharif crops at Rs 764; this is due to the fact that in rabi all of MDs 200 acres are cultivated whilst in kharif 50 acres are left uncultivated. The cropping intensity is 175 compared to 151 for the village as a whole.

The ratio of costs of production to income is 0.58 for kharif and 0.32 for rabi, giving an average yearly ratio of 0.48. For the initial outlay of capital, MD borrows approximateley Rs 30,000 for 6 months from banks, i.e., Rs 60,000 for one year, which is repaid after sale of produce. The yearly short-term loans from banks comprise about 41 percent of the total yearly costs of production; the other 59 percent come from his own savings [4].

In 1973 MD considerably enlarged a dairy farm. He spent a sum of Rs 10 lakh on the dairy plus another Rs 70,000 on extension, modern equipment and a veterinary clinic. The major portion of this investment (Rs10 lakh) came from the state via the Agricultural Development Bank (ADBP), and Rs 70,000 from his own resources.

The farm has about 300 cows, buffaloes and calves. In 1978 MD sold 8 maunds of milk at the rate of Rs 70 per maund, to a dealer in Lahore. In some ways MD is also a monopsonist in that he buys milk from individual sellers at a lower than market rate [5]. The total yearly income from milk is about Rs 102,200 which represents a considerable accumulation of capital in Mallian.

*Ahrth* shop: MD is also an *ahrthi* (commission agent) and has an office-godown in the Sheikhupura grain market, in partnership with three other persons. MD sells his own and other cultivators produce through his ahrth as I have described in chapters 5 and 6 [6].

*Case study* 2 CB is a jat of the virk clan. He is the second largest resident landowner in Mallian with 137.5 acres. Of this 37.5 acres is parcelled out to 4 sharetenant households in parcels of 8, 7.5 10 and 12 acres. In 1977/78, 7 acres were left uncultivated due to waterlogging and salinity, which leaves CB with 93 acres for self-cultivation.

The agricultural equipment owned by CB includes one tractor with a trolley bought in 1972 with a loan from ADBP. He owns only one tubewell but has access to canal water which meets most of his irrigation needs. On average CB uses 1.5 bags of fertilizer for rice and 1 bag per acre for wheat. CB cultivates 93 acres (about 68 percent of the land) with 4 full time workers, and as in case-study 1, additional workers are hired during the peak agricultural periods. Excluding the tractor driver who is paid in cash, each worker is paid in kind according to the following rates:

17 maunds of rice per year
17 maunds of wheat per year
2 meals per day
2 pairs of shoes per year, and cash advances
of 2000-3000 rupees.
One tractor driver: paid Rs 200 per month,
plus 2 meals a day.

CB also has sep relations with the carpenter, blacksmith, shoemaker and barber households who are also paid in kind.
As tables 7.9 and 7.10 show the net average income per acre of kharif crops is Rs 404.5 and Rs 637.5 for rabi. The ratio of costs of production to net income is 0.7, with 0.8 for kharif, and 0.6 for rabi. That is, the total costs of production of crops is more than half the total net income, which is higher than MDs ratio of 0.41, reflecting CBs less efficient cultivation. The cropping intensity is 149.4 which is a little below average for the village.

*Ahrth* shop As with the first case study, CB is also an ahrthi and has an office-godown in the grain market in Mallian. In addition to buying and selling produce, he advances loans to cultivators - mainly poor or small peasants for growing vegetables. The loans are either for purchase of seed and fertilizer or these materials are advanced as loans [7]. In return the borrowers market their produce through his ahrth.

According to CB 80 percent of his customers, including some large landowners, are from Mallian and market their produce through him [8].

Among other assets CB has livestock of 50 animals, of which 15 are milch cows and buffaloes; the rest are draught animals such as donkeys, horses and bullocks. Unlike MD, CB does not sell milk on a commercial basis because a large part is processed into *ghee* (clarified butter) for household consumption. Reputedly, he does not sell milk which is generally consumed freely by guests and often, the needy; this might change in the future, and milk might also become commoditized along with other changes in Mallain [9]. A large part of CBs investible surplus goes towards the upkeep of a guest house [10] as we shall see in chapter 9 [11].

*Case study* 3 This is an absentee landowner who lives in Lahore. With 259 acres he owns the third largest holding in Mallian; in addition he has 55 acres in another village in the district. He is also a businessman and has distribution rights from a cigarette manufacturer.

The absentee's land in Mallian is managed by a *munshi* (manager or agent), who in turn apportions the 259 acres in the following manner:

| | acres |
|---|---|
| Land cultivated by the *munshi* | 100 |
| Rented to sharetenants (parcels of 25, 25, 25 and 16 acres) | 91 |
| Leased for rent in kind | 17 |
| Leased for fixed money-rent (parcels of 8,8,12 and 13 acres) | 41 |

According to the munshi, only marginal land is rented out to sharetenants, relatively more fertile land is given to tenants on fixed rental, and the most fertile land is kept for himself.

One tractor and 2 tubewells are deployed on the absentee's holding, purchased in both instances with loans from the ADBP. The fertilizer input is 1.5 bags per acre for rice and 1 bag for wheat. The munshi employs 3 permanent full time workers for cultivation, and casual labourers are hired on a daily basis when needed; in addition, seasonal labour is hired during harvesting and sowing.

In kharif 1977, 50 acres were cultivated with rice, 5 acres with vegetables, and 20 acres with fodder of the high value shaftal variety; in rabi, 45 acres were given to wheat, 4 acres to vegetables, and 8 acres to fodder. The cropping intensity is 132.

## Comparison of large landowners' production

### *Capital in the production process*

The role of both constant and variable capital is significant for the three households, though the extent of capitalization differs in each. In case-1, 4 tractors are deployed giving a tractor-land ratio of 1:50; in case-2 this is 1:93, and in case-3, it is 1:100 [12]. In case-1 there is one tubewell for every 25 acres; in case-2 there is only one tubewell for 93 acres, and in case-3 one for 50 acres. Similarly, case-1 uses 2 bags per acre on rice and 1.5 bags on wheat.

Average output per acre for case-1 is 50 maunds; for basmati variety, 24 maunds; for HYV wheat the yield is 40 maunds per acre. On CBs farm the yields are 30 maunds for HYV rice, 20 maunds for basmati and 25 maunds for HYV wheat.

### *Wage labour*

Case-1 has a worker-land ratio of 1:12.5 acres; for case-2, it is 1:23.5; and for case-3, it is 1:33 acres.

### *Tenancy*

Different forms of surplus appropriation underlie tenancy relations: money rent, rent in kind and labour rent. Money rent is paid only to case-1 and case-3, from 50 and 40 acres respectively. Especially in the case of money rent tenancy, the rent appropriated is capitalist ground rent since capitalist labour process underlies this tenancy. The tenant pays rent to the landowner and appropriates profit for himself, which is similar to the classic situation described by Marx (1976:905/7).

In case-1, 125 acres are parcelled out to sharecroppers on half; this accounts for 27.7 percent of this household's land in Mallian. In case-2, rent is appropriated on 37.5 acres on half share and constitutes 27 percent of his holding. In case-3, it is 91 acres and constitutes 35 percent of the holding.

Rent in kind constitutes approximately 13.8 percent of total income from land for case-1, 13.5 percent for case-2 and 17.5 percent for case-3. In addition all three households appropriate unpaid labour services from their tenants: occasional work on their farms, repairing houses, tending animals, and other similar work.

From the foregoing it can be concluded that production on large landowners holdings are constituted by different labour processes; on the self-cultivated portions these are capitalist, but non-capitalist labour processes exist on some of the tenanted portions.

**Small landowners**

These own between 50 to 100 acres. Three households are included in the sample which is 100 percent of the subcategory in the village. Households 1 and 2 own 75 acres each, all of which are self-cultivated; household 3 owns 60 acres, of which 17 are self-cultivated, 32 are sharecropped and 11 rented out for a fixed sum of money.

All three households have one tubewell and one tractor each and ploughs are used in conjunction with these [12]. All employ labourers who are paid in kind: household 2 employs 4 workers on 75 acres; household 3 employs 4 workers (two workers are the head of household's own sons) on 17 acres. Household 1 has a worker/land ratio of 1:15; household 2, 1:18.75 and household 3, 1:4.25 acres. It is apparent that land is exploited more intensively here than under the larger landlords.

Table 7.11: Crops grown and fertilizer use by three small landowners in Mallian

| Crops | Fertilizer (bag per acre) | Acres cultivated | Total fertilizer (in bags) |
|---|---|---|---|
| Wheat (HYV) | 2 | 101 | 202 |
| Rice | 2 | 100 | 200 |
| Fodder | 2 | 20 | 40 |
| Fodder (shaftal) | 2 | 48 | 56 |
| Tobacco | 3 | 7 | 21 |
| Peas | 3.5 (incl.manure) | 11 | 38.5 |
| Potatoes | 5 (incl.manure) | 1 | 5 |
| Sugar cane | 3 | 3 | 3 |

Cropping intensity:174

Given that the labour process of this subcategory is relatively more intensive, one would expect similar intensity in the use of other resources; this in fact is the case as table 7.11 shows. Three important points emerge from the table; firstly, the average fertilizer use of 2.8 bags per acre is higher than that of the larger landowners'average of less than 2 bags; secondly, this category has a greater crop mix that requires more intensive labour and fertilizer input and also has a shorter production time than wheat and rice; thirdly, the initial costs are higher because their inputs are greater; fourthly, they have a lower incidence of sharecropping which reflects, in this instance, greater intensity of cultivation.

On can look further into the role of capital in the production process of these households by focussing on the 'purpose wise' loans obtained from the ADBP in 1977. The size of loan is in rupees.

| Size of loan | Source of credit | Reason for borrowing |
|---|---|---|
| 55,000 | ADBP | bought land |
| 52,000 | ADBP | bought tractor |
| 10,000 | relatives | marriage of son |
| 37,000 | ADBP | bought tractor |
| 37,000 | ADBP | bought tractor |

Apart from Rs 10,000 for marriage expenses the loans are for productive investment in agricultural equipment and land on which a cattle shed was built. These households show that their production is increasingly capitalist, though sharecroppng still exists among some, and others have shed this only recently. Also, these households pay wages in kind, which, though not constitutive of noncapitalist relations *per se*, shows that the economy is not fully monetized; therefore masses of use values are kept out of the market by not being converted into exchange value and extending the circuit of capital, thereby constraining capital formation.

*Rich peasants*

These own between 25 to 50 acres of land. There are 8 households in the sample constituting 24 percent of the landowning category and 26 percent of the total (31) subcategories in Mallian. The sample households own 398 acres at an average of about 49 acres per household.

The households own 4 tractors between them; those without have their fields ploughed through tractor-hire. There is one household among the rich peasants that hires out its tractor or ploughs fields on hire on a regular basis. The group owns 5 tubewells and water is sold from these to cultivators in the village. Fertilizer consumption at 2 bags per acre is similar to the large landowners; however, this average obscures the variation among these households for fertilizer use, as well as for other resources, as I point out below. The yields are above average: 30 maunds per acre for wheat and 35-40 maunds per acre for rice.

Of the 398 acres, 108 or 26 percent are rented out to sharetenants on half-share; this gives an average of 15 acres per household that are rented out. Conversely, there are 12 sharetenant households renting-in land at an average of 8.8 acres. Of course these averages hide the variations in land rented out, which is from 1 to 17 acres. Only one household rents out land for a fixed cash rent: 18 acres for a three year period for Rs 11,000. The rental is low because it is rented to a member of the family to pay off debts.

The 214 acres are cultivated by 8 hired workers which gives a worker/land ratio of 1:26; if household labour is included (only two households do not use their family labour) the ratio then becomes one worker per 11.8 acres. This labour input is more intensive than the large landowners, but considerably less than the smaller ones. Of the 8 workers, 7 are paid in kind and one in cash.

Six of the 8 households reported debt; the sources and use of these were: a loan of Rs 2000 from the ahrthi for seed and fertilizer, an average of Rs 333 per household. Money was also borrowed from a bank and from relatives to have a tractor repaired, and to set up a rice-husking mill in the village. The money borrowed is thus mainly for productive purposes.

The rich peasants cropping pattern is similar to the small landowners and cultivate mainly cash crops such as tobacco, sugar cane and market garden produce. But their labour process differs from that of the rich peasants: whereas the small landowners tend to employ wage labourers, the rich peasants tend to engage juts on half-share for a significant part of their cultivation. This is probably linked to the the high proportion of cash crops that they cultivate and the fact that they do not have ready cash, most of which is put back into cultivation as circulating capital.

One might ask why the rich peasants do not invest more in vegetables which yield higher profits (but which also carry greater risk)? The response of these households was that given the size of their holdings they try to maximize their income by balancing the low risk extensive cultivation (wheat and rice) with high risk intensive cultivation (vegetables and tobacco). Their holdings are too large in relation to their limited access to credit from the ADBP, and to non-family labour, for an exclusively intensive cultivation; on the other hand their holdings are too small to rely only on extensive cultivation.

One of the most significant issues regarding the rich peasantry is whether it can transform itself from 'rich' to 'capitalist', a process that is integral to the agrarian transition. As we have seen, capitalist production underlies the groups production as a whole and especially particular households within it, though this is a recent development and carries stigmata of non-capitalist production.

*Middle peasants*

This class of peasantry owns 10-25 acres. Eight households are included in the sample which constitute 24 percent of the sample and 42 percent of the total (19), households in the village. These households are able to generate a surplus given that they own land which is two to five times larger than a subsistence unit of 5 irrigated acres. Generally, these households are least dependent on the market for reproduction and can supposedly continue to exist even after capital has penetrated the rural areas (Bernstein, 1982:170; Banaji, 1976) [13]. We shall see the extent to which this assertion holds true for Mallian.

A total of 119.5 acres are owned by 8 households at an average of 15 acres each. Only one tractor and 2 tubewells are owned in this group. The tractor was bought in cash by mortgaging land, since the amount of land they own falls short of the 25 acres required (in 1978), to be eligible for a tractor loan from the ADBP.

Six households farm with family labour. Two households rent out land to sharetenants; and 92.5 acres are self-cultivated, which is an average of 15.4 acres per household. The higher average of self-cultivated land compared to average owned per household is due to two households which rent in a total of 22 acres in portions of 12 and 10 acres.

As I have mentioned two households rent out land to sharecroppers, which is paradoxical given their relatively small holdings. However, a number of interpretations were offered as to why these households do not self-cultivate with wage-labour in preference to renting out on share: first, they do not have easy access to working capital (wages, fertilizers, HYV, tractors) because the relatively small size of their holdings makes them eligible for some state loans, such as tubewells and fertilizers, but precludes them from others such as tractors. In any case, their access to these loans is often not adequate in relation to need. In such a situation sharetenancy is a method of cost-sharing. An alternative interpretation is that the middle peasants preferred leisure to work, since they seem to be in the forefront of the village sporting and leisure activities. It is possible that both interpretations contain an element of fact.

Unlike the groups I have discussed, whose relatively large scale of production necessarily implied market relations, one cannot assume the same for the middle peasants. What and how much they buy and sell is an empirical question given the range and possibilities inherent in their economic behaviour.

These households market 38.5 percent and 25.8 percent, respectively, of their total rice and wheat production, an average of 33.3 percent by the group as a whole. (A relatively greater marketed surplus would show if the sale of milk and shaftal seed were included in the calculations, but these are marginal to their production.

A deficit in wheat occurred in three households and 85 maunds were purchased from the ahrthi. The average quantity of rice and wheat retained for consumption are: 100.6 maunds rice and 91.3 maunds wheat. The average consumption is 36 maunds of rice and 48 maunds of wheat per year. From these, sep payments are made and a certain amount of surplus is stored and the rest is marketed.

It should be noted however, that the averages conceal individual differences in market relations among the households: for wheat there is a variation from a deficit of 40 maunds to a surplus of 70 maunds; for rice there is surplus from 30 to 70 maunds. The different relationship to the market shows that these households are undergoing a process of differentiation, which I shall discuss in detail in chapter 9.

Ferilizer use averages one bag per acre for rice and wheat, which is less than the rich peasants, and so is water application and pesticide use. Consequently the middle peasants' yield per acre is also lower, at 25 maunds wheat and 30 maunds rice rice. However, since about 30 percent of their produce (produced mainly with family labour) is marketed they can be considered petty commodity producers, though a few are emerging as rural proto-capitalists. As compared to Mallian, the middle peasants in Sahiwal show much greater tendency to capitalist production, whilst those in Sargodha show the least.

The dilemma of the middle peasant is summarized by one middle peasant who urged that 'we are not big enough to rent our farms profitably, nor are we small enough to labour on the the farms of others'. It is precisely this structural position of the middle peasants which makes them relatively impervious to capital, a situation reinforced by state policies which denies them access to adequate quantities of credit and therefore the market. Even with this, however, I have indicated the opposing tendency reflected in the process of differentiation among these households.

*Small peasants*

This category is defined as owning 5-10 acres, and relies to a greater extent on the market than the middle peasant households. The sample includes six households, comprising 18 percent of the sample, and 40 percent of the total 15 households in the village (16.5 percent of the village households).

These households own a total of 57 acres at an average of 9.5 acres. But as we shall see, not all of this land is cultivable, in some cases due to inadequate irrigation facilities.

Only one household rents out land to sharecroppers, because the head of household is too old to work and his two sons work in nearby mills. One household employs a wage labourer paid in kind; two households rent in a total of 32 acres in portions of 6 and 25 acres. Another household rents in two acres at Rs 700 per acre. A sixth household has members working in nearby mills in addition to work on their farm.

In general the character of small peasant production resembles that of the middle peasant: little land is rented in or rented out; production is family based, relatively small-scale and relatively independent of capital. However, as we shall see, small peasants have a greater intensity of production than middle peasants. This is a response and adaption to constraints imposed by access to smaller quantity of land and other resources. These responses are of three kind: first, as in the case of two housholds, land is cultivated at the normal pitch of intensity and additional income is derived through off-farm work, or work on other farms in the village. The second response is to cultivate more intensely but within the traditional forms of the labour process; that is, to cultivate crop 'mixes' with family and additional hired labour; or work with a partner (*seri*) on a crop share basis. Thirdly, the response is to cultivate with juts.

An analysis of the first and second responses is not necessary in that they do not represent qualitative change in production relations or the labour process. Changes in these have occurred in the third response exemplified by household 6 in the group. This household owns 10 acres and rents in an additional 25 acres on half-share. The land is worked by the head of household, his brother, son and one full time worker.

The land is divided up for cultivation to accommodate a diversity of crop mixes, some of which have higher market value, but require a greater capital outlay and intense labour input. The crops grown in kharif and rabi 1977 are:

| | |
|---|---|
| Rice | 16 acres |
| Fodder | 4 acres |
| Vegetables | 4 acres on half share |
| Wheat | 12 acres |
| Shaftal | 8 acres |
| Vegetables | 6 acres on half share |

The jut employed for vegetable cultivation consists of 7 persons and provides the intensive and timely labour input for half share of the produce. For some other type of work however, the jut is paid in cash, on average Rs 15 per person and two meals a day, with other members of the household assisting in the work as well.

Credit, seed and fertilizers are obtained mainly from the ahrthi and the extended family. None of the households own tractors or tubewells; all own traditional ploughs and land is sometimes prepared with hired tractors, or by a combination of the two.

Fertilizer use in this subcategory is below the optimum, with 1.5 bags urea and 0.5 bag of DAP for wheat and one bag of urea and no DAP for wheat or rice. In household 6, however, the average fertilizer use is 4 bags per acre for wheat, 2 bags per acre for rice, 6 bags per acre for vegetables, and 6 to 8 bags per acre on tobacco. In this household fertilizer use is the highest *per capita* than for any other household in Mallian, and is matched only by some households in our survey in the Sahiwal district.

In order to see the market relations of this class of peasant households, household 6 is not taken into account as it distorts the averages. For the other five households, total rice production is 628 maunds which is 125.6 maunds per household; of this 430 maunds are marketed, an average of 86 maunds per household or 68.5 percent of the produce. For wheat, 335 maunds, an average of 67 maunds per household is produced, none of which is marketed; three households are deficit in wheat which is off-set by a surplus in rice. In addition to agriculture, two households have a member working in nearby industry and one member of another household operates a *tonga* (horse-drawn carriage) in Sheikhupura.

*Poor peasants*

These households own between one to 5 acres, which is the minimum subsistence unit for irrigated land. There are 5 households in this subcategory comprising 15 percent of the landowning households sample, and 20 percent of the 18 households in the village.

The group owns 18 acres of land, an average of 36.6 acres per household; in addition, 25 acres are rented in by 3 of the 5 households, an average of 8.3 acres on half share. One household had had its tenancy revoked in 1977 whilst another was evicted in 1978. It is generally from this category that tenants at will are drawn.

Among this group, capital equipment consists mainly of ploughs, bullocks, scythes, spades, hoes and other traditonal technology worked manually or by animals. All households own a plough as it is a precondition for obtaining a tenancy. Loans for production are rarely obtained from outside of the wider kinship network, therc is little resort to the ahrthi or banks.

On average fertilizer use is lower than that of the middle and small peasants; consequently average yields of rice and wheat are low: 20-25 maunds of the former and 15-25 maunds of the latter. A total of 473 maunds of rice is marketed, an average of 94.6 maunds per household; and in individual quantities of 12, 40, 26, and 135 maunds. The high average is due to one household which owns 4 acres and rents in an additional 12 acres on half share. These households are deficit in wheat by about 7.4 maunds per year each, which is made good by purchases on the market.

It is clear that for all smallholding categories, cultivation and market relations can differ significantly with the transformation of some households production into a more intensive type, though overall it is the size of their family which determines their defict or surplus status in production.

Additional sources of income for this group consists of sale of milk and milk products and work in local industry. A few members of the family work in juts or do casual work in the village. This diversification of household economic activity is different from that of the small or middle peasants; unlike these, the poor peasants cannot significantly change their cultivation practice since access to modern production inputs is limited by their small holdings.

**Landless agricultural households**

These households do not own land but the major portion of their income is derived from agriculture. Twenty-four households have been included in the sample which is 18.4 percent of this category of households in Mallian. These are further classified into tenants and wage labourers' households.

*Tenants*

The sample contains 18 tenant and 6 wage labourers' households. The tenants cultivate a total of 230.5 acres, an average of about 12.5 acres per household. Some tenants rent from more than one owner, and cultivation is sometimes joint and cooperative with members of their biraderi. Most of the tenants in this category are hereditary, who, as I have said in chapter 5, have a lower socio-economic status than tenants at will, in the local social division of labour.

No household in this category owns a tubewell or a traditional plough, and their average fertilizer use is the same as that of the poor peasant. Of the 18, 13 households own and use the traditional plough; though hired tractors are increasingly used: In 1978, 5 households had their land ploughed by tractors and in 1987 this had increased to 9 households.

The yields among these households are the lowest in the village: an average of 12 maunds of wheat per acre and 11 maunds per acre for rice. The variation in the yields is large, from 5 to 20 maunds per acre for wheat, and 11 to 31 maunds per acre for rice. The reasons for the low yields are that, on the whole, only marginal land or land of low fertility is rented to hereditary sharetenants.

For working capital 4 households depend exclusively on ahrthis in Sheikhupura for credit in return for selling their produce through them. Three households depend entirely on non-institutional sources (friends and relatives) for credit; 4 households depend exclusively on landlords for credit. The remaining 7 households depend for half their credit needs on landlords from whom they have rented land.

In 1977, 237 maunds of rice and wheat were marketed and 50 maunds were bought, giving a net marketed surplus of 187 maunds. There was a deficit in wheat - 214 maunds were bought on the market. In money terms, the income from the sale of rice was Rs 5,610 whereas purchases amounted to Rs 6,868, giving a deficit of Rs 1,238.

Income from the sale of milk and milk products is negligible; where these items are sold, this is at a cost of considerable self-deprivation of essential nutrients for the whole family. The main source of income apart from agriculture, is work in industry, which I shall discuss in chapter 8.

Given the small size and low fertility of the land which these households are constrained into renting, and minimal use of modern inputs, it is not surprising that they are barely able to meet their subsistence needs, and many are indebted. The total debt for the 24 households is Rs 24,800 or Rs 1,033 per household. However, 15 households did not report any debt of significant magnitude, and among the 9 that did, the average was Rs 2,755 per household. Among the 15 reporting very little debt, 6 are wage labourers households, and another 6 had one member of the family working in industry. Of course, the debt among these households is qualitatively different from the debt of the larger owners; the latter ostensibly are used for purchasing elements of production, whereas the tenants on the whole borrow to meet consumption needs. All 18 households in the sample give over 50 percent of their gross produce to the landowners. Hence rent in kind is the dominant form of surplus appropriation. Rent in kind is surplus labour in the form of surplus product (Marx,1974:634) and can be constitutive of different production relations. Rent in kind does not *a priori* signify non-capitalist relations for it can be 'no more than an extension of money-rent in medieval garb' (ibid.:788). Rather, it is the labour process underlying sharetenanat production that determines the capitalist or otherwise nature of production, which I shall come back to shortly.

In Mallian tenants also do *corvee* (unpaid, forced) labour (ibid.) in such work as weeding, supervising irrigation, or building and repairing landowners' houses. The tenants rarely refuse to do this because of the threat of revoking their tenancy, and the burden of debt coerces them to acquiesce to such demands. The labour process of the sharetenants in the sample is basically non-capitalist for the following reasons: the appropriation of surplus labour occurs through extraction of rent from tenants who organize the labour process, i.e., ploughing, planting, weeding and harvesting, with their household labour. The landowners or merchants do not own or control the tenants' labour process (Marx, 1976:1023). The scale of production is small; only household labour is set to work; they own part of their means of production such as oxen, scythes, hoes, and so on. The aim of course is to maximize production, but in effect half of their household production is appropriated by the owners, and they are often left with less than subsistence. Following what I have said, the low output of these households is correlated with low integration into the international economy as reflected in the minimal use of fertilizer and other agro-chemical inputs.

*Wage labourers*

There are 6 wage labour households included in the sample out of the village total of 36. As we have seen in the previous chapters, the wage labourers can be paid in cash and/or in kind. Five workers are employed on the landowners intensively cultivated portions. Among the 6, 3 are permanent labourers who are paid Rs 150-200 per month, plus clothes and meals. Two work in juts or do casual work. One wage labourer works exclusively on MDs dairy and is paid cash wages of Rs 150 per month, including meals and one *seer* (about 32 ounces) of milk daily. His work consists of feeding, washing, grazing, and collecting dung from the herds. Generally, members of these households work either as part of a group under a superviser who instructs them at the start of the day on the work to be done: clearing ditches, irrigating fields, weeding, ploughing, sowing, cleaning machinery and equipment, and so on. Thus the 6 wage labour households are separated from their means of production and are engaged in relatively large scale socialized form of production set in motion by capital and elements of production originating in the developed countries.

## Non-agricultural households

There are 18 households in this category which is 24 percent of the sample and about 10 percent of the total non-agricultural households in the village. The major portion of their income is derived from non-agricultural sources. These comprise a variety of occupations such as shop retailers, artisans and traders, and can be broadly classified into two broad subcategories: those who work in their traditional occupations under sep, like that of the carpenter and blacksmith, or those who work outside of this.

*Sep production*

There are 10 households employed in their traditional occupation, of which 4 are in sep. Of these, 2 (carpenter and and blacksmith), are the linchpin in the reproduction of sep and small-scale production in the locality. For example, the carpenter is on sep with about 30 agricultural households and also works on a job basis. His work consists of making ploughs, tips for furrows, hoes, spades, scythes and saw handles, among other traditional manual and animal operated machinery and equipment. The blacksmith has 20 households on sep which is less than households on sep than the carpenters' 30.

Both forms of production is based on family labour. The products are not sold on the market as commodities, but are bartered with agricultural households produce under sep. Additional workers, if at all hired, are incidental to their production, and generally no items are produced which have not been ordered beforehand. Both households own their own means of production which consist of simple non-mechanical products: the carpenter has the iron bits of his plane or chisel made or maintained by the blacksmith who in turn has the wooden handles on his tools (soldering rod, grinding wheels) made by the carpenter. This production originates from and is confined to the household; capital has not intervened and taken control of the production process, though a very small part of some of their 'superior' machine tools are gradually but increasingly being produced by national or international firms, as we shall see in chapter 9.

One household of shoemakers in the sample makes and repairs shoes and leather goods, which they barter or sometimes sell in the village. Production is based on household labour and the raw materials (mainly leather and cloth) are generally produced locally by leather workers or cured by the shoemaker himself. The tools and instruments of labour are rudimentary: buck-sewer, scissors, hammer, colouring, chisel, anvil, and so on, but these too are increasingly produced from outside of the local economy mainly by Pakistani firms using nationally produced machine tools sometimes with imported components.

The labour process of the shoemaker is self-activated, and like the carpenter and blacksmith, controls his own labour and its products.

Another household included in the sample is that of the barber: he has sep with only 6 households, and works mainly for cash. He operates both from his 'salon' in Mallian and in the evening goes from house to house for work. The barber owns his tools of work and his work is also household based. Some of the tools of his trade are made locally but most are manufactured by modern machine tools industry in Pakistan or in the devloped countries. The razors and other equipment is generally made in Pakistan, whilst the finer quality ones are made abroad. As we shall see rather more systematically in chapter 9, the same artisan/service households production connects the local national and international economy in similar ways to the agricultural households, but to a far lesser extent. Their main structural role is that they are an obstacle to the extension of the home market.

*Trade and commerce*

There are 6 households in this subcategory in the sample. Three are potter households who work in their traditional secondary occupation - the carrying trade. They transport all kinds of goods between Mallian and Sheikhupura market and within and between villages. They operate with pack animals, mainly with donkeys and horses, which is their major capital investment. Their work is household based: men, women and children work though additional labour is also hired on an *ad hoc* basis for bundling, loading, unloading, packing, unpacking and delivery of goods.

The potters, like the blacksmith and carpenter, own their means of production. But the difference between the two groups is crucial: The potters buy, sell and transport goods which they have not produced, whilst the artisans produce for barter.

One of the potter households has diversified its work: he works together with an ahrthi in transporting agricultural produce from Mallian to Sheikhupura. This household also engages in trade, buying up grain during harvest or immediately after, when prices are low, and selling when prices are high (buying cheap to sell dear). An example of one transaction will illustrate this: The trader bought 50 maunds of shaftal seeds from a number of small producers in Mallian at Rs 200 per maund and sold them in Sheikhupura for Rs 300 per maund [14]. The same household has a retail shop in Mallian, where goods can be bought on credit and loans can be repayed in grain; this attracts the poorer sections of the village population whose income fluctuates appreciably during the year. The repayments in grain are invariably made at harvest time when prices are low so that, in effect, an interest surplus is appropriated. This household does not control any aspect of the labour process in Mallian and operates in the sphere of the circulation of commodities.

There are two washer/dyer/tailor households in the sample. One works as tailor on a cash basis only; the second household had stopped working on sep since 1960; his work is now mainly washing and dying clothes and cloth. This household is under contract to wash and dye clothes for a large laundry/dry cleaning contractor in Sheikhupura. Work is done by household labour only, and only partly owns the means of production, some of which are forwarded by the contracting firm: soap, dyes, and utensils in which clothes/cloth are washed or dyed.

In terms of our theoretical scheme, this household has come under the formal subjection to capital; real subjection would be signalled when many workers, dyers and washers are brought together by capital in one place; and the labour process and its technical conditions of production are involved in large-scale production.

Finally, a goldsmith household of which there are 3 in the village. The goldsmith biraderi jointly owns a jewellery shop in Sheikhupura which has enabled the household in our sample to rent in 25 acres of land for Rs 40,000 for 5 years, from an absentee landowner in Mallian. In turn they have rented out this land to tenants which brings them an income of Rs 12,000 per year. The land has been parcelled out to tenants, on the old mode of cultivation without bringing changes in the labour process. This household has also bought a tractor for cash and ploughs fields on hire at Rs 20 per acre.

In this chapter I have described the process of production of a representative sample of households in Mallian. I have shown that many households' production is increasingly dominated by capital but the extent of this differs between households and producer groups some of whose production is still largely non-capitalist. This process is contradictory in that whilst the most productive units are those with the highest input of modern elements of production, such as fertilizers, it is precisely these which create a situation of dependent relationship since these inputs are either imported or manufactured with imported technology and raw materials. Conversely, the units of production with the lowest output and productivity use the least amount of these inputs and depend for their production on inputs from within the local economy. In other words, the most productive units in general are those which have been incorporated most into the international economy, by the international circuit of capital, and which in turn restricts national and local development.

**Notes**

1. That is, during the land reforms under Z.A.Bhutto regime, 1972/77.
2. The relatively high yields are attributed by MD to the Irri varieties of rice and to increased other inputs of water, pesticides, and better quality of his self-cultivated holding.
3. Shaftal, a superior variety of fodder crop cultivated by MD and others in Mallian for its seeds, which fetch a high market price, and as a forage crop for animals.
4. Short term loans are given to meet the costs of fertilizers, seeds, ploughing, water rate, land revenue; these loans are often 'cornered' by the larger owners.
5. MD claims he buys at a lower than market rate because the milk is adulterated with water; but of course he is a monopsonist.
6. MD also charges for weighing, storing, quality of the grain, 'adulteration factor' (amount of dirt on the grain); moreover, he buys up at harvest prices and sells at the 'normal' government procurement prices or even higher; because when harvests are relatively poor, little wheat is sold to the government depots at the procurement price (in 1978 this was Rs 37 per maund for wheat and Rs 30 per maund for rice).
7. CB and other ahrthis either buy up fertilizer and sell it on credit or they give a letter of credit to cultivators who can obtain fertilizer from shops on presentation of the letter.
8. I was able to obtain the following specimens of the quantity of grain marketed by Mallian households through CB's ahrth, in maunds: 800, 800 and 500 for rice; and 300, 300, and 50 for rice.
9. When questioned about making milk a saleable commodity, CB stated 'milk is for consuming not selling'.
10. CB's workers gather in the courtyard of the guest-house for meals and receiving instructions for the days work.
11. This expenditure is made out of the income of all his land (included the sharetenant portion) and is not confined to deduction of income from his self-cultivated holding.
12. The proportions in the relative use of tractors and ploughs is assymetrical, for those who own tractors; ploughs supplement tractor use when the latter are not in working order, or when ploughing small areas.
13. There is of course extensive literature on this issue including: Lenin (1960); Patnaik,U. (1979); Vergopoulos (1978); Hill,P. (1983).

14. Similar other transaction in grain and other agricultural products are carried out by this household, where small quantities of produce at low prices are bought from several producers and sold in larger quantities at the prevailing market.

# 8 The impact of modern industry on the local economy

The economic and social development that I have analyzed in Mallian so far has been the result of a complex configuration of processes both internal and external to the local, mainly agrarian, economy. In this chapter I shall focus on another aspect of this relationship, the impact of modern industry on Mallian's economy. This impact has contributed significantly towards further internationalization of the local economy and to some extent has facilitated the agrarian transition; though, at least in the short run, this process has also reproduced structures that impede the transition.

This articulation has two related but distinct aspects: first, and for our purposes the most important, is the influence of local industry on Mallain; second, the effect of Mallian's political economy on the industrial unit in question. The first aspect includes the impact of industry on the village social formation as a whole, especially on particular households and groups; on increasing the monetization of the local economy, on sep, and the realization of surplus value produced in Pakistan and in the developed countries. I shall deal with the second aspect of the relationship first.

Small-scale industry has been present in the district of Sheikhupura (but confined exclusively to the town) during the 1950s and 1960s and even earlier. These enterprises were confined on the whole to processing raw materials (cotton gining) rather than more complex labour processes involved in yarn-spinning or weaving. More importantly, these enterprises were small-scale and their impact on the surrounding economy was minimal. This situation was to change, for beginning in the late 1950s and maturing in the mid-1960s, modern large-scale industry was established in the area which was to have a much greater impact, including that of introduction of sytematic wage labour and money into the local economy.

This industry was set-up under the aegis of the import-substituion industrialization undertaken in the 1960s which I have discussed in previous chapters. The technology and other equipment is almost entirely produced in the devloped countries, with a minimal local content which is generally confined to manufacture of spare parts of relatively simpler components. Whilst not entirely an enclave within the larger national economy, modern industry has extremely weak linkages with other manufacturing industry in the region and in Pakistan, as we shall see.

However, as I indicated in the Introduction and chapters 2 and 4, there are linkages between industry and agriculture but these are relatively weakly developed and asymmetrical; for whilst industry utilizes agricultural production in the form of food (wage goods) and raw materials (such as cotton fibre), agriculture receives few inputs from from Pakistan's industry. There is thus a lack of integration between agriculture and industry in Pakistan. This is certainly the case in the Sheikhupura industrial complex which I discuss below. Here, a large part of the industry is comprised of textile firms producing yarn; their raw material, cotton, is imported from the cotton-growing districts of Pakistan, processed into yarn and sold to indigenous firms producing cloth for domestic consumption or for export. In contrast, the inputs for cotton are directly or indirectly imported. This asymmetrical relationship between agriculture and manufacturing industry, and between different sectors of manufacturing industry, significantly curtails capital accumulation as I have suggested earlier, and which I shall discuss further in chapter 9. Of course, modern industry in the locality does create employment and earn foreign exchange in the short run, but as I have indicated, this mode of industrialization creates a dependency situation and does not deepen the national economy, and does not lay the basis for its future development.

### *The industrial complex*

The industrial complex in Sheikhupura district is located around the Lahore-Sheikhupura road, which constitutes a strip running 26 miles in a north-west direction from Lahore. In 1978 there were approximately 53 industrial units of various sizes ranging from a factory making rubber sandals and employing about 25 workers to a large modern textile mill employing 2,600 workers [1].

Data were collected from a random sample of 54 manual workers from Mallian employed at STM Ltd., a cotton textile mill. A very large proportion of workers employed at STM are from Mallian as I point out below. The mill started production in 1969 [2]. In 1978 it had 1,200 employees including clerical staff. About 720 were manual workers classified according to skill levels: fore-runners, starters, helpers and substitutes, which corresponds in descending order of skilled, semi-skilled and unskilled work. However, the skill required (excluding the technical staff) is not high and little more than fourteen days training and a very basic or no education is needed to acquire the requisite working skills [3]. Hence the majority of the labour force can be drawn from amongst the population of the surrounding areas which have literacy rates of less than 20 percent.

Of the 720 manual workers 683 come from the Punjab Province, of which 562 were from Sheikhupura district. Of these, about 250 were from Mallian and about 200 from Chuharbad, a small market town about 10 miles from the factory. The rest came from other villages in the area. The majority of workers were recruited from within a 16 mile radius ('cycling distance' to use the management's phrase) from the factory [4]. In 1978 all the work force was male, but in 1987 a dozen females from the lower castes had been recruited into the labour force for unskilled work like cleaning and washing.

*Method of recruitment* A brief outline of the method of recruiting the labour force is essential as this has important consequences both for Mallian and the mill. Before a worker is employed at STM, he/she has to obtain a *sifarish* (a request or recommendation) by a 'notable'. Since the policy of STM management is to recruit mainly from nearby villages, the notables are invariably local landlords. Of course the management does recruit some workers without reference to the landowners, but this is not generally the case.

The significance of this method of recruitment, which allows landowners to influence events in the factory is discussed in a later section. Before this however, I need to describe the characterisitics of the labour force at STM as it reflects some of the socio-economic processes at work in Mallian and in the local economy in general.

## Socio-economic characteristics of workers from Mallian

A random sample of 54 workers was drawn from a list of about 250 workers from Mallian. This revealed that Mallian workers at STM came mainly from three types of households: non-agricultural, tenants/sharetenants, and peasant proprietors. A further classification reveals that that out of 54 workers, 27 are from households owning land; 9 are from households that both own and rent land; 12 are from sharetenant households; and 16 are from non-agricultural households. Thus the largest number of workers, 27, are from households owning land. If one adds to this workers from households that both own and rent land, the number of workers owning some land is 36, which is more than half the sample.

However, out of the 27 workers, 17 are from households owning 5 acres or less; and 5 are from households owning between 5 to 10 acres [5]. Of the workers from the sharetenant category, 4 are from households which rent in 6 acres or less, which is below the subsistence unit of 5 irrigated acres, since their share would be half of the 6 acres. On the other hand, 8 households rented in over 10 acres which is on or a little above subsistence level.

For households that own land, work in industry represents a source of supplementing their income; for the sharetenants this work allows them to diversify their economic activity and to meet their costs of production in agriculture.

Of the 16 workers from non-agriculttural households, 9 are from artisan/service households; though only 4 households are actually employed in their traditional occupation. These are: oilpresser (1), weaver (2), and barber (1). Households where the traditional occupation has terminated are: oilpresser (2), potter (2), and tailor/dyer (1).

Among the 16 non-agricultural households, 12 are proletarianized and depend solely on work in industry for their livelihood; workers from the 4 artisan/service households that I have mentioned, and who are still working in their traditional occupation, are technically not separated from their means of production, and therefore have an alternative to industrial employment. But judging by the trends (slack demand, increasing costs of production, competition from modern manufacture) their occupations are on the whole in a precarious situation, compared to other artisan households of carpenters and blacksmiths.

Evidence suggests that artisan/service households' employment at STM has contributed to, but was not the initial cause of decline in their occupation. Indeed, employment at STM was a source of income supplementation, without which they would be seriously underemployed. However, once industrial employment was taken up their traditional occupation either ceased to exist, or as in the case of 5 households just mentioned, became a peripheral activity. In this sense, alternative employment in modern industry has eased the process of proletarianization among these households.

*Proletarianization and diversification*

The recruitment of an industrial labour force or the subjection of some sections of Mallian's population to industrial capital did not pose any problems for STM. Local industry did not have to break up a natural economy to obtain an adequate labour force. On the contrary, in Mallian there is keen competition for jobs at STM by many members of household who do not have sufficient land, or possibility of other employment.

For the landless, industrial employemt was something of a liberating experience: they did not have to put up with the tutelage of the local landowners; the work was regulated in terms of hours worked and at least formally, carried no subservience or bowing to caste and status hierarchy; though as we shall see, these aspects were by no means absent in the 'social system' of STM.

For a small number of workers from landless households, but more so for those from peasant proprietor households, work in the factory was second best. Their preferred choice is to own and make a living off the land. This would raise their socio-economic status (at least it would not fall) within the traditonal social hierarchy. As it is, work in the factory is seen to have an ambiguous status, both by the incumbents in the factory and the better-off peasantry in Mallian.

As I have mentioned, the demands for labour were met largely within the existing socio-economic structures in Mallian. For even though about 250 workers from Mallian were employed at STM, no radical transformation of Mallian's economy was needed to recruit the required quantity of workers. However, particular categories of workers at STM did reflect changes in the socio-economic structure of Mallian. For example, among the workers from non-agricultural households, 3 had been evicted by their landowners who had resumed land which they were cultivating with wage labourers [6].

The relationship between Mallian and STM is further illustrated by the Christian households who, as I have mentioned in chapter 5, are grossly under-represented at STM.

With 60 households in Mallian they had only 6 workers in the mill. This under representation has a number of causes, which are located both at the level of production relations and ideology.

Landowners in Mallian prevent christians from working at STM because they are more dependent upon them, than on any other category of tenants in Mallian. As I have mentioned in previous chapters, the christians form the majority of hereditary sharetenants in Mallian; they do not and have not owned land in the locality; they are often *de facto* not allowed to own land and no one sells land to them, even when in a negligible number of cases, they are able to purchase land.

This 'tradition' of keeping the christians landless also makes landowners confident to engage them as sharecroppers: they did not lay effective claim to land when land reforms were instituted under the Ayub regime in 1960 and the Bhutto regime in 1972. They are thus safer tenants than tenants at will, who are invariably Muslim and generaly from high status biraderis. Because of this situation almost all the large owners in Mallian are able to keep the christians in a state of servitude under 'feudalistic' production relations. Under these conditions the landowners have a wholly dependent work force to cultivate their land, which, as I have indicated in the previous chapters, is of low fertility. This prevents more christians from working at STM.

The mechanism by which this is done is that landowners withold their *sifarish*, or recommendation, which is a precondition for getting a job at STM.

There is another reason for the exclusion of christians from STM: the mainly Muslim work force attempts to monopolize the jobs by preventing a relatively powerless ethnic minority from sharing scarce jobs (Morris 1969) [7]. In contrast to the christians, the dependent Muslim peasant households operate within less severe structural constraints imposed by local landowners [8].

*Trade unions in the locality*

The effect of Mallian's political economy on STM is further shown by trade union activity, recruitment policies and labour-management relations at STM. As I have indicated, before an individual from Mallian is offered employment at STM, a sifarish has to be obtained from a local 'influential' which in Mallian means mainly the two largest landowners, MD and CB.

The management offers the job to the recommended person on the understanding that he will not be a 'trouble maker', i.e. take part in trade union activity, and that the recommending landlord will be responsible for the workers conduct. The landlord is willing to be a guarantor of good behaviour because as a regulator of the labour supply and with close connections with the STM management, he has power and influence over allocation of jobs: these are scarce and competition for them is great, a necessary cause of the landowners' power, authority and influence.

Before giving a recommendation landowners expect prospective employees to work *gratis* on their farm or household; they are also expected to show gratitude to the landowners from time to time by siding with them in disputes and local factional politics. Moreover, before either of the two or more landowners in Mallian recommend workers, they elicit guarantees of 'good behaviour' from the older members or head of kin-groups of the recommendees.

In 1978 the trade union leadership at STM was 'elected' according to the number of workers from the two main areas of recruitment, Mallian and Chuharbad; about 200 workers come from the latter compared to Mallian's 250. The general secretary of the CBA (collective bargaining agent) union - the officially recognized union at STM, was from Mallian, a man of weaver biraderi household that cultivated 25 rented acres. The president of the union was a jat of the virk clan from Chuharbad and member of a household that owned about 50 acres of land.

Prior to the formation of the CBA union in 1973, there had been many years of violent and bitter conflict between the two factions for the domination of the union at STM. In this the landowners from the two areas had played a significant part; they wanted 'their' men to be dominant in the factory, for this increased their power and influence. The interference took the form mainly of police protection, in cases of serious assault on rivals, of monetary help and legal advice, and occasionally providing their factions with arms. In 1973 a compromise was arrived at between the STM management, the landowners, and the workers.

There is one particularly noticeable feature about the trade unions: the majority of the leaders came from the middle or richer sections of the peasantry, and their following often rested on biraderi or village loyalties. Many who were active locally during the Z.A.Bhutto regime 1972-77, were generally from this class of the peasantry. However, after Martial Law was declared in 1977, and trade union activity was curtailed a number of trade union leaders including some from Mallian turned strike-breakers, especially in the Karachi textile mills.

The political consciousness of the trade union leaders at STM was limited and was permeated with careerism and opportunism. The political consciousness of the rank and file members was limited too. If that were not the case then union leaders would have been chosen irrespective of biraderi or village affiliations. Moreover, the trade union leaders would have clearly seen the landowners in Mallian as people with whom they are in struggle, and viewed their interference in trade union politics with alarm.

As it was, the trade union leaders, and to a large extent their rank and file members, the landowners and the STM management, were involved in a check-and-balances situation as well as a pecking order.

*Political culture of STM workers* There is another area which highlights the effect of Mallian on STM, specifically on trade union activity - the reproduction of culturally relevant political practices of the village, among the trade union members. Notably, the offering of animal sacrifice at the shrines of saints.

When a trade union faction is involved in a power struggle with other factions, or after success in an election, as happened in 1978, trade union leaders go to a local shrine to sacrifice goats or lamb and also consult *pirs* or holy men to thank or to pray for their victory. In fact some factions had a pir whom they would consult and solicit for advice on a regular basis. All this is taken with great seriousness and clearly falls within, and is the effect of cultural-ideological processes emanating from Mallian social formation.

This rather brief summary shows that there is a process of mutual influence of local industry via STM, and Mallian. This should not be taken to mean, however, that no change has occurred as a result of this interaction. Clearly, whilst the trade unions compete for power within the traditional cultural-ideological idiom, on the basis of faction, village and biraderi, the fact is that trade union organization and holding of office within this organization has created a new source of power and authority, however circumbscribed this may be.

Trade unions at STM owe their power to bureaucratic organization as well as to struggles within modern industry, even if this power is shared with other competing individuals and institutions; and this is clearly the effect of opening out or enlarging the local political economy.

Moreover, whilst workers and union leaders from Mallian bring their social and political practices into STM, these are modified by the structure of industrial organization in the mill: no trade union leader can create an hereditary office, or a new caste/biraderi of industrial workers. In this sense, Mallian workers at STM have brought a new factor into the socio-economic and political organization in the locality: individuals who are relatively autonomous of Mallian's internal economy, whilst still being located within its social formation.

## The effect of STM on Mallian and the local economy

The location of modern industry in general and STM in particular, has had a significant impact on Mallian and the local economy. In summary this is constitutive of:

1. Alternative employment for Mallian households.

2. Increased money circulation and monetization of Mallian's economy; the realization of surplus value.

3. The preservation of small holdings in Mallian.

4. Diminished distinction between the economy of Mallian and the external economy.

5. Development of the informal sector in the local economy.

6. Emergence of a new category of households in Mallian, the industrial workers.

7. STM itself - an enormous penetration of the international economy into the national and local economy in the form of technology and capital, which is realized locally.

First, at least one member from about 150 households is employed at STM; industrial employment thus represents alternative sources of income which is relatively independent of Mallian' socio-economic structure.

The second effect of STM is that 250 or so workers draw in about Rs 100,000 per month (average wage of a little over Rs 300 per month) into Mallian. This means a further monetization of Mallian's economy, and realization of surplus value produced in Pakistan and other countries. The link between the two is provided by the 6 retail shops in the village. These sell consumer goods which are produced both in and out of the village and are purchased by wages earned at STM: rice, wheat, *ghee*, edible oil, pots and pans, spices, and so on.

The purchase by wage-earning households of goods produced elsewhere in Pakistan or in the developed countries (electric bulbs, cloth, clothes, cigarettes, watches, bicycles, radios. tea, soft drinks, medicine, kerosene oil) links the local with the national and international circuits of production and consumption, that I discussed in chapter 2 [9]. The important point about households that depend mainly on wages from STM is that they buy more even though they might consume less than some peasant producer households in Mallian, since they are more or less separated from any other means of subsistence.

In the absence of money-wages from STM, the economy of Mallian would have much less of a commodity character, and its incorporation into the national and international economy would be much less complete. This penetration by, and incorporation into, the international economy of course creates the basis for the further extension and penetration of capital.

The third effect of STM on Mallian has been a tendency for the reproduction of smallholdings in Mallian. In the absence of alternative sources of income, smallholders might be compelled to sell or mortgage their land in order to meet their expenses. As it is the additional income from STM has enabled these households to meet most of their costs of production in agriculture; under different circumstances, where there was no additional income, they would have to borrow from landowners or merchants - with the risk of default in repayment and possible loss of land.

Fourth, wages from industrial employment has contributed towards blurring the lines between the village economy and the market in Sheikhupura and Lahore, which connect the local and regional to the national and international economy. With increase in monetization through development of the wage the movement of resources and commodities is now much easier; in the absence of money wages there was much greater *immobility*, as resources first had to be transferred physically from the point of production to the market and exchanged for money or for other produce.

Fifth, money-wages has meant a certain loosening and opening up of the local economy, reflected in the development of the informal sector linked to local industry. A large number of small-scale 'enterprises' have developed as a direct result of local industry: hawkers of various sorts, tea and food stalls, cigarette shops, bicycle repairs, and other mainly consumption-oriented business. These mop up surplus production and extend the penetration of capital rather than directly contributing to capital formation, as we shall see in chapter 9.

Sixth, STM workers and their trade union organization represents a potential new force in the political economy of the village; this is inspite of the constraints imposed by the village social structure and the STM management, under which the trade unions exist and operate.

Seventh, as I have said, international capital in the form of technology and capital equipment for modern industry, self-expands or is valorized in the developed countries but is realized locally. This also represents a drain of resources, not withstanding the creation of employment and the foreign exchange earned; more importantly, it epitomizes almost an enclave economy with few linkages to other manufacturing industry in Pakistan (but it does have linkages with other foreign manufacturing sectors). This relationship is epitomized by STM: apart from the most rudimantary spare parts which are manufactured locally, the capital equipment is wholly imported. The situation is somewhat different with regard to STM's relationship to Pakistani agriculture: raw cotton is obtained from Sargodha and other cotton growing districts in Pakistan, and whilst linkages are created between agriculture and industry the relationship between the two is still asymmetrical. Of course, an increase in cotton production would expand the productive capacity of Pakistani agriculture; but this would necessitate an increase in inputs of capital and intermediate goods which are directly or indirectly imported. An expansion of the industrial unit, however, would depend wholly on import of equipment and technology, without inducing a corresponding development of Pakistani industry, hence reinforcing a dependent form of development.

## Notes

1. This does not include the various motor mechanic-repair shops, which employ less than five workers, or the numerous food and hawker stalls that are situated near the mills.

2. The mills has 25,000 spindles, making it larger than the average mill; it produces about 7,808,400 lbs of cotton a year.

3. The labour process takes place in three sections of the factory: the back process, where cotton is put through a cleansing process; ring spinning, where the thread is made; and cone-winding, where the yarn is wound into cones and bales.

4. In 1978 the wage levels were largely determined by, among other things, state legislation; the minimum take-home pay at STM was about Rs 300 per month.

5. As I have indicated in previous chapters, in Pakistan 5 acres of irrigated land is considered to be the mininmum subsistence unit of land for an average size household.

6. The labour force displaced by the introduction of tractors in Mallian has been about 5 workers per tractor; in 1978 there were 17 tractors in operation in Mallian which means that at least 85 workers have been displaced from work in the village.

7. Morris (1969:79), argues on similar lines vis-a-vis the untouchables workers in Bombay: 'We may at least raise the possibility that the exclusion of the Untouchables was not entirely a caste phenomena but was also a device to preserve the monopoly of particularly advantageous but very limited opportunities against newcomers'.

8. Alavi (1973:418), is partially right when he suggests that: 'Poor peasants in peri-urban villages, especially those that are situated near large industrial centres, do have an alternative means of livlihood that is accessible to them. They enjoy, therefore, a relatively greater autonomy in political action'. But as I have suggested, different groups among the poor may have unequal access to resources and the labour market.

9. This can be said of the purchase of tractors, fertilizers, pesticides and other capital and intermediate goods in Mallian - these represent the realization of surplus value produced outside of Mallian, through their consumption Mallian.

# 9 Local and national development in the international economy

As I have indicated the process of local development is contradictory: it is dependent on imported technology and intermediate inputs which further integrates the local into the international economy and structures a relationship of dependent development. In a sense the distinction between national, international and the local economy becomes less clearly demarcated, an outcome of the international circuit of capital, which incorporates and integrates different economies. And in one sense the separation of the national, international and local economies is largely conceptual; though each of these levels has a specificity whose configuration with other levels establishes and delimits local developemt including that in Mallian.

In this chapter I shall analyze this development by focussing on Mallian's economy at three different levels of relationships, to establish the tendencies facilitating or impeding capitalist development: 1) the structure of relationships within Mallian; 2) Mallian's relationship with the national economy; 3) Mallian's relationship with the international economy.

I have indicated that, looked at over an appropriate period of time, there has been significant capitalist development in Mallian which has involved, among other factors, increased role of capital in the production process, the development of commodity production, and expanded reproduction based on wage labour and new technical conditions of production. A process which has expressed itself in, and including the differentiation of the peasantry, the development of a new social division of labour, development of productive forces, increase in profits and rents and of capital accumulation by the larger landowning households.

However, capital has not taken complete command of the labour process of all productive activity in Mallian and non-capitalist structures remain; therefore the agrarian transition, the theoretical concept in which local development is analyzed, is not complete.

These non-capitalist structures cannot be accounted for by focussing solely on one level of explanation or one general theory of development or underdevelopment; as for example, the world-systems approach, which would seek the cause of underdevelopment in Pakistan as a result of its incorporation into the world economy or due to unequal exchange at the global level (Wallerstein, 1979; Amin, 1974, 1979; Frank, 1969, 1980; Emmanuel, 1972). Though, as I have indicated, these relationships have important consequences for local and national development in that they set the parameters within which, in the short run, possibilities of development are determined. These theories are useful (even though each is different in important ways), insofar as they point to important dimensions, which are substantive, historical, conceptual and contextual in attempting to account for development. However, in another sense they are too general and operate at too high a level of abstraction, to explain, by themselves, concrete processes and specific instances of development at a local, that is, empirical level.

Nor can the existence of these non-capitalist structures be attributed to any single empirical condition such as sharetenancy (Bhaduri,1973; 1983); which is much too specific to account for the complex process of development and underdevelopment.

One influential work that attempts to explain capitalist development/underdevelopment in concrete terms and at the same time partially overcomes some problems of the world-systems approaches, is that of Brenner (1977:16):

> What accounts for capitalist economic development is that the the class (property/surplus extraction) structure of the *economy as a whole* determines that the reproduction carried out by its component 'units' is dependent upon their ability to increase their production accumulate and thereby develop their forces of production...[In] contrast, precapitalist economies, even those in which trade is widespread, can develop only within definite limits, because the class structure of the economy as a whole determines that their component units -specifically those producing the means of subsistence and means of production...neither can nor must systematically increase the forces of production, the productivity of labour, in order to reproduce themselves.

Brenner's analysis emphasizes the internal class relations which facilitate or impede capitalist development, according to whether absolute or relative surplus value extraction is the dominant form within the structure of class relations.

The extraction of absolute surplus, which, as I discussed in chapter 2, involves qualitatively greater productivity of the labour process, comes about according to Brenner, as a result of competition between units in agriculture (ibid.:32); the outcome of which is the development of capitalism. Further, according to Brenner, smallholding peasant households impede this process since they are not separated from their means of production, are kept out of market competition and the field of investment (ibid.:73-4).

Brenner's analysis does offer a correct view of the way smallholders in Mallian impede or at least pose problems for the agrarian transition, but as I indicate below, this approach cannot account for their conditions of existence.

Moreover, Brenner's heavy focus on a class frame of reference cannot account for the complexities of development or underdevelopment in Mallian. Here, as we have seen, one of the major constraints on the development of productive forces and hence of capitalist development in agriculture were the forces of production themselves. Of these water and fertilizers were the main lack, which were partially overcome by tubewell irrigation and chemical fertilizers.

Whether it is the forces of production or production relations that impede agrarian development, is an empirical question. Other things being equal, production relations can and do impede this development. But 'other things' are not necessarily equal, where the means of wetting the land is a major constraint. In the absence of water in semi-arid conditions, no combination of class relations can overcome a constraint imposed by the lack of a major productive force, water.

Brenners theoretical framework is thus only partially relevant for our analysis. His emphasis on the relations of production or 'class relations' as the major determinant or obstacle to capitalist development assumes, *a priori,* that factors other than class relations (e.g. water) cannot impose a serious constraint on that development. In this sense Brenner's approach is not concrete enough.

Of course, once a major constraint (such as water) has been removed then relations of production may well impede further development of capitalist agriculture - but this an issue that requires an empirical investigation. In fact, as I have pointed out, the increase in water availability changed in important ways, the labour process, which became more intensive, increased productivity, and brought about changes in the local social division of labour.

Also, whilst it is true, as Brenner suggests, that the conditions for accumulation and development of the productive forces are signalled when the social relations of production are premissed on free wage labour; that this creates the potential for capital and labour to combine at the highest level of productivity; and only under these consitions is this combination deemed feasible or necessary for generalized commodity production: 'where both labour and capital are commodities, will the continued increases in productivity be necessitated'(ibid.:30-1). Nevertheless, as I have argued, the conditions in which capital and labour can combine in the manner prescribed by Brenner do not exist, and thus sometimes have to be created.

Of course, the attempt to formulate a general primacy of either the forces or relations of production as primary social economic determinants has been a longstanding one. The generation after Marx's death tended to emphasize the primacy of the forces of production (Plekhanov, 1969; Bukharin, 1926); as also the relatively recent work of Cohen (1978). Whilst western Marxists, among others Lukacs, tended to accord primacy to the relations of production: '*all economic or "sociological" phenomena derive from the social relations of men to one another*', (1972:136; emphasis original).

I have suggested that both these schools are wrong insofar as they hold there can be a general primacy of any kind. In fact, as I have said, there can be no general primacy of either relations or forces of production. The primacy, if any, must be established on an empirical investigation and concrete analysis and not *a priori*.

It is with this methodology that I shall analyze capitalist development in Mallian and account for the incomplete agrarian transition. But first, a review of the development that has taken place in Mallian.

## Agrarian development in Mallian: a review

As we have seen, Mallian's economy has undergone important quantitative and qualitative transformation, signified by the extension of agriculture and changes in the labour process underlying this; which is characterized by both relative and absolute relative surplus value appropriation.

During the period under study, especially from 1967 there was a significant increase in land under crop, extension of cultivation, and higher cropping intensity, which rose from about 140 in 167 to 151 in 1977. This change, however, 'conceals' the increases that had occurred before 1967. If one takes 1962-3 as the base year then cropping intensity, as I have indicated in chapter 6, rose from less than 100; this is similar to the cropping intensity of 84 in Sheikupura tehsil in 1962/63.

The changes from 1965 onwards were due to both the extension of irrigation to overcome water constraints, and use of fertilizer, adoption of HYVs, and other inputs. For example, private tubewells increased from 8 in 1967 to 26 in 1978, in addition to the 6 installed and operated by the government. This increase in water resources allowed more land to be brought under cultivation, and increase in the cultivation of crops such as vegetables, wheat, rice and fodder. Previously these crops had 'competed' for water which thus prevented some crops from being cultivated. Increased water also laid the basis for the subsequent increase in the use of fertilizer and HYV.

Economic activity in Mallian became altogether more intensive and continuous instead of being fragmented into seasonal activity: multiple and double cropping increased significantly during most part of the year. Of course, the increased use of these inputs was in turn premissed on the state making available credit, largely money from the World Bank or under bilateral agreements, for the purchase of these subsidized inputs.

There was an increase in tractor use too: these increased from 6 in 1967 to 17 in 1978, and were adopted mainly by the larger owners who were eligible for long and medium term loans; that is, those owning more than 25 acres of land. This technological innovation was again premissed on increased irrigation, and together with other inputs, greatly transformed the labour process in the locality. Labour, now combined with its new technical conditions of production, marked the development of relative, in addition to intensified absolute surplus value appropriation. This development signalled a qualitative change in the production relations in Mallian, the emergence of 'free' agricultural labourers.

These structures and processes emerged out of an economy that was largely non-capitalist; although as I have shown, increase in output and some capital accumulation had occurred previously. The relations of production were dominated by sharetenancy and bonded agricultural labour; the surplus being appropriated largely through pre-capitalist ground rent in the form of rent in kind and labour rent.

The sep relations were an integral part of this structure of production and formed the unity between handicraft industry and agriculture which characterizes non-capitalist production.

The transformation of labour/production processes in Mallian during 1967 to 1978 are reflected in increased production: upto 200 to 300 percent increase in per acre output, mainly of rice and wheat. There was increase in marketed surplus of many households, though amongst the smaller owners this did not increase to any great extent, since the costs of production, in the form of modern inputs, increased too, and were often used in less than optimal quantities by the smaller producers. Moreover, these inputs had to be bought on the market, as separate elements entering the process of production, as commodities, and not as previously, as a portion kept over from previous production.

Similar transformation occurred in production relations: compared to the situation before 1967 when there were no wage labourers on cash, by 1978 these had increased to 36; and formed part of a social organization of production which comprised the following:

| | |
|---|---|
| Tenants of various kinds | 130 households |
| Agricultural workers on sep | 76 persons |
| Wage labourers (on cash) | 36 persons |
| Workers in juts | 60 persons |

The different categories of wage labourers can be analyzed both together and separately to show in concrete terms the labour process specific to each subcategory.

The workers on cash are almost always employed on the most intensively cultivated and technologically most modern part of a landowner's holdings. That is, the portion where modern machinery and other inputs such as tubewells, tractors, fertilizers and HYV combine with wage labour in production based on capitalist labour process. On this portion, as we saw in Mallian, the output per acre is higher than on portions where this form of production is absent. This capitalist production invariably takes place on the self-cultivated portions of land. Here wage labourers on cash engage in relatively large-scale socialized production at a higher level of technical efficiency and productivity.

The agricultural labourers on sep are paid in kind and include two different categories, though I classify both under sep, as this is the terminology used in Mallian and because they also have some features in common.

In the first category, of which there are 30 in Mallian, are the hereditary landless agricultural labourers who are in a relationship of personal dependence to the landowner; of course this does not preclude them from being exploited under capitalist production, in addition to the basically non-capitalist forms of exploitation to which they are subjected.

The other 45 workers are wage labourers who are paid in kind, and as we saw in chapter 7, are employed on the farms of the small landowners and rich peasants, who have a shortage of circulating capital and therefore pay wages in kind.

The work of the juts reflects too the emergence of capitalist labour processes: a relatively large-scale socialized form of production, but one where the technical conditions of production, that is, the application of machinery, is still rudimentary. Moreover, as we have seen, workers bring themselves together to engage in socialized labour which is reflective of early stages of capitalist production; a higher form of the social organization of production would be signalled when capital itself brings isolated workers together to engage in capitalist production.

Thus there has been substantial capitalist transformation of Mallian's economy during 1967 to 1978, pointing towards a process of the agrarian transition in the locality. Yet, as I have indicated, inspite of impressive development, Mallian' economy is not under the complete command of capital. There still exist small-scale non-capitalist structures which have not been transformed by this development. In order to account for these, one needs to analyze Mallian's internal relationships, as well as relationship to the national and international economy.

## Relationships within Mallian

### *Modern technology*

Whilst there has been a considerable increase in the use of tubewells, fertilizers, tractors and HYV and other inputs, there is still a relative shortage of these inputs in relation to the needs of the village economy as a whole. For example, inspite of increase in tubewells, there is still a water shortage in Mallian, especially in rabi.

There are 26 tubewells in Mallian with an average capacity of 1.5 cusec; that is, they can pump water at the rate of 1.5 cubic feet per second. During kharif the tubewells can provide about 330 acre-feet of water each; during this period, however, the water table is high and canal water is abundant so that water supply is relatively adequate.

During rabi on the other hand, there is a natural lowering of the water table, and less water is pumped to the surface. With a decrease in water supplied from the Upper Chenab Canal during winter, Mallian faces a seasonal water shortage. In rabi, each tubewell can provide only about 100 acre-feet of water; this means that of the 3258 cultivable acres in Mallian, only 2600 acres can be cultivated. Moreover, about 25-35 percent of water is lost in both seasons due to seepage in the water courses, and mismanagement and lack of control of the water supply.

Another constraint, though the efficacy of this is disputed as we saw in chapter 4 (because it is held by some that animal-drawn ploughs are more efficient and cost effective for small-scale cultivation), is the relative lack of tractors in the village.

In 1978 there were 17 tractors of standard unit work capacity (between 40-60 horsepower), each with an optimal capacity to plough about 100 acres per season. With a cropping intensity of about 150, approximately 4,900 acres are ploughed every year, not counting the land poughed as a result of the multiple and double cropping which continues throughout the year and which is not accounted for in the official statistics compiled by the revenue department. For optimal cultivation in Mallian, at least 49 tractors are required for good cultivation of the 4,900 acres.

Another constraint on agrarian production is that of sub-optimal fertilizer use. For the village as a whole, fertilizer use barely reaches the minimum requirements of 1.5 bags of urea and 0.5 bag of DAP plus some application of superphosphates. In fact, the average use for the village would be far lower if some of the small number of households using larger quantities of fertilizers were excluded from the calculations.

Thus, there still exist technological constraints in expanding agricultural output in Mallian. However, I have looked at these constraints for the village as a whole, in the abstract, without taking into account the differential access to these resources by the various producer groups in Mallian.

### *The large landowners*

In chapter 7, I described how the cultivation practice of the three large landowners was comprised of two or more distinct but related labour processes. On MDs farm this consists of sharecropping, a fixed-rent tenancy and a self-managed portion where wage labour and capital was combined in the production process. It is only on this portion that production is premissed on capitalist labour processes under real subsumption to capital.

Similarly, the two other large owners had self-cultivated and sharetenant portions where both capitalist and non-capitalist labour processes are extant. Why is it that these landowners did not bring all their holdings under capitalist self-cultivation? In other words, what are the incentives for these landowners which makes them continue to appropriate rent in kind (through sharetenancy) and absolute surplus value - since the self-cultivated portions have greater output per acre and higher profitability. There are two sets of factors involved here, but one must separate at the outset, the discussion on the nature (capitalist or otherwise) of the sharetenant's labour processes, from the reasons for their existence.

*Sharetenancy*

Land in Mallian is tenanted for a number of quite different reasons: due to the low fertility of the land which is uneconomic under present conditions to bring under modern capitalist production; so this land is rented to tenants who have no alternative means of employment and are often under debt bondage to the landowner; to keep a pool of labour attached to the land and under the landowners control; absentee landowners who rent out land because they find this 'efficient' in terms of opportunity cost of other employment, especially in Sahiwal; fragmented and scattered holdings which are not amenable to profitable cultivation because of high supervision costs, and so on.

Among the large landowners especially, one can discern two main distinct but related reasons for the existence of sharetenancy: first, low fertility of land where profitable cultivation is not possible; and second, the process of land re-fertilization by the large owners. In fact, I shall indicate that the connection between the reproduction of small-scale production and the agrarian transition is in part the existence of sub-fertile land.

During fieldwork it was observed that most of the land rented out was generally sub-fertile, especially that rented to hereditary sharetenants: the average yields from their cultivation are about 12 maunds per acre for wheat, and 11 maunds per acre for rice; compared to yields of 35-45 and 30-35 maunds of rice and wheat respectively, on the self-cultivated portions of the large owners land. In some instances, the yields on sharetenant farms are as low as 5 maunds per acre for both rice and wheat.

The land has low fertility due to three main factors and three types of sub-fertile or ecologically damaged land are in existence in Mallian. Since this is the major reason behind the large amount of land which is sharetenanted in Mallian (but not in Sahiwal as we shall see), I shall explain the factors that affect the soil in some detail.

The three categories of sub-fertile soil are those due to waterlogging (standing or perched water); land affected by saline salts; and land damaged by alkaline dust.

*Water logging*: this prevents germination of the seed and is the result of inadequate drainage, due in part to the fact that the canals distributing water from dams/barrages and rivers are located above ground level. These were constructed in the nineteenth or early twentieth century and lacked the appropriate hydraulic technology to lift water from below ground level.

*Salinity*: here the salts from the earth have percolated to the top-soil, and when dried by the sun, form a top layer on the soil that prevents germination of seeds.

*Alkaline dust:* this again is due to biochemical processes which form an impervious layer of dust on the soil which can also affect the deeper soil.

Generally, the land rented out to sharetenants has varying degrees of the types of damaged soil which I have described. In many cases, as part of their work, sharetenants have to grow special grasses (*argemona mexicon, sueda fruticosa*) either on their own or intermixed with other crops; these are grown all the year round, and ploughed back successively into the soil to increase its fertility.

During fieldwork one of the sharetenants told me that he had, through the processes I have described, nursed a few acres back to fertility, only for these to be taken back by the landowner for self-cultivation.

There are other ways of restoring damaged soils back to fertility, but these are relatively costly and the treatment involves rather more complex operations which are carried out under the aegis of an internationally funded national organization, the Salinity Control and Reclamation Programme (SCARP).

*For water logged land*: the water is removed by lifting through tubewells and drained away through pipes; the soil is then drilled through the impermeable strata to enable perched water to seep through to join ground water; this is then drained away by pumping out by tubewells.

*For alkaline soils*: the dust or white encrustrations on the top soil are removed by scraping; these are then flushed away via drainage channels; later gypsum (*hydrate calcium sulphate*) is added to the area. The other operations then include furrowing and green manuring and mulching the area; or alternatively, spreading some artificial material on the soil to reduce evaporation; then draining to lower the water table.

*For saline soils*: huge quantities of gypsum are added to neutralize the salts and all the other operations for treatment mentioned for alkaline soils are carried out.

The second (SCARP) method is more costly in restoring fertility to land and landowners in Mallian prefer the first method. This takes longer, often several seasons, but control is retained over the land, during the treatment.

Be that as it may, this attempt to treat the land back to fertility among the larger owners through the work of their sharetenants, is itself reflective of an extremely important development: the profitability of self-managed capitalist production and the attempt (of whatever degree of enthusiasm) to extend this by investing in sub-fertile land.

Another reason for the existence of sharetenancy in Mallian is the scattered and fragmented holdings even of the larger owners. This problem is epitomozed by the statement made by the largest landowner in Mallian, MD, who said that because only about 100 acres of his 500 acres were in one contiguous piece, he was not able to profitably install a combine harvester. In fact this points up a generic problem in Mallian (and in Pakistan). In general it is rare to find more than 50 acres of land owned by the same household, in one piece. The rest are scattered from one side of the village to another, consuming time and energy to cultivate each portion. These fragmented and scattered holdings also incur high supervision costs in self-cultivation, thus making sharetenancy a relatively economical undertaking.

The reason behind fragmentation and scattered holdings are complex, but have their roots in the history of land tenures and the lack of adequate development in Pakistan (and the origin of this development under colonial rule); which did not provide alternative employment to the rural poor, and who thus hang on to the dwarf-holdings under any circumstances.

Of course, the immediate cause for fragmentation and scattered holdings is the Islamic law of inheritance, which stipulates equal division of land among all male offspring, and a smaller portion for females (Nazir, 1981). But the fragmentation also occurs because land is bought and sold wherever it is available in the village. The various attempts to consolidate these holdings via the Land Conolidation Act have largely failed; the reasons for this are complex and are not of direct relevance here.

There are other reasons for the existence of sharetenancy in Mallian: there are portions of land in Mallian which do not receive adequate water from tubewells or canals; either because they are on elevated land, or there are no channels leading from the waterhead to distribute water to these fields.

In addition there are some specifically 'sociological' reasons for the existence of sharetenancy: some landowning households rent out land to landless members of their own biraderi, ostensibly for humanitarians reasons. However, I found evidence to the contrary as well: members of a biraderi did not want to rent land to other members of the same biraderi in case they laid claim to its ownership; as for example under the 1913 Land Preemption Act which allowed members of a biraderi to make such a claim, if land had been alienated without full consent of members of a family.

Different reasons for renting land to sharetenants is provided by evidence from Sahiwal and Sargodha, which is included in the appendix, and which I shall summarize here.

In Sahiwal the largest owner in the sample owns 204 acres and rents in an additional 184 acres, giving a self-cultivated holding of 388 acres, which is twice the size of MDs self-cultivated holding in Mallian. This is cultivated with 18 permanent wage labourers; in addition, labour is hired during the peak agricultural periods. This household owns 3 tractors and 3 tubewells plus other equipment, which facilitates, rather than explains his large scale of cultivation.

Note that land is rented in by this household, rather than rented out, to sharecroppers, because all of this household's land is fertile. This illustrates that it is not the relatively large size of the holdings which prevent landowners from extending their self-cultivation, but as I have emphasized, in many instances it is the low fertility of the soil, among other factors.

Evidence from Sargodha supports this assertion. Here one landowner with 150 acres rents out 50 acres to sharetenants, in portions of 12 to 20 acres. One sharetenant household, renting in 16 acres from this landowner, displays the following characteristics: the wheat yields are 10 maunds per acre and 12.50 maunds per acre for rice, which is very similar to the sharetenants output in Mallian. If land in Sargodha were amenable to modern cultivation and given greater yields, then self-cultivation would be extended.

There are reasons other than ecological ones for the existence of sharetenancy in Mallian, Sahiwal and Sargodha. In Sahiwal especially, many (including hereditary) sharetenancies are under the formal subsumption to capital: large amounts of capital and intermediate inputs enter into the process of production for the market, based on the tenants' household labour. In this district, owners and tenants participate much more in the decision-making process and organization of production for mutual benefit, than in Mallian or Sargodha.

I am arguing in line with what I said earlier, that there can be no general theory of sharecropping. This criticism applies equally to some writers within the Marxist tradition (Pearce, 1983; Bhaduri, 1973, 1983), whose work I have mentioned in previous chapters.

Attempts to account for sharetenancy in terms of a 'specific form of surplus appropriation' and 'one mechanism through which owners of means of production acquire access to others' labour' (Pearce, 1983:53), leads to the formulation of a formal theory of sharetenancy. This is too general and devoid of any content, and subsumes qualitatively different production and labour processes, and therefore conceals very different reasons and conditions for the existence of sharetenancy.

Sharetenancy as a specific relation of production constitutive of a mode of production that is semi-feudal is suggeted by Bhaduri (1973, 1983). This is untenable. It is too specific and precludes different processes (relation to capital, labour process) underlying sharetenancy; as well as different conditions in which it can exist, including under the formal subsumption to capital (Gupta,1980; Pearce, op. cit).

In my view sharecropping cannot be conceptualized as constituting either a specific relation of production (constitutive of a specific mode of production) or in general and formal terms of 'mobilization' or 'appropriation' of labour. In this sense, sharecropping can only be seen as an altogether variable, whose conditions of existence must be established empirically by a concrete analysis. Such an approach can relate the existence of sharetenancy to its wider relationships in the economy and also enable one to characterize the labour processes underlying its production in terms of whether these exist within or outside of the capital-relation. And hence whether these contribute to or impede the agrarian transition.

But as I have said, the characterization of the labour process (capitalist or otherwise) underlying sharetenancy must be separated from the reasons for its existence. I have argued that in Mallian sharetenancy does pose a problem for the agrarian transition, but that its existence can only be explained within the empirical conditions in Mallian, and not in terms of *a priori* theorizing, which would see sharetenancy as the same under all conditions.

As I have said, there is no *a priori* basis for assuming either the primacy of production relations or forces of production in conditioning social economic relations, Brenner's assertion seems weak: 'The manner in which any ruling class can or does best maximize its surplus may not at all correspond with the objecive requirements for the development of the productive forces',(1977:60).

Brenner neglects the constraints which preclude all but a limited mode of surplus appropriation; so that landowners do not carry out some alternative forms of surplus extraction because the existing method maximizes their suplus; this is certainly the case where constraints on water availability severely restrict re-organization of labour for expanding production, as in the case of the sharetenants in Mallian.

Thus in Mallian, on the whole, it is not sharetenancy (relation of production) that explains low productivity (underdevelopment of productive forces) but low productivity of sub-fertile soil that explains sharetenancy. In other words the productive forces constrain the relations of production.

On a similar theme to Brenner's, Bhaduri (1973, 1983) suggests that the existence of sharecropping can explain agricultural backwardness in south Asia, because it acts as a disincentive for the landlord to innovate technological improvement. The result, according to Bhaduri, is agricultural backwardness, since he equates sharetenancy with semi-feudal production relations. Specifically, the reasons for the existence of sharetenancy is that:

> Since the semi-feudal landowner derives his income from both property, and right to usury, he will be discouraged from introducing any technological improvement so long as his gain in income from increased productivity brought about by technological change falls short of his loss of income from usury due to reduction (or incomplete elimination) in the level of consumption loans required by the *kishan* (peasant)(1973:135).

This of course is a tautology. But even if Bhaduri's assertions were accepted, he would still have to explain why landowners innovate and bring technological improvements in their cultivation? And equally important, why does land continue to be sharecropped? This, as I have argued, is an empirical question, which in Mallian is related to ecological factors.

*The smallholders*

The relationship of the smallholders to capitalist development and the agrarian transition in Mallian is complex; for as I have said in the foregoing chapters, this is not a homogeneous category, and reflects many different relations to capital. Nevertheless, a process of differentiation and diversification is noticeable among these households (constituted mainly but not exclusively by middle and small peasants), so that the effect of these processes on the agrarian transition are somewhat complex.

The smallholder, whose production is premissed largely on household labour, is able to reproduce himself, inspite of differing relationships to capital, because it is least dependent on the market. It owns enough land to subsist on without having to rent in additional land. Similarly, its engagement with the labour market is minimal - hiring in or hiring out of labour occurs at peak periods, but this is generally incidental to its conditions of production (Banaji, 1976). Put another way, the smallholder persists because it can engage in production without receiving profit or rent, or accounting cost to itself, though it is increasingly subject to market forces, as I have indicated.

Looked at historically, however, the smallholder does disappear as in England (Johnson, 1979), and this is one of the tendencies and processes to which it is subject to in Mallian. I shall describe this process below, but I shall describe first why smallholdings in general impede the agrarian transition.

The smallholders are attached to their means of production, which are small-scale, consequently the scale of production is small; no wage labour is exploited to any sigificant extent, and no expansion of capital takes place, though in years of good harvests surplus produce does accrue which can sometimes be converted to capital. By owning their means of production and subsistence, they hinder the concentration and centralization of the means of production; and they prevent these from being converted into capital thus precluding a higher rate of capital accumulation; this hinders the polarization of the countryside into wage-labourers and capitalists, that is, capitalist development and the agrarian transition.

According to Marx:

> Proprietorship of land parcel by its very nature excludes the development of social productive forces of labour, social forms of labour, social concentration of capital, large-scale cattle raising, and the progressive application of science (1974:804).

I shall come back to these general characteristics of the smallholders later, but first I need to describe the structure of smallholding peasant households in Mallian and relate this to the existence of petty production in Mallian as a whole.

In fact as I indicated in the Introduction and in chapter 5, the size of holdings in Mallian is relatively large by Pakistani standards; consequently, the smallholders (middle, small and poor peasants) constitute about 50 percent of landowning households but own only 16 percent of the land. On its own this quantity is not a high proportion, but in conjunction with sharetenancy it constitutes a barrier to the penetration of capital.

What keeps the smallholder extant in Mallian and what are the possibilities for its dissolution? There is no unilinear process but a number of processes at work often reflected in opposing tendencies that tend to reproduce or dissolve these small-scale structures.

There are two main tendencies which tend to reproduce the smallholders. First, money is borrowed by the smallholders when necessary from ahrthis to meet production costs or for consumption during poor harvests, when small producers are particularly vulnerable to indebtedness which can result in loss or mortgage of their land. These loans are generally paid back through distress sales or in surplus product during harvest, and the holding remains the peasants property.

The fact that merchant capital tends to bolster the smallholders is in line with evidence from other situations (Lenin, 1960:185). Secondly, smallholders are reproduced by local modern industry. In chapter 8 I described how one of the consequences of Mallian's articulation with local modern industry was the diversification of economic activity, rather than proletarianization of some peasant households. This enables additional money to flow into these households and precludes or postpones indebtedness; which in other circumstances could lead to mortgaging and ultimately loss of land, forcing the smallholders to join the ranks of the rural poor (Banaji, 1976:38).

There are a number of processes in Mallian that tend towards dissolution of the smallholder rather than its reproduction. First, the smallholders are subjected to a tendency to successive fragmentation of land over generations so that it becomes too small even for subsistent cultivation. These dwarf-holdings can sometimes be sold and employment sought in industry. Second, the market relations of the smallholder: he now relies increasingly on the market for agricultural inputs such as HYV seeds, fertilizers, pesticides, and irrigation technology. These are obtained either from the ahrthi or banks; so that, whilst he is still relatively less dependent on the market, he has nevertheless been increasingly drawn into the vortex of market relations.

If, as is the case in Mallian, the ahrthi is a local landowner and the borrower is a member of the same biraderi, the smallholder can be separated from the land with less difficulty, than would be the case if this were not so. This is because the legal restrictions on land alienation and sales under the Punjab Alienation of Land Act of 1901, are not effective if land is being alienated within the biraderi. In fact MD, the largest owner in Mallian, is supposed to have accumulated his holdings largely through buying up land from within his biraderi.

The third tendency dissolving the smallholders is located at the level of demand: there is evidence that in Mallian capitalist penetration and integration into the world market has imposed new cultural demands/norms of consumption on the smallholder: including consumption of radio-cassettes, televisions, bicycles, scooters, cigarettes, cologne, after-shave lotion, tea, bottled drinks, and watches. As well as: going to the cinema, visiting urban areas and relatives, and so on. These have to be paid for either by increasing production or from other sources of income including from work at STM, or through loans. As Gudeman's (1978:131), informant stated in another context: '"In the old days there were no radios and people made their own clothes and hats. Today people want money to buy these."'

It is difficult to establish the dominant tendency from the complex ongoing processes; but taking all factors into account and looked at historically, there might either be no definite dominant tendency, with the situation likely to be expressed in some sort of 'blockage' or stasis, with agriculture and industry blocking each others development. Or the tendency is for the dissolution of the smallholder. The latter, paradoxically, is related to the same tendency which in the short-run prolongs its existence - local modern industry.

The smallholder will find it easier to part with his holdings if alternative means of industrial employment is available. This, of course, will be a configuration or combination of other processes such as fragmentation of holdings, development of market relations, and most importantly development of industry. But this is likely to be a prolonged process.

**Artisan production and sep**

In chapter 7 I described the production process of artisan and service households. It was apparent that these households' production impedes or slows the agrarian transition as it is part of, and contributes to, the unity of agriculture and relative self-sufficiency of the village. The demise of sep is thus crucial for the further penetration of capital into the Mallian economy, and the agrarian transition.

I have described how artisan production is constitutive of small-scale production based on household labour, in which the worker owns his own means of production. These are simple tools and instruments of production operated manually and incapable of producing on a large scale.

The artisans products are generally bartered with those of the agricultural households; that is, exchange takes place outside of the market. In this economy, capital is kept out of the sphere of production and circulation. And the worker treats his materials and elements of production 'simply as the object of his creative activity, and not as capital...[and in the labour process] consumes the means of production as mere means of subsistence of labour', (Marx, 1976:1007).

There are a number of conditions for the existance of artisan production in Mallian. First, it is appropriate to Mallian's traditional non-capitalist agrarian economy based on sep; second, it is premissed on the existence of small-scale production of the smallholders who use relatively simple technology; this means that the demand for artisan production is likely to remain as long as small-scale agriculture exists; third, artisan production is required for peasant dwellings which are constructed out of mud and wood; but this is not a regular or continuous demand; fourth, artisans are partially adapting to the new conditions by acquiring skills appropriate to the new technology.

As with the smallholders, there are a number of processes at work which tend to erode or assist the demise of artisans' production, or conversely, facilitate the reproduction of sep relations.

In fact there are five ways in which artisan production can, or has been, eroded: First, the labour processes of some artisans can come under the formal subsumption of capital: the artisan produces on the old basis but capital intervenes and takes control of the labour process and its products. As we saw this tendency is weak in Mallian; only one household has come under this form of capitalist penetration. This is where a large laundry/dry cleaning enterprise in Sheikhupura town brought clothes to the tailor/washer/dyer household in Mallian for cleaning. Second, artisan production is becoming increasingly dependent for its raw materials and instruments of production on the larger market; this weakens the interdependence and reciprocity between artisan households, whereby these produce and exchange materials and instruments for each other's production, such as wood handles, iron tips, levellers and so on. Clearly, this process occurs in the early stage when artisan interdependence diminishes, thus creating the conditions for its eventual demise.

In chapter 7, I indicated a third way in which the basis of artisan production and sep is being changed: increased work on a job basis, paid for in cash and conducted outside of sep. This opens up artisan production, more so than before, to the vagaries of supply and demand and also to a more monetized economy. This, in addition, curtails the paternalistic 'security' under a relatively undynamic economy in which the artisans operate under sep.

Fourth, as we saw in chapters 6 and 7, the way certain artisan occupations had already eroded or had become subsidiary occupations, such as that of the weaver and water-carrier; a direct result of the development of large-scale modern machine production: textile mills and water pump-sets. Similarly, technologically more sophisticated instruments of production have come in use since the 1960s, such as tractors, threshers, tubewells, and other equipment, which require production and maintenance work on a different basis to that which the artisans skills can offer. Hence, increasingly, work is diverted away from artisans, to more complex labour processes of engineers and technicians.

Fifth, as I indicated in chapter 8, alternative means of employment in nearby modern industry facilitates the possibility of artisans giving up their traditional occupations, especially such as those of the weavers and oil-pressers. However, as I will discuss shortly, the alternative employment opportunity offered by industry is limited, given the dependent nature of industrialization in Pakistan.

### Relationship with the national economy

The relationship between Mallian and the national economy as a factor in local development is less transparent than the relationships within Mallian. And the causal process is not symmetrical: the structure of dependent capitalist industrial development slows the process of agrarian development in Mallian and in turn the latter (in aggregate with other similar social formations), hinders a faster rate of capitalist development nationally, but only in a partial sense. For, as I have indicated, the process of agricultural and industrial development is accompanied by dependence on the international economy, which restricts an integrated development and formation of a national economy.

There are a number of underlying reasons behind national-local relationships which results in the reproduction of underdevelopment in the latter. First, Mallian's agriculture is not integrated into the national economy, in particular into industry; the latter is dominated by cotton textiles and other agriculture dependent manufactures, and cannot adequately supply the major inputs for agriculture, as we saw in relation to the producer groups who used less than optimal quantities of inputs.This is clearly illustrated by the fact that the green revolution was critically dependent on imported agro-chemicals and technology.

I have described how the use of inputs for agriculture are below the minimum requirements for Mallian as a whole. For not only is the supply of important inputs inadequate in quantity, but the process of production in Mallian largely bypasses the national economy: because these are either provided by the local economy (such as farmyard manure or simple technology) under sep, or by the international economy, as we shall see. For example, in 1978/79 about 59 percent of fertilizers in use in Pakistan had to be imported (Burki and Laporte Jr.,1984:53); the 40 percent produced domestically relied not only on foreign technology for production, but a significant proportion of the raw materials were imported as well. This is even more so with other inputs such as irrigation technology, tractors, pesticides and HYV seeds. Of course this represents a loss of foreign exchange; but of greater consequence is that the circuit of productive capital, and in particlur the moment of self-expansion occurs in the developed countries, thus depriving the national economy of a higher rate of capital accumulation.

The lower productivity that results from the lower inputs means that the potential for increasing agricultural resources (raw materials and food in the way of wage goods) to industry are also diminished. Though it must be stated that even if greater resources were released by agriculture, under conditions generated by dependent industrialization, the deepening of the economy would not occur to the *extent* it would if the capital goods and technology generating sectors (Department 1) were located in Pakistan and integrated into Pakistani agriculture.

There is another way in which a weakly developed industry limits agricultural development: the relative lack of industrial employment means that agriculture is congested and employs over half of the labour force, and the rural areas house more than 70 percent of the population. There are more people looking for employment in industry than there are jobs as we saw in relation to STM and Mallian. The result is that inspite of low wages poor agricultural households hold on to fragmented, subdivided and sometimes ecologically damaged land which they cannot reclaim. If regular and secure employment opportunities were available through rapid industrial development, then it is likely that many owners with extremely small holdings would be more likely to part with them, creating the possibilites for consolidating these into more economical units. Moreover, if agriculture was less congested, then larger owners in Mallian would be compelled to re-organize their production to extract relative surplus value. In such a situation rack-renting would not be possible because both tenants and wage labourers would be harder to recruit. So that instead of relying on 'labour squeezing' practices, landowners would have to increase output through a re-organization of the labour process.

Another relationship with the national economy which impedes capitalist development and the agrarian transition in Mallian is artisan production, some aspects of which I have already discussed in the previous section. Artisan production under sep limits the size of the home market by reproducing a certain amount of self-sufficiency in the local economy. Outside capital, and products of modern industry only partially manage to supplant artisan production, a situation that restricts the extension of the home market to a considerable degree.

It might be objected that what is needed are more favourable government policies, such as higher subsidies for inputs and higher procurement policies for agricultural produce. To an extent, the subsidies already exist; in the late 1970s these were from 30-70 percent for fertilizers, tractors, irrigation technology and pesticides. And whilst higher prices would undoubtedly increase output, this could only be done by increasing the consumption of imported inputs, which would increase the costs of production and dependence. So that agriculture would tend to lose on the roundabout what it gained on the swings.

## Relationship with the international economy

The international circuit of capital incorporates Mallian into the international economy, and increasingly controls its conditions of production, concretized in the consumption of tractors, irrigation technology, fertilizers, pesticides and other chemicals and HYVs, that form the basis of the green revolution. This has occurred simultaneously with the centralization and concentration of finance, commodity and productive capital at the global level, and embodied in the operation of international banks and multinational corporations.

The significance of this relationship is not just the physical provision of internationally produced goods for the local economy, but the importance of the local economy for the completion of the circuit of expanded reproduction of capital of the developed countries. The international economy, dominated by the developed economies and their multinational corporations, sell elements of production and consumption to the local economy in Mallian via the national economy in Pakistan, thus appropriating and re-incorporating the surplus production, and re-constituting this into the international circuit of expanded reproduction.

The net result of this incorporation into the international economy is the structuring of dependent local development. And other things being equal, the greater the development the greater the incorporation into the international economy, as happened during the period of the green revolution. This is illustrated by the following: Even though the capacity to produce domestic fertilizer increased by 240 percent from about 400,000 product tons in 1970/71 to 950,000 product tons in 1978/79, the proportion of imported to domestic fertilizers increased from 43 percent in 1970/71 to 59 percent in 1978/79 (Burki and Laporte Jr., op. cit.:53) Taking into account, as I have mentioned, that domestic fertilizer production relies heavily on imported technology and raw and intermediate materials, the extent of dependence on the international economy is enormous. The same would hold for other machine equipment and chemical goods which are imported and form the basis of local development.

The international economy, in the main, links Mallian to itself, in large part bypassing the national economy, which cannot supply the elements of agricultural production, thus creating the disjuncture between agriculture and industry which I discussed in the Introduction and chapters 2 and 4.

It is a paradox, therefore, that the process of Mallian's incorporation into the international economy, which in an immediate sense facilitates development by providing the vital inputs, also retards development and the agrarian transition locally and at the national level, by increasing dependence and thus restricting further development.

The mechanism by which this situation comes about takes two distinct but related forms. Under the first mechanism, the money borrowed to purchase inputs for production, and the debt servicing that follows, creates a drain of capital and hence contributes to underdevelopment. The second mechanism creates a structural dependency due to a lack of a capital goods and technology generating sector in the national economy.

Undoubtedly the increasing commercialization of agricultural production has expanded opportunities for international capital investment in the sphere of circulation locally (a process by which the surplus value produced in the developed countries is realized), while opening up new possibilities in fertilizer production and in other items that comprise the new technology of the green revolution.

Since the mid-1960s, the needs of the green revolution, on which Pakistan's agriculture development strategy is based, has been fashioned through technology rooted in the developed countries. This ensured the sale of large quantities of the new technology including fertilizers to Pakistan; for example, in 1978/79 about 0.7 million tonnes were imported into the country(Government of Pakistan, 1980).

Though the need for the new technology, and especially chemical fertilizers, could be met through expanding domestic production, this development would be accompanied by a technological and financial dependency. In other words, whilst less fertilizers and other intermediate goods might be imported by expanding domestic production, more capital goods and technology would have to be (and have been) imported to produce these.

This suggests that the degree of structural economic integration between the local, regional and national economy is even further eroded. If this is the case it would suggest that there exists an inverse relationship between the degree of integration into the international economy and the level of structural independence it has achieved.

The second mechanism is related to the first, but has more substance. It follows Marx's analysis of the relationship between Department 1 which produces the means of production and Department 2 which produces the means of consumption. The argument is that the first department is located mainly in and its goods are produced by the advanced industrial countries, which hinders the accumulation of capital in Pakistan, as in other developing countries (Cardoso, 1972; Byres, 1982, 1980, 1974).

The inability to produce capital goods and production technology nationally, imposes constraints on Mallian's development, because the expansion of local development does not feed back into Mallian or the national economy; rather it serves more the international economy, through the expanded reproduction of the international circuit of capital, which draws in surplus produced in Mallian but does not re-enter and expand Mallian or the national economy.

In a situation where the Department 1 goods producing sector was more developed in Pakistan the national economy would be deepend (Marx, 1961/62, vol.2: part III; Dobb, 1967; Byres, 1974). The international economy could be entered into more selectively or it could become a complementary or supportive factor in the expansion of national and local development. As it is the international economy mediates local development and precludes a more profound transformation of the local economy.

# 10 Conclusion

This study has stressed the centrality of capital goods and technology in the development process in Pakistan and *ipso facto* other similarly placed developing countries. I have indicated that the use of imported technology has been highly contradictory, in the sense that whilst considerable growth has been achieved in the short run by the use of this technology, this has created a dependence on the international economy dominated by the developed countries. This is because the strategy of development which has relied so heavily on imported technology has created a disjuncture between agriculture and industry. Each relies on the outside economy for its inputs for production. This has also slowed the process of capital accumulation and transformation of the national economy because the production of capital goods and equipment and therefore capital expansion (valorization) takes place outside of the national economy.

The role of the capital goods and technology generating (the producer goods) sectors is analytically useful: in Pakistan's large economy, which in the long run must inevitably supply the bulk of its requirements for intermediate and capital goods, it is the industrial branches included in the producer goods sector whose output is essential to the transformation of the country's production possibilities. In this sense, the development of producer and capital goods sector is central to the overall economic development of the economy as I have indicated especially in chapter 2.

I have suggested that imported technology may solve some problems in the short-run, but a long-term expansion of the economy can only take place within an integrated national economy supplied by a domestic producer goods sector. In the absence of this the future obstacles to development, without recourse to outside help, will be impossible. In order to achieve a high degree of self-reliance at the national, regional and local level, a strong and versatile capital goods and technology producing sector is needed, which is also fully integrated into Pakistani agriculture. In the medium and long run these objectives can be achieved through the modernization of Pakistani agriculture. This modernization can be accomplished by changes in the social organization of agricultural production and a more equitable land distribution, and through a continuous expansion in the capacity of the machine-building industry to provide large quantities of agricultural machinery and intermediate inputs.

In Pakistan, as in many other developing countries, the capital goods and technology producing sectors of industry has to play a very important role in the development process in general, and industrialization in particular. Being key industries, these can have a high linkage effect to other industries, such as metallurgy, rubber, glass, plastics and so on. These industries can increase the supply of new machinery and stimulate the rapid growth of several new industries including chemical fertilizers. Moreover, owing to its high capacity for generating new products, the capital goods and technology producing sectors can grow faster than industry as a whole. The rapid growth of this sector can bring about a significant change in the pattern of manufacturing output.

## The role of capital goods in the development process: India, China and Pakistan

In a comparison of Indian and Chinese development strategies, (with China emphasizing capital goods and machine building rather more than India) Raj states:

> The much more striking difference in [Indian and Chinese] performance has been the fairly high rate of investment maintained in China in recent years with only marginal dependence on imports of machinery and equipment. Complete industrial plants and other equipment had accounted for 60 percent of China's total imports in 1958, and 63 percent in 1959...[Moreover] China was repaying loans taken from the Soviet Union and completed full repayment by 1965 (thus gaining the distinction of being perhaps the only developing country now not to have any foreign debt. In these circumstances, if China had not already built up the machine-making sector to the extent it did, the cut in the rate of domestic investment necessitated by foreign exchange shortage is likely to have been very much sharper than has actually been effected during this period. [India] presents a

> sharp contrast. It has been heavily dependent on foreign aid, both on account of the difficulties it has faced in raising the domestic saving and its continued reliance on imports of machinery and equipment on a large scale (for sustaining a lower rate of investment than in China. Imports of machinery alone account now for about 30 percent of India's total import bill...[So that] for raising the rate of capital accumulation, India faces both a saving and a foreign exchange problem, while China has not only succeeded in raising the rate of saving much above the level of India but has very nearly broken the foreign exchange bottleneck as far as investment is concerned (1969:224/26).

During the comparable period, Pakistan's development strategy presented a picture which was different to both India and China, with an almost total neglect of the capital goods and machine building sectors, which both India and China in their particular ways, attempted to develop (the indigenous capital goods sector which I discussed in chapter 4 is a minor exception.)

In a classic study, Hoffmann (1958), suggests that in the first stage of industrialization, net output of consumer goods industries is on the average five times that of capital goods. In the second stage, the ratio is reduced to about 2.5 to 1, while in the third stage the net output of these groups is approximately equal. Most developed countries followed this progression, but they operated in an altogether different historical and economic context. But most important of all, the production of consumer goods, which initiated the industrialization process (e.g. textiles in Britain), were produced with domestic technology, unlike the situation in the currently developing countries, including that in Pakistan.

Thus in order to create a self-reliant and integrated economy, Pakistan needs to reverse the classic path of consumer goods led industrialization. However, since consumer goods industries exist to a large extent, Pakistan needs to rapidly equalize the two industries - to use Hirschman's phrase it has to work its way from 'last back to intermediate and basic industries'.

Pakistan (and other comparable developing countries) needs a high rate of investment in capital goods by re-allocation of foreign loans and remittances, as well as tapping new sources of investible surplus by taxing agricultural incomes; these are critical issues but a detailed analysis of these is beyond the scope of the present work.

Because machinery and technology are a major component of fixed capital, the demand for it is a function of the rate of investment. The rate of investment also influences the rate of expansion of its production capacity. As technology and equipment (for example for agriculture), are more complex in structure, these require more sophisticated production technology and machine-bulding industries, which have so far largely been imported.

Of course, capital goods take a longer period than for textiles and other light industry to build facilities and get operations under way; and the opportunity cost of domestic production of capital and producer goods may be higher than for imported items, but the latter only add on to structural problems in the long run, by creating bottlenecks.

During the early phase of capital investment in producer goods, the amount of real income created may be close to zero, and there may be no profit in investment. This is inevitable, since there is a long gestation period before there are returns to capital (or capital recovery), which makes the expansion of the capital goods and technology generating industry rather capital-intensive, therefore costly for most developing countries.

However, as I have stated in different words, the producer goods industry cannot be satisfactorily measured merely by the costs or quanitity of output. The industry provides capital goods for other industries and this is a major factor in productivity, the technical level of its productive capacity, and it determines the overall level and pattern of national development. Because the machine-bulding and technology generating industry is a major supplier of producer goods, there is an obvious correlation between its development and the development of a national economy. From a static point of view, the contribution of this industry can be measured by its share in the total value-added of industrial output or its share in total employment. From a dynamic view, it has to be measured by the upstream/downstream or linkage effects, and their repercussions for the whole economy.

In Pakistan, with the exception of the Karachi Steel Mill established in the early 1980s, and with a few other exceptions, no such recovery from capital investment are needed; instead, loans and interests on loans have to be paid. For example, in 1961, during the high tide of import-substitution for consumer goods, the share of machinery and equipment in Pakistan's total industrial output was 7.1 percent; compared to 12 percent for Argentina, 16.3 percent for India, and 11 percent for Mexico [1].

The central problem confronting Pakistan's development is the critical shortage of capital, which in turn is due to two factors; first, low productivity in agriculture: as in most developing countries, agriculture remains the main source of saving. Despite the growth of a modern textiles and some other industries, it retains the dominant share in the GDP in 1990.

In 1988, for example, agriculture's contribution to the GDP was 26.2 percent, whilst manufacturing accounted for 16.9 percent of the GDP. Agriculture provides about 80 percent of the raw materials for at least 60 percent of the manufactures.

Cotton and rice comprise the largest single export items, and a large percent of fiscal revenue comes directly or indirectly from agriculture. This is indicative of the vital importance of the contribution that agriculture can make to capital accumulation. Conversely, stagnation or slow growth of agriculture sets limits to the growth of light industry, exports, and revenue, which in turn affects the rate of savings.

In the 1980s Pakistan's, agriculture grew at about 4 percent annually; and during the 1950s, 1960s, and 1970s, it grew at 2.3, 5.2, and 2.3 percent per annum. Population increased by 2.2 percent in the 1950s, 2.4 percent in the 1960s, 2.8 percent in the 1970s, and 3 percent in the 1980s.

On average, during the last four decades Pakistan's agriculture grew at about 3.4 percent annually, whilst population increased at an annual average of 2.5 percent, which means an annual average increase in agriculture of around one percent per capita. Since about 85 percent of consumer goods are composed of agriculture and derived products, a 2 percent annual increase in per capita consumption easily uses up most of the agricultural surplus, leaving very little room for increases in saving, and for endogenous capital formation. In order to increase the rate of capital formation, agriculture needs to become much more productive, and its surplus transformed into investment.

Second, the other source of capital accumulation has been light industry; and profits and revenues from the processed food and textile manufactures could be increased. But the shortage of raw materials and increased competition have forced these industries to slow down. In the 1970s for example, about 20 percent of textile industry was idle.

It is clear that a rapid increase in the producer goods industries may, through the linkage effects, raise the rate of growth in industry. But because Pakistan's industry and agriculture are not integrated, industry has failed to exert any substantial linkage effects on the agricultural sector and its need for inputs. As a result, savings and capital formation has grown more slowly than capital goods, thus creating a disjuncture between the demand for and the supply of capital goods. In Pakistan, the supply of capital rather than the ability to invest is the limiting factor in the country's development process.

Of course, the existence of a capital goods sector by itself is no guarantee that linkage effects will developing in the economy: it is paradoxical that the Karachi Steel Mill in Pakistan, which has a production capacity of 1 million tonnes, is underutilized, and is consistently working under full capacity. This is due to two main factors. First, the connection between capital goods and their transformation into usable inputs is mediated by the technology generating or machine-building industry; in Pakistan this is lacking and without this capital goods remain in their unfinished form. Secondly, a large part of Pakistan's economy has already been tied and subordinated to the international economy, through multiple ties of financial, legal, and technological dependence, which makes it very difficult for Pakistan's capital goods industry to make inroads into its own economy, even if it had the technological capacity. However, with short, medium, and long term plans the capital goods and technology generating sectors could bring about an integration of the national economy.

Other strategies of development, such as export-led industrialization are likely to come across barriers of competition on the world market, but especially the lack of producer goods needed to expand production. But in addition:

> It may look on the face of it quite plausible that "exports" can play a strategic role in the whole [development] process. On the one hand, it can provide a market for sectors where output has increased and, at at the same time, it can provide the capacity to import additional capital goods. Thus, both the demand problem and the capacity problem can be taken care of through the mechanism of international trade...[But] the ability to expand exports as well as to secure favourable terms of trade have usually depended on on rather

> exceptional circumstances. These include the phase of the economic cycle through which developed countries are passing, the nature of the product demand and the course of technological change (Chakravarty, 1979:1236).

Similar arguments would apply to market-oriented strategies which suggest that output can be increased through the manipulation of the market; for example, by merely raising prices, price-support for produce, or other incentives to increase production. These policies may increase output in the short-run, but these will definitely be confronted by structural problems in the economy, especially by the inability of a weakly developed producer goods sector to supply inputs to meet increased demand for these.

The capacity to generate technology and machine-building sectors premissed on a capital goods industry is a long term prospect; in the meantime, as Hirschman (1971), suggests, in order to maximize growth the developing countries could need an appropriate alternation of contact and insulation, of openness to the trade and capital of the developed countries, to be followed by a period of nationalism and withdrawal. I have indicated in this study a need for selective involvement in, rather than isolation from the international economy, and for a selective rather than no use of imported technology, which complements instead of constraining national development.

**Notes**

1.Compiled from: United Nations (1965), *Industrial Development in Asia and the Far East*; ESCAP, Bangkok;; United Nations (1963), *Production and Export of Mechanical and Electrical Engineering Goods, Geneva;* United Nations (1962) *World Economy Survey 1961*, New York.

# Appendix 1: Development of Sahiwal and Sargodha

Data were also collected from two socio-economic and ecologically contrasting districts of Sahiwal and Sargodha, to include a comparative perspective on local development. Sahiwal lies to the south-west of Sheikhupura and is considered to be one of the most developed districts of the Pakistani Punjab. This is characterized by a wider variety of crops grown, relatively large landholdings, use of larger quantities of inputs, and good water resources comprised of canal and tubewell irrigation. Sargodha district lies to the west of Sheikhupura; and though it has relatively large landholdings, its development is hampered by inadequate quantity and quality of water availability, which is reflected in, among other things, an important crop which is not grown: rice.

## Sahiwal

Capitalist development is relatively more developed in Sahiwal, than in any other areas of our research. This is reflected in, among other factors, rent, which varies from Rs 1,500 to Rs 6,000 an acre per year, with an average around Rs 2,500. The relatively high rents reflect higher output based on both good water availability and fertile soils. The higher fertility is due in part to the fact that this district was opened up to agriculture on a large scale after the construction of irrigation canals during and after the second half of the nineteenth century.

The Sahiwal district, and Okara tehsil where the survey was carried out, is favourably disposed to capitalist development in agriculture in other ways too: relatively large holdings, with an average of about 9 acres for the district, compared to about 7 acres for the Punjab as a whole. Here one finds, more so than in any district, the 'classic' English pattern of land tenure: many large landowners rent out to tenants who pay rent to the owners, wages to labourers who work the land, and appropriate profits for themselves.

However, an important difference between the English system and that prevalent in Sahiwal is that in the latter, tenancy arrangements are rarely entered into legally, and normally do not run for more than two years. The reason for the short tenancy contracts is that with rapid price rises, owners consider it in their interest not to rent out for longer periods. Of course, in the English system, where leases are for relatively long periods, sometimes of 99 years duration, the tenants have incentives for making investment in land; in Sahiwal the shorter periods of tenancy contracts preclude such investments in land on a significant scale.

*The survey*

Eighteen households are included in the sample from the Sahiwal tehsil (of Sahiwal district): 11 in the large, 4 in the medium and 3 in the small and landless categories.

**Large landowners**

These are defined somewhat loosely as those owning over 25 acres; this follows the way cultivators in this district classify themselves; and as we shall see, the income derived from this quantity of land is large enough (and comparable to the larger owners' in Mallian) for these owners to be included in the large owner category.

The total quantity of land held by the 11 households amounts to 1,638.5 acres, an average of 150 acres per household. Total land rented in by these households is 86.4 acres. The 9 self-cultivating households hold 1,357.5 acres, an average of 150 acres.

*Sharetenancy*

The reasons for the existence of sharetenancy among two households is that in one case the owner is a retired army officer who was alloted 50 acres in Sahiwal; but because he owns over 300 acres in another district (which are self-cultivated) he rents out to sharetenants in Sahiwal. In the second case the landowner is also a retired army officer, who lives in the North-West Frontier Province (about 700 miles away), who finds it more convenient to rent out to shartenants in Sahiwal. An important point is that the conditions for the existence of sharetenancy are quite different to those in Mallian where it was largely the least fertile land that was given out on share.

*Employment of labour*

A total of 48 full-time workers are employed by 8 households giving an average of 6 workers employed per households and a worker to land ratio of 1:20 acres. The 48 workers do not include workers employed on a temporary basis, which I shall describe below. The wages of the full-time workers range from Rs 125 to Rs 250 per month plus grain.

*Crops grown*

The figures below show the crops grown and acreage under cultivation in 1977 and 1978, based on the sample of large owners in Sahiwal. In all cases HYVs and other improved varieties of seeds are used:

| Crops grown | Acres |
|---|---|
| Wheat | 310 |
| Rice | 291.5 |
| Potatoes | 352 |
| Tobacco | 253 |
| Other crops (cotton maize,sugarcane,fodder, other vegetables) | 251 |

Cropping intensity 178

It can be seen that not only is there a greater crop mix, but there is also a relatively high cropping intensity of 178, compared to the cropping intensity of 152 of the self-cultivated portions of large owners in Mallian. This is higher because tobacco is doubled-cropped whilst there are three crops of potatoes a year.

These two crops constitute about 41.5 percent of all crops grown, and the figure would be higher if other vegetable crops were included in the calculations.

In this area a significant proportion of potato seeds are obtained from Belgium and Holland, and are kept refrigerated in the cold storage plants built in the area since the early 1970s. The imported seeds give higher yields and a more regular shaped potato; however, I was told that some of the indigenous varieties of potatoes were being selectively bred at Agricultural Research Stations in Pakistan to give improved varieties.

*Capital input*

The criteria of capital use is the same as for Mallian and includes both divisible inputs such as fertilizers, seeds, water and pesticides, and indivisible ones such as tractors, tubewells, threshers and other equipment.

The 11 households own 14 tractors, 5 of these since 1966, and 15 tubewells. Only the two households that rent out to sharetenants have their land prepared by ox-drawn ploughs. There is of course a variation in the number of tractors and tubewells owned; for example, one household owns 3 tractors and 3 tubewells, whilst others own only one of each.

The overall fertilizer use in Sahiwal is higher than in Mallian: rice and wheat are given applications of 3 bags, and for potatoes and tobacco, 5 bags of fertilizer each per acre. In addition 20 cartloads of farmyard manure per acre is used on tobacco and vegetables. The cost of production of tobacco and vegetables is about Rs 3000 per acre and net profit is between Rs 6000 to Rs 10,000 per acre, which is considerably more than in Mallian.

*Crop yields*

Yields per acre are some of the highest in the country, and only one cultivator in Mallian from amongst the small peasants has a similar output. Moreover, the yields in rice and wheat are comparable to those in Japan and Britain. In Britain the average yield for wheat is 41.3 100 kilograms per hectare (Palmer, 1972:2), which is about 38 maunds per acre. The sample from Sahiwal shows yields of about 49.05 100 kilograms per hectare, which is about 45 maunds per acre. For rice, Japan produces an average of 42.5 100 kilograms per hecatare (ibid.:3), which is about 39 maunds per acre; in the Sahiwal sample the average yield is 52.32 maunds per acre.

Of course, I am comparing national averages of Britain and Japan with the averages of a small sample drawn from large-scale farmers in a highly developed district of the Punjab. Nonetheless, the figures show the intensity of cultivation in the district. This is further shown by the following case-study of the largest landowing household in the Sahiwal sample.

*Case study*

MMS owns 208 acres in a village in the area; and he rents in an additional 184 acres from absentee owners, and supervises the cultivation himself.

*Capital input* MMS owns 3 tractors, 3 trolleys, one disc plough, 6 tubewells and two automatic threshers; capital equipment which was bought in 1969. In 1977 the following crops were grown in acres: wheat 130, potatoes 40, rice 130, cotton 120, maize 40, fodder 15; plus 5 acres of vegetable crops such as tomatoes and chillies, and some tobacco for self-consumption.

Fertilizer use is high: an average of 2 bags of DAP and 2.5 bags of urea per acre for all crops except tobacco and potatoes; on these 8 to 9 bags per acre are used. The average production costs are Rs 2000 per acre.

Capital for the high initial costs of production are obtained from an ahrthi, to the tune of Rs 150,000 per season; in addition MMS contributes Rs 200,000 from his own resources.

*Employment of labour* MMS employs 18 full time workers who are paid Rs 250 per month; in addition he sells his workers 3 maunds of wheat each month. During the peak sowing period, 50 additional workers are hired on a cash basis; and during the harvest period about 50 additional workers are hired (including 20 women for picking cotton), and these are paid mainly in kind.

The production on this farm is clearly capitalistic, being based on large-scale socialized labour processes, which are set in motion by capital, in a process of capital accumulation within the parameters of dependent capitalism.

The yields on MMS' farms are high and the average of 46 maunds per acre for wheat and rice, which, as I have indicated, is higher than those in Britain and Japan. Of course, I have drawn this comparison with Britain and Japan here, because it is only in Sahiwal that the average productivity is high for the whole district.

*The medium owners*

These are classified as those households owning between 6 and 24 acres. The households in this category own a total of 43.25 acres, in portions of 6, 5.25, 11 and 21 acres, giving an average of 10.8 acres per household. In addition another 119.5 acres are rented in, giving a total of land held at 163.75 acres, which is an average of 40.75 acres per household.

*Crops grown* The main crops grown are, in acres: wheat 53, tobacco 49, potatoes 26, rice 16, maize 28, fodder 18; giving a total of 190 cultivated acres. Potatoes and tobacco account for 39.5, and rice and wheat for 60.5 percent of the acreage.

*Market relations* Among these owners almost 90 percent of the wheat and rice and 100 percent of all other crops except fodder, are marketed; about 40 percent of the fodder is retained for domestic cattle.

*Capital input* None of the households own a tubewell: all rely on canal water or water bought from tubewell owners in the area. One household owns a tractor, and another household is part owner of a tractor. In both instances, the tractors were bought with cash because these households do not own 25 acres which would make them eligible (in 1978), for a loan from the ADBP to purchase a tractor. For ploughing their fields, all households use tractor hire, though one houshold uses the traditional plough.

Fertilizer use is higher than the average for Mallian: 3 bags per acre for rice and wheat, and 5 to 6 bags on potatoes and tobacco; this is also higher than the larger cultivators' fertilizer use in Sahiwal for rice and wheat, but lower than the average for potatoes and tobacco.

Each household spends an average of Rs 30,000 per season towards production costs, an average of almost Rs 3000 per acre. This high outlay is due to the fact that potatoes and tobacco, which require high fertilizer use, account for about 40 percent of the crops grown, though fertilizer consumption is high for other crops as well. These households have little recourse to loans from the ahrthis; some loans are obtained from banks, but the cultivation is largely self-financed through savings.

*Employment of labour*

Four full time labourers are employed by three 3 households; and one household relies exclusively on its family labour for cultivation. However, most of these households' labour use is met by the juts who are employed to cultivate potatoes and tobacco, on a job or piece-rate basis, in the same way as in Mallian. Additional labour is hired during the peak period of sowing and harvesting.

Among most of these households, capitalist production is clearly present with capital organizing and controlling a socialized labour process based on wage labour, reflected in high output and profits. As of 1978 no process of proletarianization among these households was observed, in the way we saw among this category of owners in Mallian.

Proletarianization is warded-off largely as a result of renting in additional land, which is made possible by the relatively large number of absentee landowners in the area. For example, two households that own 6 and 11 acres each, rent in 37 and 40 acres, which enables them to carry out a relatively large-scale production and capital accumulation.

This situation may change, however, as resumption of land by owners increases; but as yet this has not happened to any significant extent. In any case, given that most of these households have accumulated large sums of money, they could, if the situation arose, either purchase additional land, or diversify their economic activities, and thus ward-off proletarianization.

**Smallholder and landless households**

These are classified together as their number in the sample is too small to be considered separately. Smallholding peasants own less than 5 acres. There are three households included in this category; one owns 3 acres and the other two households are landless.

The smallholding household owns 3 acres of land of which only one acre is cultivated, the other two are infertile. Wheat was grown on the single acre of land; and the owner does casual work on a daily wage basis in the locality.

The second is a landless sharetenants household. Here 4 brothers jointly cultivate 25 acres on half-share; the land is owned by an absentee owner who has a job in the civil service in Lahore. The land is ploughed by the sharetenants themselves with the traditional plough. Wheat, rice, maize and sugarcane are the main crops grown. Fertilizer use is 4 bags per acre for all crops; production costs are met by the sharetenants themselves, though the owner provides seed and pays the revenue.

The sharetenants cultivate land which is of average or good fertility, unlike that in Mallian, where most of the sharetenanted land is sub-fertile; and unlike Mallian, the sharetenants cultivation is intense, with high fertilizer input and use of HYVs. Clearly, this form of tenancy is suggestive of the 'formal subsumption' of labour to capital (Gupta, 1980); and goes against Bhaduri's theory that sharetenancy is constitutive of feudalistic production relations.

The landowner takes an active interest in cultivation which is carried out at the highest level of productivity. For example, I was told by this sharetenant that he had come to an agreement with the landowner to cultivate tobacco and potatoes during the 1978 season, for which the owner would provide the seeds, and all other costs of production would be shared in half. The production of tobacco and potatoes and other vegetable crops requires a much more intensive and socialized labour process, and to meet these labour requirements, an agreement had been reached between the owner and tenants that any labour costs additional to those of the four sharetenants, would be shared equally between the owner and the tenants.

The third household in this category works in a jut comprised of 8 persons who work collectively on tobacco and potato cultivation and are paid by the job: for example, this jut worked on 8 acres of potato at the rate of Rs 300 per acre, and their income amounted to Rs 300 each. It took the jut about 1.5 days to complete the job of harvesting potatoes. Similar procedure applies to work on a job basis in tobacco cultivation, which involves pruning, trimming, cutting, uprooting, bundling and loading.

There were three other juts operating in the locality, comprised of 34 persons and covering a cultivated area of about 350 acres. Other juts in the area can vary in size from 6 to 60 workers, though the typical jut is comprised of about 12 persons, which is somewhat larger than the typical jut operating in Mallian.

Work for juts in this locality is available for almost every day of the month, whilst as we saw in Mallian juts find work for about 20 days in the month; therefore, a far more continuous and uninterrupted production cycle exists in this area. This clearly shows that capitalist forms of production have developed here to a greater extent than in Mallian.

But smallholder property (less than 5 acres) still exists. However, the exact impact of smallholdings on capitalist development and the agrarian transition is difficult to assess given the small size of the sample. On the one hand, these no doubt prevent their means of production from being converted into capital and thus preclude a higher rate of capital accumulation; on the other, the smallholdings 'tie' the small owners to the land and thus constitute a valuable source of labour, in an area where labour can be relatively scarce. Evidence from the survey suggests that the existence of smallholders does not prevent capitalist development and the agrarian transition, but it does slow down this process, especially if seen within the context of dependent development and the incorporation of the local into the international economy.

This retardation of capitalist development becomes clear when we analyze artisan production and sep, which still exists in this area, in a reciprocal relation with smallholders' production. These still depend, to a large extent, on the traditional method of cultivation using the ox-drawn plough, and for this the work of artisans is important as we saw in Mallian.

What are the processes tending towards the reproduction or dissolution of smallholders, sharetenants and artisans? I have already discussed sharetenancy, and have suggested that in this area, this is under the formal subsumption to capital. However, the conditions for its dissolution are likely to become dominant, and it may no longer exist in the near future; local inhabitants in fact anticipate its demise by about about the mid-1990s. Given the profitability of cultivation, landowners in this area are likely to extend their self-cultivation by transforming their landless sharetenants into wage labourers; a process that already has taken place to a considerable extent, aided during the early 1970s by the impending or anticipated land reforms.

The opposing tendency (and these are tendencies and not inexorable laws), is that since a large number of landowners live out of the district and hold other jobs, they might still find it more convenient to rent out their land to sharetenants. However, this arrangement is diminishing, and the trend I observed during fieldwork in 1978, and again in 1987, was for landowners to increasingly appoint munshis (managers, overseers), to supervise their cultivation. Thus the dominant tendency in Sahiwal is for sharetenancy to dissolve.

The smallholder is subject to a number of complex, and at times contradictory, processes and tendencies; for instance, given the high production costs, the smallholders are subject to being squeezed out of the market. This is offset by renting-in land from absentee owners, a situation that is likely to change as resumption by landowners increases.

It is unlikely, given the high status attached to land, as well as lack of regular and secure alternative employment, that smallholders will relinquish ownership: more likely, they will diversify their household economic activity by renting out their land and seeking off-farm employment. If this happens then the smallholders' land is likely to come under large-scale capitalist production; and an important part of the obstacle to capitalist development and the agrarian transition would have been overcome. Though it is also possible that the smallholders are much more likely to hang on to and cultivate their land and seek additional work outside of agriculture.

Among the artisan households the same set of complex processes are at work; some tending to reproduce and some dissolve sep relations. But in Sahiwal there is another process which is absent in Mallian and Sargodha: modern brick-built houses. These are fairly common in the district and are generally owned by households owning or cultivating 25 acres or more. These houses require modern skills and rather more complex technology to construct, and the work of the artisan is thus in relatively little demand here. In this situation, the artisans, who have traditionally built and maintained the peasant dwellings made of wood and mud, find that the demand for their work is decreasing.

Also, this district is more mechanized than Mallian with greater use of modern technology; so that more specialist engineering skills are needed for repair and maintenance of this equipment, than the artisans possess; hence a further curtailment of demand for their work. Given these complex processes at work, artisan production is likely to erode and be supplanted by goods produced under modern relatively large-scale production, but this is likely to be a gradual process.

Finally, I should like to consider other developments in the economy of this area, which are related to the transformation of agrarian production. For instance, the construction of large modern cold storage plants for storing both fruit and vegetables, and particularly for potato and tobacco seeds. These plants now make available some out-of-season fruit and vegetables, all the year round.

During fieldwork I observed that about 6 of these cold storage plants had been set up in the Okara tehsil by individuals who generally owned over 150 acres of land. Whilst these plants were constructed largely on the basis of long-term loans obtained from the ADBP, a high initial down payment of about Rs 20 lakhs was required before the loans were advanced. Of course, these plants are wholly constructed from imported technology.

There are developments also in the sphere of large-scale dairy farming and processing of milk products such as cheese, and processing fruit and products derived from this; developments which reflect important capitalist transformation of the local economy, and its incorporation into the national and international economy. In fact the greater extent of capitalist development is premissed on greater integration into, and dependence upon, the international economy; and the extent to which non-capitalist production remains is also determined by this (weak) relationship.

International capital links itself to the local economy and largely circumvents the national economy which cannot provide the modern means of production due to the absence of a capital goods and technology generating industries.

### Sargodha

There are eight households in the sample from Sargodha. As the sample is small the respondents are divided into only two categories: large owners owning over 25 acres, and medium owners, owning 6 to 25 acres. Six households are included in the first category, each owning land in portions of 31.5, 54, 80, 150 and 150 acres respectively. The two households included in the second category own 8 and 12 acres each. The aim of the survey is to see, as in Mallian and Sahiwal, the extent of local capitalist development and its relationship to the international economy. As we shall see, capitalist development has taken place in the locality, but it is weaker and more unevenly developed than Sahiwal and Mallian.

### Large landowners

The six households in this category own a total of 550.5 acres; in addition 52 acres are rented in and 25 acres rented out, in both cases for a fixed money-rent of between Rs 500 to Rs 1000 per acre a year. This gives a net total of land held at 577.5 acres, or an average of 96 acres per household. All except two households are self-cultivating: the two rent out 89 acres to sharetenants in portions of 39 and 50 acres.

#### *Capital input*

These households together own 6 tubewells in addition to the two owned by the government. This group owns 3 tractors, and those without have access to these through tractor-hire, or use a combination of tractors and traditional ploughs.

Evidence suggests that on the whole, relatively little money is borrowed from banks or ahrthis for meeting production costs, which are met from their own sources. The use of fertilizer varies significantly within the group: from a high input of 4 bags per acre for wheat and rice, to 6-8 bags for vegetables and sugarcane; to a low one bag per acre for wheat and rice.

*Employment of labour*

Five households employ full time labourers and one household relies for its cultivation on a cooperative or reciprocal exchange of labour between households known as *vingar*.

The five households employ a total of 32 workers or 6.4 workers per household, which is one worker per 18 acres of cultivated land. Seasonal and casual labour on a job basis is hired by all households. The average, however, distorts the uneven spread of labour use between these households: this ranges from one household employing 2 workers to another employing 13 workers.

*Sharetenancy*

The two sharetenancies need to be accounted for: in the first case the owner self-cultivates 41 acres with 7 workers and rents out 39 acres. Why does he not extend his cultivation, since this is more profitable? The reason given by this owner is that he has 17 acres in Multan district which is about 300 miles away, to which he goes frequently to supervise cultivation, which he could not do if he were to self-cultivate all his land in Sargodha. Moreover, the land rented out to sharetenants is of low fertility, hence renting out land is the most convenient way of managing his land under present conditions.

The other household self-cultivates 100 acres with 7 workers, and rents out 50 acres. The reasons for sharetenancy here are somewhat complex but the quality of the soil is the major reason, though other reasons, which I shall discuss shortly, are important too.

This household owns a rice-husking and a flour-mill as well as a petrol station in the nearby town of Bhera. The head of the household is also active in politics which, he claims, leaves him little time to adequately supervise more than 100 acres of his land.

In my opinion, the main reason why this household rents out land on share is that it cannot be exploited profitably by modern methods because of low fertility and inadequate water resources. For, if need be, self-cultivation can be extended by appointing a munshi. In spite of the landowner offering other explanations for sharetenancy, the next category, which I shall discuss below, the small owners, prove my hypothesis to be correct.

*Crops grown*

The main crops grown by this producer are wheat (172 acres), rice (65 acres), cotton (30 acres), sugarcane (38 acres); other crops grown are vegetables, fruit (particularly oranges), and henna. It will be noticed that significantly less rice and vegetables are grown in this area, reflecting a water shortage and also a relatively long distance from the market. There is greater variation in crop yields than in Sahiwal, but similar to Mallian: from 20 to 40 maunds per acre for wheat, and 25 to 45 maunds per acre for rice. In almost all cases HYVs are used. The average yields are lower than for Mallian and Sahiwal.

**Medium owners**

There are two households in this category. One owns 12 acres which is cultivated by sharetenants; the second owns 8 acres and rents in an additional 16 acres. The first household owns one tubewell, but it pumps out brackish water and therefore is not suitable for cultivation; the problem of brackish water is fairly common and exacerbates the water shortage of this relatively arid area.

The reasons for renting out land to sharetenants is that the head of household is 70 years old and is unable to cultivate or supervise the cultivation himself. He has two sons who are employed in clerical jobs in Sargodha town. This owner stated that if his land was more fertile his sons might have given up their jobs for self-cultivation. As it is, they can maximize their income through diversification of their economic activities.

The second household owns 8 acres and rents in 16 acres on share. The sharetenanted land is of poor quality as the following yields show: 6 acres of wheat with a total yield of 60 maunds, i.e., 10 maunds per acre; 4 acres of rice with a yield of 50 maunds, or 12 maunds per acre.

In both instances land is cultivated on half-share, with equal share of production costs and the gross produce between the owner and tenant.

*Capital input*

I have already mentioned that one household owns a tubewell which pumps out water which is unsuitable for irrigating crops. Both households own 2 ploughs each, and a number of draught animals as well as milch cows and buffaloes.

Fertilizer use in the first household is 2 bags per acre for all crops grown; in the second household, one bag is used for all crops. The main crops grown are wheat, rice, fodder, and cotton; the first household also has 2 acres of citrus orchards.

*Market relations*

Only the household owning 12 acres marketed any produce: 16.5 maunds of cotton for Rs 2,310; the fruit from his orchards had already been mortgaged to a large owner to pay off a debt. The second household with 8 acres, had no surplus; and had to purchase 17 maunds of wheat to meet household consumption needs.

Given the small sample it is difficult to say anything more than I have on capitalist development and the persistence of the smallholder within the context of the international economy. As I have said, the cultivation practice and the extent of capitalist development in agriculture varies significantly in Sargodha between different categories of owners. Amongst the larger owners, capitalist production is significantly developed though sharetenancy and small peasant and artisan production has a significant role in the local economy.

Here, as in Mallian, ecological factors such as quality of the soil, water resources, land distribution and extent of incorporation into the national and international economy has a crucial determining effect on processes that facilitate or impede local capitalist development. However, from the limited data, it can be seen that apart from specifically local factors, the low productivity reflects the low level of integration into the international economy than either Sahiwal or Mallian. Though in broad terms, the same processes and structural factors delimiting or facilitating Sahiwal and Mallian's development are at work in Sargodha.

# Appendix 2: Economic and social development of pre-colonial and colonial Punjab

This chapter is divided into two parts: the first describes and analyzes some aspects of economic and social structure of pre-clonial Punjab; and the second deals with some aspects of social and economic transformation of the Punjab under British rule.

As I shall indicate, colonial rule had a profound impact on the economic and social organization of the Punjab: the enactment of absolute individual ownership of landed property; structuring of systematic linkages with, and incorporation into the national and internationl economy, commercialization of agriculture, increased peasant indebtedness, class formation, new political forms and ideologies, and so on; some aspects of which have been well-documented (Bannerjee, 1980; Mukherjee, 1980; Nazir, 1981; Darling, 1947, Calvert, 1936).

A discussion of some of these changes will enables us to see, firstly, the continuities and changes between pre-colonial and colonial Punjab, and secondly, the subsequent transformation of the Punjab economy and society after independence and especially during the period of the green revolution.

## Pre-colonial Punjab

Between the period of Mughal decline and the rise of British power in the Punjab, there was a relatively short period of Sikh rule. During this period (1750 to 1849) there was no radical departure from the land/adminstrative policy of the Mughals. But there was relative instability as the Sikh confederacies were struggling to establish their hegemony and the Punjab was often in a state of turmoil. After 1810 the consolidation of the Sikh *misls* under Ranjit Singh restored some measure of stability to the province.

The main elements of Ranjit Singh's fiscal policy was two-fold: parts of the districts of the province were parcelled out to local hereditary chiefs of clans (*jagirdars)* or to appointed officials from among his own followers, in return for provisions of men, arms and horses to provide military service. The other system was to reallocate land in groups of villages or estates to *kardars* or revenue collectors who then contracted to pay the treasury fixed payments. The *kardars* and *jagirdars* in turn parcelled out the land in a number of tenurial systems to cultivators for the extraction of the surplus product.

The complexity of the method of revenue collection and forms of tenurial systems was compounded by the complexities of caste/class and their relationship to land control and landownership. The traditional hierarchical structure of caste system was almost uniform throughout the province; the dominant caste being the one that owned or held more land. And whilst the traditional 'abstract' caste hierarchy correlated with the local real hierarchy based upon landholding strength, this correlation was weak during times of rapid social and economic change.

Instances of this change are, for example, when non-landowning castes or lower status castes such as blacksmiths, potters and carpenters obtained land and achieved upward socio-economic mobility - this occurred during the rise of the Sikhs in the Punjab (Van Den Dungen, 1968:70); or when land passed into the hands of the money-lenders, a phenomena which assumed great proportions under British rule, especially in the closing decades of the nineteenth century.

During this period the Punjab villages, on which the economy was based, were characterized by largely self-sufficient but not subsistence production; and by and large they consumed what they produced within the locality.

Products imported into the villages generally were crude iron and other metal products, cotton or cotton yarn, and salt, which were then transformed into finished goods within the village or cluster of villages (Nazir, 1981). The export from the villages depended largely upon the specialization prevalent in the area. Some areas such as Wazirabad had for long specialized in metal products, but generally agricultural produce and hides were the main village exports.

There was considerable inter-regional and intra-regional as well as international trade both over land and river-bound with the Middle East and Central Asia, and with other parts of the world, a trade often mediated and controlled by the East India Company.

Much of the manufactured goods were produced in the towns. In most of the villages, the degree of specialization was largely circumbscribed and delimited by the local social division of labour conditioned by caste. In most instances, specialization depended on the quality of soils, climate, and distance from the urban market.

Because of the relative dearth of reliable material on the Punjab economy under the Mughals and Sikhs, it is not clear as to the extent to which the economy was commercialized. Reliable and systematic data on the economy and society of pre-colonial Punjab is even more scarce on the socio-economic organization of Punjab villages. With the exception of Kessinger's (1974) *Vilyatpur*, there is little to draw on insofar as village level data on pre-colonial Punjab is concerned.

*Kessinger's Vilyatpur* This is a detailed study of one Punjab village, Vilyatpur, from 1848 (one year before the annexation of the Punjab by the British, in 1849), to post-independence (Indian) Punjab in 1968. Kessinger's description of Vilyatpur prior to annexation shows the village to be a more developed type of a village in pre-colonial Punjab.

In 1848 the village consisted of 123 households with 565 persons. These were organized into clans who were differentiated in terms of caste and occupational groupings. And the major factor in social differentiation was, as it is now, land. Accordingly, the primary socio-economic division in the village was between cultivators and non-cultivators.

The cultivators (mainly *Sahotas* a landholding *jat got* or sub-caste), consisted of 60 lineages or groups (to use Kessinger's terminology); 12 service castes' groups, 15 groups of artisans, and 14 groups of agricultural labourers.

Most of the land was held and cultivated by the Sahotas; the tenants and other groups cultivated 25 acres as compared to the *Sahotas'* 475 acres (out of the village total of 500 acres). The majority of landholding households fell into the middling category of 10 to 20 acres. But what separates the landholding structure of pre-colonial Vilyatpur from that in 1968 is the relatively smaller number of households in pre-colonial Punjab that owned or held less than than 4 acres of land. In 1968 these households formed a much larger proportion.

In pre-colonial Vilyatpur cropping patterns were different to those in 1968. In pre-colonial Vilyatpur, for rabi crops, wheat constituted 38 percent, barley 5 percent and pulses 3 percent of the cultivated area. For kharif, maize constituted 3 percent, pulses 9 percent, fodder 27 percent and sugarcane 8 percent of the cultivated area (ibid.:65). Rice, a major crop in 1968, was not cultivated in 1848. Then, as now, the social division of labour was organized under sep.

There also seems to have existed some form of merchant and usurer capital in the economy. Kessinger suggests that revenue was paid in cash and that in order to convert produce into cash the cultivators resorted to merchants from the urban areas who bought up the produce in cash. This seems unlikely. Because it is not clear to what extent merchant and usurer capital dominated the economy of the rural Punjab as a whole. Kessinger could have arrived at his erroneous conclusion as a result of confusing the assessment of revenue in cash with actual payments in cash; for even under the Mughals, revenue was assessed in cash but paid mainly in produce.

The significant commercialization of Vilyatpur suggested by Kessinger, could be due to the relatively large production of *gur* (crude sugar) from sugarcane which is a less durable consumer good than grain. This would have made a rapid sale on the market necessary, and might well explain the monetization of the village economy and the presence of the merchants and money-lenders.

However, as I have suggested, Vilyatpur could be classified as a more developed type of Punjab village at the advent of British rule, though one cannot from that fact alone generalize the characteristics of this village for all Punjab villages. Whatever the extent of monetization or market orientation of pre-colonial Punjab, the important point is that the economy was largely self-sufficient and its conditions of reproduction lay mainly in the local rural economy, and not on the larger regional or world economy.

Vilyatpur, as a microcosm of pre-colonial rural economy, displayed features which are both familiar and unfamiliar in relation to Vilyatpur in 1968 (and to Mallian); the familiar features being: unequal distribution of land, tenancy, existence of landless agricultural labourers, production for consumption, and rather weak market orientation. Other features did not exist in Vilyatpur in 1848 and emerged much later: greater penetration of capital in the production process, especially after the green revolution of the 1960s, and greater development of market relations which gained momentum after independence.

**Punjab agriculture during the colonial period**

After the annexation of the Punjab by the British in 1849, there followed a series of important changes in the economy and society of the province. These can be periodized into a number of phases according to the kind of changes that took place.

These phases can be dated as falling between: 1849-1870; 1870-1900; 1900-1925; and from 1925 to independence in 1947. The period upto 1870 was one of adminstrative, legal, and economic reorganization and innovation: investment of absolute private property in land; requirement for payment of revenue to be made in cash and setting up of adminstrative and judicial structures for carrying these reforms.

The second phase marked a period of important structural changes in the Punjab economy. It ended with the enactment of the Punjab Alienation of Land Act of 1901; this piece of legislation was aimed at controlling the social and economic change that had followed in the wake of colonial rule, especially indebtedness and alienation of land among the peasantry to the money-lenders and other landowners.

The third phase, from 1900-1925, was also one of relative development and expansion of Punjab agriculture, based on the the capital investments of previous decades. This included extensive irrigation networks of barrages, dams and canals, which harnessed and increased water availability and opened up the canal colonies to settlement.

The period from 1925 to independence was one of relative stagnation if not actual decline in agricultural productivity (Mukherjee, 1980). Whilst the phases I have mentioned marked different cornerstones of Punjab economic history, it is not necessary to deal with each phase separately since, for our purposes, they are not equally important.

The most important period of colonial Punjab, in fact spanned two phases - from 1870s to the 1920s. During this period there were important changes in the rural Punjab, with agriculture going through important transformation of commericalization and extension of cultivation. This was related mainly to the incorporation of the Punjab into the international economy, and in particular to serve the needs of Britain's industry. This established the colonial economy and placed the Punjab in the world division of labour; a process greatly facilitated by the extension of communications networks, particularly railways and trade through the Suez canal via steamships. The following developments show this:

*Railways* In 1872/73, there were 410 miles of railways in the Punjab, and in 1892/93, 1,725 miles; 4,441 miles in 1922/23 and 5,500 miles in 1932/33 (Calvert, 1936:107).

*Roads* For the same years as the railways, the mileage of metalled roads was: 1,036 miles; 2,142 miles; 2,938 and 3,904 miles (Ibid.:107).

*Irrigation works* In 1872/73 there were 2,744 miles of canal; in 1893/93, 12,368 miles, in 1922/23, 19,664 miles, and in 1932/33 there were 19,601 miles (Ibid.:107).

*Cultivated area* The amount of cultivated area of course is related to the increase in irrigation. In 1872/73 there were 18.8 million cultivable acres; 26.7 million in 1892/93; 30 million in 1922/23 and 30.9 million acres in 1932/33.

*Exports* An important consequence of the above developments was the large increase in exports from the Punjab. The main item of export was wheat. Its value in 1871 was about Rs 11,448 lakhs. Cotton and some oilseeds were also exported, but these were much less important than wheat (ibid.:107).

*Population* During the period under consideration, there was an appreciable population growth, a factor which had an important impact on the agrarian relations in the province. For inspite of extension of irrigation works and cultivable area, there were tenants looking for land instead of landlords looking for tenants.

Between 1856 and 1881, the population of the Punjab increased from 11,500,000 to 17,270,000, and increase of over 50 percent (ibid.:218). In 1921 the population had risen to 20,680,000 and in 1931 to 23,580,000 (ibid.:218).

The population of the province then, as now, was mainly rural, though some towns, such as Lahore and Multan expanded rapidly. For example, in 1881 the population of Lahore was 149,369 and in 1931 it had risen to 429,747. For the same years, Multan's population was 6,874 and 119,457 (ibid.:57). No more than 10 percent of the total population was urbanized; in the contemporary Punjab about 75 percent of the population lives in the rural areas.

*Characteristics of the colonial economy*

The Punjab became an extension of Britain's economy, and whilst there was capital accumulation (which could have been far greater under different social, economic, cultural and institutional structures), the classic dependency relationship with the industrialized centre economy was established during this period. The circuit of capital which linked the Punjab to Britain's economy was completed in the Punjab. A part of Britain's capital was realized in the Punjab, represented by the import and use of Britain's manufactures in the form of railways, transport equipment, dams, and other technology for processing agricultural produce. In turn the Punjab became a supplier of raw materials and food to the centre country (Britain), thus bypassing the subcontinental economy and in particular the Indian textile industry located in other provinces.

Not all regions of the Punjab were equally affected by these changes; the irrigated areas were far more affected by these changes than the rain-dependent areas. It can be claimed that the subsequent regional social and economic differences were accentuated during this period.

However, despite the development of, and increased responsiveness to the market, agriculture in the Punjab remained small-scale and peasant based - but a more 'active' one than was the case prior to British rule. With the extension of demand, the smaller landowners and cultivators in general took greater interest in the crops grown, paid more attention to cultural practices, to timely sowing, harvesting, and inter-cropping. This was especially the case in the canal colonies and other irrigated districts of the Punjab.

Moreover, the increased agricultural production and expansion of the market meant that surpluses were now marketed to a greater extent than before. Inspite of this, however, it has been estimated that no more than 20-30 percent of the food grains entered into a market economy, outside of the village economy (Calvert, 1936:7). These figures would be somewhat higher in the case of cash crops such as cotton and sugarcane, but these were not as important as wheat, and were not grown on a very large-scale in all districts of the Punjab.

*Land and credit* Land, as I have indicated, was unequally distributed in pre-colonial Punjab, and was possessed or held under restricted ownership rights. After annexation, when absolute private property in land was instituted, landownership displayed inequalities as before, except that with the development of a market in land, there was now a greater propensity for land fragmentation, for sale, mortgaging, and so on. In other words, land became a relatively unrestricted saleable commodity.

In 1925 about 17.9 percent of the owners of cultivated land in the province owned less than one acre of land; this accounted for one percent of the total cultivated area (ibid.:172). About 40 percent of cultivators owned between one to less than 5 acres, which is 11 percent of the total land. Twenty-six percent of the owners possessed from 5 to less than 15 acres, which is about 26.6 percent of the land. About 12 percent of the owners held 15 to less than 50 acres, which accounted for 35.6 percent of the land; and 3.7 percent possessed from 50 acres or more, which is 25.7 of the land (ibid.:172).

During this period, the average cultivated holding was about 8 acres, though this would be higher if holdings of less than one acre were left out of the calcualtions. Thus it can be seen that whilst the overall pattern of land distribution in contemporary Pakistani Punjab conforms in many ways to that of the colonial period, the average size of the holdings has been getting smaller through successive generations: for example, from the average holding of 8 acres in 1925 to about 5 acres in present-day Punjab, though the average differs between districts.

There was a great expansion in the availability of rural credit in the rural areas, which was an aspect of, and was accompanied by, the commercialization of agriculture during the early decades of the twentieth century. In addition to usury and merchant capital, there was also a rudimentary development of productive capital, whose sources were savings and modern banking institutions. However, then as now, the majority of cultivators borrowed from within the village: from money-lenders, ahrthis, and relatives. But, whilst credit facilities and disbursement of credit increased during the period, most of the loans were expended on consumption and alleviating distress, including loss of cattle, spoliation of crops, floods, drought and so on (Calvert, 1936; Darling, 1947).

As I have said, one of the main sources of credit were from money-lenders (agricultural and non-agricultural; the former being wealthier landlords who also lent money since the money-lending activities of the non-agricultural money-lenders, the *banias*, were curtailed by the Punjab Alienation of Land Act of 1901; and because alternative avenues for investment were restricted) and co-operative societies. But generally, the co-operative societies were insignificant compared to the activity of the money-lenders as the following figures show.

The total working capital of the Co-operative Societies in 1929 was Rs 72,300,000; this is in contrast to the invested capital of Rs 220 million of only 6000 out of 55,000 money-lenders in the Punjab who had been assessed for income tax (Mukherjee, 1980:51).

The Report on the Co-operative Societies in the Punjab (conducted in the 1920s), revealed that 15 percent of the loans advanced had been for the purpose of paying land revenue, and about 18 per cent to make good loss of cattle by disease (Calvert, op.cit.:158). This mode of borrowing by the cultivators was strikingly similar to that which took place in the 1960s and 1970s, where 12 per cent of the loans from money-lenders were used for paying land revenue and 11 per cent to make good the loss of cattle. These figures clearly show that the loans were borrowed for largely unproductive purposes, but were nevertheless important because they alleviated distress. In fact the considerable investible capital available never made a breakthrough either in agriculture or in industrial development, a fact which needs to be analyzed systematically: whether this was due to the constraints of colonial structures and policy, or the socio-economic institutions prevalent in the Punjab at that time; or indeed a configuration of the two. But this is beyond the scope of the present work.

*Capital and technology in the production process* According to Darling the tools and implements of cultivation in the Punjab were of a rudimentary sort:

> The plough looks "like a half-open penknife" and just scratches the soil; the hand-sickle made more for a child than a man; the old fashioned winnowing tray that woos the wind to sift the grain from the chaff; and the rude chopper with its waste of fodder, are indisplaced from their primitive but immemorial function (1947:149/50).

Improved quality (but still modelled on the traditional variety) of hoes, drills, harrows, reapers, fodder-cutters, and other manual equipment whilst available, were not purchased in any significant number by cultivators. For example, in the 1920s and 1930s, out of a total of 2.25 million ploughs in use in the Punjab, less than 100,000 were of the 'modern', that is, of the improved traditional variety (ibid.:150).

The use of chemical fertilizers in production was minimal and only farmyard manure was used. According to Calvert, the cultivators 'put hardly any animal manure back on the land and no artificial manure' (op.cit.:77).

There was rather more use made of new improved varieties of traditional strains of wheat and some other crops, but these were used more for their robustness in combating disease than for achieving the large increases in yields.

During the last decades of colonial rule the cultivation of the larger owners was largely extensive and based mainly on sharetenants, who cultivated about 50 per cent of the land in the Punjab. The other 50 per cent of cultivation was comprised of owner cultivators, and to a small extent, self-cultivation with wage labour.

Unlike the situation we have observed from our 1978 study, during the 1920s and 1930s, Calvert saw that the

> [Big] owners took little trouble to develop the latent potentialities of their land and to insist on a higher standard of cultivation; and since half of the cultivated land in the province is held by tenants who do not possess the capital, the intelligence or the initiative to venture on any improvements of methods (op.cit.:9).

Darling came to the same conclusion:

> The landlord...lives on his rents. He has little desire to develop his lands, as his rents are generally sufficient to maintain him in comparative ease, and more than this he does not desire' (op.cit.:257).

The smallholders' cultivation too differed at that time in many respects from what I found in 1978. Apparently, they looked down upon intensive type of cultivation such as the cultivation of vegetables as a menial agricultural activity; so that intensive cultivators such as *malis* (market gardeners) who had accumulated wealth actually gave up market-gardening to raise their social status (ibid.:78).

The important point in all this is that whilst Punjab agriculture during the last decades of colonial rule became intensive and more 'active' and responsive to the market (though it fluctuated along with fluctuations in the world market, as during the depression), it did so without radical transformation of the old mode of agricultural production and the labour processes underlying this. The question remains, however, as to what the major constraints on Punjab's development were. Whether these are to be sought in the the incorporation of the Punjab into the colonial economy, the lack of investment in industry which was not encouraged to develop under colonial rule, or in the social, economic, political and cultural processes of the Punjab; or indeed in a complex configuration of the two.

# Appendix 3: Methodology

This study has not been conceived in terms of some simple and unitary research design. It has attempted throughout to present an analysis at once theoretical and empirical and to back that analysis with data gathered by a number of techniques that seemed appropriate. Hence a 'composite' methodology has been adopted in our research though some greater weight has necessarily been given to the household survey.

*Method of data collection*

Data were collected by a survey of village households in the Sheikhupura, Sahiwal and Sargodha districts of the Punjab in Pakistan. In the main area of our research, the village which I have called Mallian, data were also obtained of all the village households on such characteristics as their relationship to land, on their place within the local division of labour, access to capital, production processes, household income, and so on.

A more detailed, intensive type of data were collected by a sample survey of households in Mallian and in Sargodha and Sahiwal. In addition, data were collected by a survey of workers from Mallian employed in a textile mill located nearby. The aim of the intensive survey is to focus sharply, in greater detail, on the production process of selected households, by drawing on a representative rather than a statistically random sample.

The intensive survey is comprised as follows:

| | |
|---|---|
| Interviews from Mallian | 75 households |
| Interview from the textile mill | 54 workers |
| Interviews from Sahiwal | 18 households |
| Interviews from Sargodha | 8 households |

The 75 households from Mallian are classified as follows:

| | |
|---|---|
| Households owning land | 33 |
| Landless agricultural households | 24 |
| Non-agricultural households | 18 |

The universe was classified according to the theoretical categories adopted for this study: landowning agricultural households, non-landowning agricultural households, and non-agricultural households. These three categories were then stratified into sub-categories of large landowners, and rich, middle, small and poor peasant households; landless agricultural labourers and tenants from the non-landowning agricultural households; and artisan/service and 'miscellaneous' households from the non-agricultural households.

From each stratum or subcategory a representative number of households were selected for the study. In Mallian this procedure was adopted for all except the large owners with over 100 acres (since the intention was to analyze holdings that were conducive to capitalist development), and the artisan/service households in the non-agricultural category; these were selected without randomness because, being few in number (16 out of 187 non-agricultural households), these could easily have been missed in a random selection. With the same intentions I included in the sub-category of large landowners an absentee landlord who owns 259 acres in Mallian but lives in Lahore.

For the other strata a random selection procedure was adopted: from the list of each stratum or subcategory (derived as I have said from the general survey of all Mallian households) the first household was selected and the head of that household was approached for interview based on a structured but open ended interview schedule; if the head of household was not available or information given was considered unreliable, then the next household was approached for interview, and so on, till the number required for 'representativeness' was obtained.

Table A.1: Classification of sample survey of Mallian households in 1978

| Households | | Sample Households No. | Sample Households % | Village Households in this Category No. | Village Households in this Category % | | Sample Sub-Category as a Proportion of Total Village subcategory % | |
|---|---|---|---|---|---|---|---|---|
| **Owning land (acres)** | | | | | | | | |
| Large and medium landlords | (100 and over) | 3 | 9 | 5 | 5.5 | | 60 | |
| Small landlords | ( 50 - 100 ) | 3 | 9 | 3 | 3 | | 100 | |
| Rich peasants | ( 25 - 50 ) | 8 | 24 | 31 | 34 | | 26 | |
| Middle peasants | ( 10 - 25 ) | 8 | 24 | 19 | 20 | | 42 | |
| Small peasants | ( 5 - 10 ) | 6 | 18 | 15 | 16.5 | | 40 | |
| Poor peasants | ( 1 - 5 ) | 5 | 15 | 18 | 20 | | 28 | |
| | Total no. | 33 | 100 | 91 | 100 | | | |
| **Non-landowning agricultural** | | | | | | | | |
| Tenants (landless) | | 18 | 54 | 93 | 71 | | 19 | |
| Landless labourers (on cash and sep, excl. Juts) | | 6 | 18 | 37 | 29 | | 16 | |
| | Total L/hlds | 24 | 72 | 130 | 100 | | | |
| **Non-agricultural** | | | | | | | | |
| Blacksmith | | 1 | 5.5 | 3 | 2 | | 33 | |
| Carpenter | | 1 | 5.5 | 5 | 3 | | 20 | |
| Shoemaker | | 1 | 5.5 | 10 | 5 | (4 wkng in trdnl occpn) | 25 | (as prpn of 4 wkng as sh.mkrs) |
| Barber | | 1 | 5.5 | 4 | 2 | | 25 | |
| Dyer/Tailor | | 2 | 11 | 5 | 3 | | 40 | |
| Potter | | 3 | 16.6 | 14 | 7.5 | (4 crryng trde & shpkg, 10 in industry) | | |
| Goldsmith | | 1 | 5.5 | 3 | 2 | | | |
| Miscellaneous (1 each in the following 8 occpns: food stall, worker in railway/coal dump, casual labourer, cleaner in factory, milk seller, worker in a carpet factory, village guard) | | 8 | 44.4 | | | | | |
| | | 18 | 100 (adjusted) | | | | | |

NOTE: Percentages adjusted to nearest whole figure

## The Mallian study

Table A.1 shows the classification of the sample survey of the Mallian households. As I have mentioned, 75 households were included in the Mallian survey. This gives a 20 percent sample of the Mallian households. As indicated above, these categories are further stratified into subcategories as shown in the table.

In terms of the proportion of the three categories in the sample to the sample total of 75 households, the 33 households owning land constitute 44 percent of the sample; the 24 non-landowning households constitute 32 percent, and the 18 non-agricultural households represent 24 percent of this category.

The sample of the 33 landowning households represents 36 percent of the 91 households owning land in Mallian. The 24 non-landowning agricultural households in the sample constitute about 20 percent of the 130 in the village. The 18 non-agricultural households in the sample represent about 10 percent of the 197 households in the village.

Some of the proportions of the subcategories in each stratum of the village total are large, whilst others are small, and vary from 100, 75 and 60 percent, to 20 and 25 percent; this is inevitable given the small size of the universe.

### *Other sources of data*

The Mallian study also drew on data from official sources collected periodically (yearly, bi-annually) by state officials operating at the district, tehsil (subdistrict) and village levels. These are kept at the district adminstrative headquarters in Sheikhupura. In addition data were collected by participant observation and case studies.

# Select bibliography

Aftab, K. and Rahim, E. (1986), 'The emergence of a small-scale engineering sector: the case of tubewell production in the Pakistan Punjab,' *Journal of Development Studies*, 23:1.

Aglietta, M. (1982), 'World capitalism in the eighties', *New Left Review*, no.136.

Agricultural Development Bank of Pakistan (1977), *Agricultural Indicators of Pakistan (various issues)* Islamabad.

Ahmad, M. (1976), 'Rural self-government in Pakistan' in Stevens, Robert D. et al. (eds) *Rural Development in Bangladesh and Pakistan*, University of Hawai Press, Honolulu.

Ahmad, S. (1973), 'Peasant Classes in Pakistan', in Gough, Katherine, and Sharma, H., *Imperialism and revolution in South Asia*, Monthly Review Press, New York.

Ahmad, S. (1977), *Class and Power in a Punjabi Village*, Monthly Review Press, New York.

Ahmed, V. and Amjad, R. (1984), *The Management of Pakistan's Economy*, Oxford University Press, Karachi.

Alavi, H. (1976), 'The Rural Elite and Agricultural Development in Pakistan' in Stevens, R. D., et al. (eds) *Rural Development in Bangladesh and Pakistan*, University of Hawai Press, Honolulu.

Amin, S. (1974), *Accumulation on a World Scale*, Monthly Review Press, New York.

Andreff, W. (1984), 'International centralization of capital and the re-ordering of world capitalism', *Capital and Class*, no.22, Spring.

Banaji, J. (1975), 'Summary of selected parts of Kautsky's "The Agrarian Question,"' *Economy and Society*, 5:1.
Baran, P. (1957), *The Political Economy of Growth*, Monthly Review Press, New York.
Bardhan, P. (1976), 'Variations in extent and forms of agricultural tenancy,'*Economic and Political Weekly*, 11 and 18 September, no.37-38.
Bannerjee, H. (1978), 'The growth of commercial agriculture in the second half of the 19th century', *Punjab Past and Present*, vol.12.
Becker, D. et al. (eds)(1987), *Postimperialism: International Capitalism and Development in the Late twentieth Century*, Lynne Reinner, Boulder.
Beidelman, T. (1959) *A Comparative Analysis of the Jajmani System*, J.J. Augustin, Locust Valley, New York.
Berry, R. and Cline, W. (1979), *Agrarian Structures Productivity in Developing Countries*, The Johns Hopkins University Press, Baltimore.
Bhaduri, A. (1973), 'A Study of agricultural backwardness under semi-feudalism', *Economic Journal*, 83: March.
Bhalla, S. (1976), 'New relations of production in Haryana agriculture', *Economic and Political Weekly*, no.13, 27 March.
Bharadwaj, K. (1972), *Production Conditions in Indian Agriculture*, Cambridge Univeristy Press, Cambridge.
Bhattacharjee, A. (1988), 'New seed policy: whose interest would it serve?' *Economic and Political Weekly*, 8 October, 1988.
Brass, T. (1984), 'Permanent transition or permanent revolution: peasants, proletarians, and politics', *Journal of Peasant Studies*, 11:3.
Brecher, I. and Abbas, S. (1972), *Foreign Aid and Industrial Development in Pakistan*, Cambridge University Press, Cambridge.
Brenner, R. (1977), 'The origins of capitalist development: a critique of neo-Smithian Marxism', *New Left Review*, no. 104.
Bukharin, N. (1926), *Historical Materialism*, London (N.P).
Burch, D. (1987), *Overseas Aid and the Transfer of Technology*, Avebury Publishers, Aldershot.
Burki, S.J. (1976), 'The Development of Pakistan's Agriculture, in Stevens, R.D., et al. op.cit. and Laporte, R. Jr. (1984), *Pakistan's Development Priorities*, Oxford University Press, Karachi.
Byres, T.J. (1972), 'The dialectic of India's green revolution, *South Asian Review*, 5:2.
(1974), 'Land reform, industrialisation and the marketed surplus', in Lehmann, D. *Agrarian Reform and Agrarian Reformism*, Faber and Faber, London.
(1977), 'Agrarian transition and the agrarian question', *Journal of Peasant Studies*, 4:3.
(1982), 'India: capitalist industrialization or structural stasis?', in Bienefeld, M. and Godfrey, M. (eds), *The Struggle for development*, John Wiley, Chichester.
Calvert, H. (1936), *The Wealth and Welfare of the Punjab*, Civil and Military Gazette, Lahore.
Cardoso. F.H. (1972), 'Dependent capitalist development in Latin America', *New Left Review*, no.74.

Cathie, J. (1989), *Food Aid and Industrialization,* Avebury Publishers, Aldershot.
Chakravarty, S. (1979), 'On the question of home market and prospects for Indian growth', *Economic and Political Weekly,* XIV, No.30-32.
Chattopadhyay, P. (1972a), 'On the question of the mode of of production in Indian agriculture', *Economic and Political Weekly,* March. (197), 'Mode of production in Indian agriculture: an anti- kritik', *Economic and Political Weekly,* December.
Chayanov, A.V.(1966), *The Theory of Peasant Economy,* (eds) Kerblay, B. et al. R.D. Irwin, Homewood, Illinois.
Cheong, K.C. and Lim, K.C. (1981), 'Electronics industry in in Malaysia: issues in transfer and development of technology', *Asian Economist,* December.
Cheung, S.N.S. (1968), 'Private property rights and share- cropping', *Journal of Political Economy,* November/December, no.76. (1969a), 'Transaction costs, risk aversion and choice of contractual arrangements', *Journal of Law and Econmics,* April. (1969b), *The Theory of Sharetenancy,* Univeristy of Chicago Press, Chicago.
Child, F.C., and Kaneda, H. (1975), 'Links to the green revolution,' *Economic Development and Çultural Change,* 23:2.
Chung, K.M.(1975), 'Commercial transfer of technology in the Korean electronics industry' *Korean Science and Technology Investment Project,* Seoul, mimeo.
Cleaver, H. (1972), 'The contradictions of the green revolution', *Monthly Review,* June.
Cohen, G.A. (1978), *Karl Marx's Theory of History: A Defence,* Oxford Univeristy Press, Oxford.
Darling, M. (1947), *The Punjab Peasant in Prosperity and Debt,* Oxford University Press, London.
Djurfeldt, G. and Lindberg, S. (1975), *Behind Poverty: The Social Formation of a Tamil Village,* Curzon Press, London.
Dobb, M. (1967), *Papers on Capitalism, Development* and Planning, Routledge and Kegan Paul, London.
(1969) *Socialism, Capitalism and Economic Growth* (ed) Feinstein, C.H., Cambridge Univeristy Press, Cambridge.
(1960) *An Essay on Economic Growth and Planning,* Routledge and Kegan Paul, London.
Dube, S.C. (1955), *Indian Village,* Routledge and Kegan Paul, London.
Ellman, M. (1979), *Socialist Planning*, Macmillan, London.
Emmanuel, A. (1972), *Unequal Exchange: The Imperialism of Trade*, New Left Books, London.
Epstein, T.S. (1960), *Economic Development and Social Change in South India,* Manchester University Press, Manchester.
(1973), *South India: Yesterday, Today and Tomorrow*, Macmillan, London.
Erlich, A. (1960), *The Soviet Industrialisation debate, 1924-1928*, Harvard University Press, Cambridge, Mass.

Feder, E. (1976), 'McNamara's little green revolution: World Bank scheme for self- liquidation of the Third World Peasantry', *Economic and Political Weekly*, 3 April.

(1977), 'Capitalism's last ditch effort to save under-developed agricultures', *Journal of Contemporary Asia*, 7:1.

Feder, G. (1980), 'Economic growth, foreign loans and debt servicing', *Journal of Development Studies*, 16:3.

Frank, A.G. (1967), *Capitalism and Underdevelopment in Latin America*, Monthly Review Press, New York.

(1969), *Latin America: Underdevelopment or Revolution*, Monthly Review Press, New York.

Frankel, F. (1971), *India's Green Revolution - Economic Gains and Political Costs*, Princeton University Press, New Jersey.

Freiden, J. 'International capital and national development', in Becker, et al.(eds)(1987), *Postimperialism: International Capitalism and Development in the Late Twentieth Century* Lynne Rienner, Boulder. (1987), 'Third world indebted industrialization', in Becker, et al.(eds)(1987) *Postimperialism: International Capitalism and Development in the Late Twentieth Century*, Lynne Rienner, Boulder.

Gardezi, H. and Rashid, J. (eds), (1983), *Pakistan: the Roots of Dictatorship*, Zed Press, London.

Government of India (1983),*Foreign Investment Policy in India*, Ministry of Industry, New Delhi. Government of India (1980), *Foreign Investments in India*, Indian Investment Centre, New Delhi. Government of Pakistan, Agriculture Division, *Agricultural Statisitics*, Various Issues

Government of Pakistan, Finance Division, *Pakistan Economic Survey*, Annual Issues.

Griffin, K. (1974), *The Political Economy of Agrarian Change*, Macmillan, London.

Gudeman, S. (1978), *The Demise of a Rural Economy*, Routledge and Kegan Paul, London.

Guisinger, S. and Irfan, M. (1980), 'Pakistan's informal sector', *Journal of Development Studies*, 16:4.

*Gujranwala District Gazetteer* (1935), Government Printing Press, Lahore.

Gupta, D. (1980), 'Formal and real subsumption of labour to capital', *Economic and Political Weekly*, September.

Harris, N. (1986), The End of the Third World. Newly Industrializing countries and the Decline of an Ideology, Tauris, London.

Hasswell, M.R. (1967), *Economics of Development in village India*, Routledge and Keegan Paul, London.

Hirschman, A.(1971), *A Bias for Hope*, Yale University Press, New Haven. (1966), *The Strategy of Economic Development*, Yale Univeristy Press, New Haven.

Hussain, S.M. (1970), *Empirical Studies on Pakistan Agriculture*, Pakistan Institute of Development Economics, Karachi.

International Bank for Reconstruction and Development (1975), *The Consequences of Farm Tractors in Pakistan*, IBRD, Washington.

International Labour Office,(1983), *Rural Poverty in Pakistan*, ILO/ARTEP, Bangkok, mimeo.

International Monetary Fund, *International Financial Statistics*, various issues.
Jenkin, R. (1984), *Transnational Corporations and Industrial Transformation in Latin America*, Macmillan Press, London.
(1977), *Dependent Industrialization in Latin America*, Praeger Publishers, New York.
Johnson, A.R. (1909,1979), *The Disappearance of the Small Landowner*, Merlin Press, London.
Johnston, D.F. and Kilby, B. (1975), *Agriculture and Structural Transformation*, Oxford University Press, New York.
Kardar, S. (1987), *The Political Economy of Pakistan*, Progressive Publishers, Lahore.
Kessinger, T. (1974), *Vilyatpur, 1848-1968:Social and Economic Change in a North Indian Village*, University of California Press, Berkeley.
Khan, M.H. (1975), *The Economics of the Green Revolution*, Praeger, new York. (1981), *Underdevelopment and Agrarian Structure in Pakistan*, Westview Press, Boulder.
Kloppenburg, J.R. (1988), *Seeds and Soverignty*, Duke University Press, Durham, N.C.
Kuhnen, F. and Haider, A.S. (1974), 'Land tenure and agricultural development in Pakistan', *Food and Agricultural Organization review*, United Nations, FAO, Rome.
Liepitz, A. (1984) 'Imperialism or the beast of the apocalypse, *Capital and Class*,no.22, Spring.
Lenin, V.I. (1960), *The Development of Capitalism in Russia*, Collected Works, vol.3, Lawrence and Wishart, London.
(1976), *The Agrarian Question and the 'Critics of Marx', Progress Publishers, Moscow.*
Lewis, S.R. (1969), *Economic Policy and Industrial Growth in Pakistan*, Oxford Univeristy Press, London.
(1970), *Pakistan: Industrialization and Trade Policies*, Oxford University Press, Oxford.
Lukacs, G. (1972), *Political Writings 1919-1929*, New Left Books, London.
Linder, S. (1986), *The Pacific Century: Economic and Political Consequences of Asian Pacific Dynamism*, Stanford University Press, Stanford.
Little, I. (1982), *Economic Development: Theory, Policy and International Relations*, Basic Books, New York.
Marx, K. (1961-2), *Capital*, Vol.II, Progress Publishers, Moscow. (1973), *Grundrisse*, Penguin Books, Harmondsworth.
(1974), *Capital*, Vol.III, Lawrence and Wishart, London.
(1976), *Capital* Vol. I, Penguin Books, Harmondsworth.
Mirza, H. (1986), *Multinationals and the Growth of the Singapore* Economy, Croom Helm, London.
Mohammad, G. (1964), 'Some strategic problems in agricultural development in Pakistan', *Pakistan Development* Review, Summer.
(1965), 'Private tubewell development and cropping patterns West Pakistan', *Pakistan Development Review*, Spring.
Mooney, J.K. (1983), 'The law of the seed', *Development Dialogue*, 1-12.
Morris, M.D. (1969), *The Development of an Industrial labour Force in India*, University of California Press, Berkeley.

Mukherjee, M. (1980), 'Some aspects of agrarian structure of Punjab, 1925-47', *Economic and Political Weekly*, June.
Muroyama, J.H. and Guyford, S.(eds)(1988), *Globalization of Technology*, National Academic Press, Washington D.C.
Nazir, P. (1975), 'Social change in Pakistani villages', *Socialist Thought and Practice*, 16:1.
(1981) Transformation of property relations in the Punjab', *Economic and Political Weekly*, XVI:8.
(1982), 'Industrial proletariat in Pakistan', *Economic and Political Weekly*, October.
(1986), 'Marxism and the national question:class and and ideology in the making of Pakistan', *Journal of Contemporary Asia*, 16:4.
Newfarmer, R. and Mueller, W. (1983) *Multinational Corporations in Brazil and Mexico*, US Government Printing Office, Washington, DC.
Organization for Economic Cooperation and Development (1979), *Technology Transfer to Developing Countries*, OECD, Paris.
Organization for Economic Cooperation and Development (1979a), *Handbook for International Trade and Development Statistics*, Paris.
Ohkawa, K. and Rosovsky, M. (1960), 'The role of agriculture in modern Japanese economic development', *Economic Development and Culture Change*, 9:2, October.
Palloix, C. (1975), 'The internationalization of capital and the circuit of social capital', in Radice, H. (ed), *International Firms and Modern Imperialism*, Penguin, Harmondsworth.
Palmer, I. (1972), *Science and Agricultural Production*, United Nations Research Institute for Social Development, Geneva.
Papanek, G.F. (1967), *Pakistan's Develoment, Social Goals and Private Incentives*, Harvard University Press, Cambridge.
Parry, J. (1979), *Caste and Kinship in kangra*, Routledge and Kegan Paul, London.
Patnaik. U. (1971), 'Capitalist development in agriculture: a note', *Economic and Political Weekly*, September.
(1972a), 'On the mode of production in Indian agriculture: a reply', *Economic and Political Weekly*, September.
(1972b), 'Economics of farm size and farm scale: some assumptions re-examined', *Economic and Political Weekly*, August.
Pearce, R. (1983), 'Sharecropping: towards a Marxist view', *Journal of Peasant Studies*, 10: 2 and 3.
Ping, H.K. (1979), 'British of the second generation', *Far Eastern Economic Review*, May.
Preobrazensky, E. (1965), *The New Economics*, Clarendon Press, London.
Plekhanov, V. (1969), *Fundamental Problems of Marxism*, Progress Publishers, New York.
Paustian, H.M. (1930), *Canal Irrigation in the Punjab*, Columbia University Press, New York.
Raj, K.N.(1969), 'Role of the" machine-tools sector" in economic growth', in Feinstein, C.H. *Socialism, Capitalism and Economic Growth*, Cambridge University Press, Cambridge.
Rajaraman, T. (1975), 'Poverty, inequality and economic growth: rural Punjab, 1960/61-1970/71', *Journal of Development Studies*, 11:4.

Rudra, A. (1970), 'In search of the capitalist farmer', *Economic and Political Weekly,* 27 June.
Saith, A. and Tankha, A. (1972a), 'Economic decision-making of the poor peasant household', *Economic and Political Weekly,* February.
(197b),'Agrarian transition and the differentiation of the peasantry: a study of a West UP village', *Economic and Political Weekly,* 1 April.
Schulz, A. (1982) 'Reorganizing deserts: mechanization and marginal lands in Southwest Asia' in Spooner, B. and Mann, H.S. (eds), *Desertification and Development*, Academic Press, London.
*Sheikhupura District Gazetteer* (1935),Government Printing Press, Lahore.
Sivakumar, S.S. (1978), 'Aspects of agrarian economy in Tamil Nadu: a study of two villages', *Economic and Political Weekly,* 6, 13, and 20 May.
Spate, O.K. (1957), *India and Pakistan,* Methuen and Co., London.
Stern J.J. and Falcon, W. (1970) *Growth and Development in Pakistan,* Harvard University Press, Cambrige.
Stevens, R.D., Alave, H., Bertocci, P. (eds)(1976) *Rural Development in Bangladesh and Pakistan,* University of Hawai Press, Honolulu.
Stewart, F.(1978), *Technology and Underdevelopment,* Macmillan, London.
Tinker, H. (1968), *The Foundations of Local Self- Government in India, Pakistan and Burma,* Praeger, New York.
United Nations (1979a), Centre on Transnational Corporations, *Technology Transfer,* Vol. III.
United Nations (1981), Conference on Trade and Development *Handbook of International Trade and Development Statistics,* Supplement, Table 7.1.
United Nations, (1975) Conference on Trade and Development, *Major Issues Arising from the Transfer of Technology to Developing Countries.*
United Nations (1984), Economic and Social Commission for Asia and the Pacific, *Transnational Corporations,* UN, Bangkok.
United Nations (1981a), Economic and Social Commission for Asia and the Pacific, *Costs and Conditions of Technology Transfer through Transnational Corporations,* UN, Bangkok.
United Nations (1980a) Food and Agriculture Organization, *Projections in Current Situation and Outlook,* Commission on Fertilizers, New York.
United Nations (1980), *Global Study of the Pharmaceutical Industry,* UN, New York.
United Nations (1982) Industrial Development Organization, *Export Processing Zones*, Vienna.
United Nations (1973), Industrial Development Organization, *Guidelines for the Acquisition of Foreign Technology in Developing Countries*, UNIDO, Vienna.
United Nations, Monthly Bulletins of Statistics, Monthly Issues, New York.
United Nations (1983), *Transnational Corporations in World Development - Third Survey,* UN, New York.
United Nations, (1979b), Industrial Development Organization, *World Wide Study of the agri- cultural machinery Industry,* UNIDO, International Centre for Industrial Studies, Vienna.
United Nations (1981b), *Year Book of Industrial Statistics 1980,* Vol.II, UN, New York.
United Nations (1981c), *Transnational Corporations in the Agricultural Machinery and Equipment Industry,* UN, New York.

White, L.J. (1974), *Industrial Concentration and Economic Power in Pakistan*, Princeton University Press, New Jersey.
World Bank (1984), *Pakistan. Review of the Sixth Five Year* Plan, IBRD, Washington.